From Hire to Liar

From Hire to Liar

The Role of Deception in the Workplace

DAVID SHULMAN

ILR Press

AN IMPRINT OF

CORNELL UNIVERSITY PRESS

ITHACA AND LONDON

First published 2007 by Cornell University Press
First printing, Cornell Paperbacks, 2007

Printed in the United States of America

Library of Congress Cataloging-in-Publication Data
Shulman, David, 1964–
    From hire to liar : the role of deception in the workplace/David
Shulman.
        p. cm.
    Includes bibliographical references and index.
    ISBN-13: 978-0-8014-4473-9 (cloth : alk. paper)
    ISBN-10: 0-8014-4473-X (cloth : alk. paper)
    ISBN-13: 978-0-8014-7331-9 (pbk. : alk. paper)
    ISBN-10: 0-8014-7331-4 (pbk. : alk. paper)
    1. Business ethics.   2. Organizational behavior.
3. Deception.   4. Work ethic.   5. Private investigators.   I. Title.
HF5387.S553 2007
174'.4 — dc22   2006023305

Cornell University Press strives to use environmentally responsible
suppliers and materials to the fullest extent possible in the publish-
ing of its books. Such materials include vegetable-based, low-VOC
inks and acid-free papers that are recycled, totally chlorine-free, or
partly composed of nonwood fibers. For further information, visit
our website at www.cornellpress.cornell.edu.

Cloth printing   10 9 8 7 6 5 4 3 2 1
Paperback printing   10 9 8 7 6 5 4 3 2 1

I noticed that the client company had completely lost its advantage in two regions of the country where last year it had showed a strong advantage. I asked my boss, "How should I update this?" to include in a report for the client. My boss said, "Leave it out."
Entry-level worker at a market research firm

I'd play solitaire and have my hand on the Alt-Tab key so that I could click over to the spreadsheets if someone walked by.
Intern at a financial services firm

My real goal at work is to do as little work as possible while getting paid as much as possible. That's it, and I don't feel bad about it at all.
Computer software consultant

She said, "Just fake the signatures," and then paused and said, "unless you're uncomfortable with that." She meant, "Just do it—what's the big deal? Don't bother me about it or you'll regret it."
Administrative assistant

A major sales producer is being recruited. Most managers want to hire her, but a major decision maker doesn't want to hire her because he doesn't think she's pretty enough. . . . He'll mask it . . . not cut her a good deal.
Manager at a large insurance corporation

If bullshit was music, I'd be the philharmonic.
Private detective

CONTENTS

ACKNOWLEDGMENTS

My first thanks go to my respondents, who generously shared their insights and experiences with me.

I have many friends and peers to thank for their advice, encouragement, readings, and suggestions during various stages of this book's earliest development. Thanks to Amy Binder, Beth Clifford, Alan Dahl, Mark Ellis, Joanne Engelhart, Brian Gran, Lisa Gurr, Lorraine Hanson, Judy Levine, Mary Lopez, John Massad, David Pellow, Lisa Staffen, Mitchell Stevens, Adam Weinberg, and Chris Wellin.

At Northwestern University, Ron Breautigam and Josef Barton were supportive administrators in the Business Institutions Program. I also owe a special thanks to Lucy Millman for her support, advice, and constant encouragement. Bernie Beck and Bob Nelson supported early inroads into this research and offered valuable suggestions. Allan Schnaiberg, with his big ear and big heart, offered constant encouragement and advice on how to tighten analytic points and expand ideas. Wendy Espeland was an invaluable source of advice on more issues than I can count. Thanks also to Mark Granovetter and Bruce Carruthers for advice and support.

Charles Ragin bolstered my confidence that this work pursued worthwhile ideas. If just a little of his sociological imagination, intellectual open-mindedness, and sense of intellectual curiosity rubbed off on me, I'd be a lucky man.

Carol Heimer and Art Stinchcombe offered criticisms that had the annoying quality of being absolutely dead-on right. Their criticisms and encouragement were invaluable. I am deeply grateful for the chance to learn from them.

I thank Peter and Patti Adler, Pete Brodnitz, Kathy Charmaz, John Deighton, Richard Leo, Dawn Iacobucci, Gary Marx, and Jim Witte for their feedback on various portions of this book. Ira Silver offered excellent suggestions on a separate book, *Talking Sociology*, and was an endless source of support. Working with Gary Alan Fine helped improve my sociological sensibility and writing. Kent Grayson's counsel, writing, and long conversations with me about this book were vital. I deeply appreciate his help.

My departmental and institutional colleagues at Lafayette College have encouraged this work. I am grateful to Dan Bauer, Bill Bissell, Rebecca Kissane, Susan Niles, the late Thomas Norton, Elaine Reynolds, Howard Schneiderman, and Andrea Smith for all of their support. Thanks also to Jackie Wogotz. The members of the Applied Probability seminar also made sober and serious contributions. Lafayette College provided me with a junior faculty leave and a publication grant. Invited talks at Clemson University, Colgate University, Wellesley College, and Northwestern University and at several professional conferences helped me further articulate some of these ideas.

Thank you also to the reviewers for their suggestions and to Nancy Ferguson, Ange Romeo-Hall, Katy Meigs, and Pam Bodenhorn for their work on this manuscript. To Fran Benson of Cornell University Press for her support of this project and for her excellent ideas—who knew that working with an editor could be such a blast?

Thank you to my father and mother, Mark and Peggy Shulman, and to my sisters, Alice Modlin and Judy Roth. Special thanks to Sherry, Sheldon, and Michael Blackman.

I owe my greatest thanks to my wife, Susan. Completing this book involved her blood, sweat, and tears as much as my own. I wish I had a poet's gift to come up with the right words to express my profound love and appreciation for you. My father once told me, "Everything good that happens to you is Susan's fault." Dad's right. Finally, I dedicate this book to Susan and our son, Alex, who is the bravest person we know. We respect and love you and want to thank you for making your Mom and Dad's hearts full of joy.

INTRODUCTION: IS DISHONESTY THE REAL POLICY?

What is the last lie or deception that you observed at your job? Was someone surfing the Web instead of working? Did someone call in sick to take the day off? Was someone sweet-talking the boss or a client? Did a co-worker ignore an inconvenient rule? Or have you, yourself, just lied about a deadline or blamed a problem on someone else?

Maybe the proverb "People are given tongues with which to speak and words with which to hide their thoughts" was inspired by what someone saw at work. In the workplace people pretend to do more work than they really do; they grit their teeth and flatter irritating customers and supervisors; they hide shortcomings and help co-workers cover up transgressions. They play solitaire on computers all morning and self-deal from the budget. The excerpts at the beginning of this book, all from my research interviews, offer some illustrations.

Some formal job responsibilities even require workers to act deceptively. Undercover officers must impersonate drug buyers and prostitutes. The first price that car dealers quote is never their closing one. Hollywood agents automatically deny any wrongdoing by their celebrity clients, even when they know that their denials ring hollow. Corporate public relations specialists state that the company is not "firing" workers but is requiring their participation in an "alternative career-enhancement program."

I became interested in studying lying in the workplace when I compared how organizations should operate in theory with my own work experiences and stories that I heard from family, friends, and students about daily life at their jobs. The organizational theory I read did not say much about the ubiquity of deception in the workplace. No studies researched why and how people lie as a normal and mundane event during their workday. Where were the people who hide their feelings by grumbling about their jobs and co-workers under their breath? Where were the studies detailing scheming and self-interested shortcuts? Who was studying how people play "blame-tag" for problems at work (I blame you—now you're "it")? Most people with work experience have encountered at least some version of exaggerated résumés, exploitative bosses, self-interested shirking, collusion against disliked colleagues, lying to clients, and countless other variants of lies on the job. In this book I aspire to tell the tale of such lies in the workplace and to examine their impact on work ethics, management, and productivity.

My scholarly goal is to describe the deceptions that people encounter and perpetrate at their jobs and connect them to theoretical explanations of how people work inside organizations. In doing so, I offer new ideas about why people lie at work and with what effect. Some people think individuals lie in the workplace in isolation. In this view, only individuals who are "bad apples" act unethically at work by lying. Others see workplace deception as a problem primarily of rogue organizations: notorious "bad apple" organizations such as Enron, which have become synonymous in the popular imagination with corporate crime. There are always some unethical individuals who lie and organizations that engage in criminal deceptions in the name of profit. Yet holding this view blinds us to the commonplace lies of everyday workers. We have to study how people routinely use lies as a tool to navigate workplace expectations and how acting deceptively is an important means of administrating work.

In this book I present the results of two qualitative case studies that detail the experiences that people have with deception in the workplace and that offer examples of deception in people's own words. The first study presents data from participant observation and interviews with private detectives, a group of professionals whose official work demands engaging in deceptive activities. The second study investigates how workers in various fields, from investment banking to environmental justice organizations, encounter and tell lies as an unofficial part of their job. Both cases offer compelling vantage points for thinking about workplace lying. I compare private detectives with everyday workers to identify a continuum of deceptive behaviors that range from lying explicitly to do one's job to breaking minor rules and shirking to get through the day. Although these case studies are different, they both illustrate how workplaces require formal and informal deceptive impression management, because there are always clients to please, rules to subvert, difficult tasks to perform, work to shirk, and job advancement to seek. The range of acts contained within these cases allows readers to assess workplace deception more extensively and should stimulate them to think about the interesting variety of lies that influence our workplaces.

Literature on Deception

Most assessments of deception by business ethicists, psychologists, philosophers, and religious traditions focus on deception as an individual character flaw rather than as an aspect of people's social environments. Business ethics prioritize moral education in the workplace in order to reduce the likelihood of lying. Social institutions, such as families, religious congregations, and schools, are ideally supposed to work to reduce lying and other undesirable character traits. The inverse proposition, that social institutions also teach people to lie, must be explored, however. How this reversed assumption operates in the daily practices and social relationships in the workplace is the central subject of this book.

Philosophers often revisit age-old arguments about the imperative to tell the truth, the nature of self-deception, and what conditions, if any, justify lying (Baier 1975; Bok 1978, 1982; Nyberg 1993). Communications scholars inventory factors involved in telling lies, such as intonation and other characteristics (Metts 1989; Miller et al. 1986; Miller and Staff 1993). Military historians assess deception as a crucial element of military strategy (Handel 1973). Psychologists tend to analyze less abstract aspects of deception, addressing such questions as: How do we detect lies? Do polygraphs work? How do children develop the capacity to lie? How do animals use deception in their behaviors? What physiological and psychological cues correlate with lying, such as facial expressions? Journalists and social scientists write case studies of deception in various settings. Examples include deceptions by advertisers, college students, con artists, corporations, impostors, government officials, scientists, husbands and wives, politicians, literary protagonists, whistle-blowers, and case studies of deception in various tribal cultures, often non-Western ones.[1] There is also a self-help literature on harmful self-deceptions.[2]

There are two reasons the above scholarly approaches get in the way of understanding workplace deception. The first reason is that these approaches use samples of deceptive behaviors that are either too broad or too narrow. Philosophical ruminations often use abstract examples to debate the morality of lying. Using hypothetical and abstract examples of lies that people might tell is less useful than considering the lies that people actually do tell. On the other hand, many studies of lying are overly individualistic, with lying only analyzed in situations in which one person lies to another person. This sampling choice neglects that more complex groups of people often lie as a team in organizations to multiple audiences. An additional sampling limitation is placing too much emphasis on studying physiological signs of deception. Although important for furthering our knowledge of how to detect lies, a physiological focus does not help uncover the social roots of why people are lying in the first place. Finally, many case studies examine exceptional and infamous deceptions, such as that of Michael Milken and insider trading, rather than more mundane occurrences.

The second reason these approaches fail to understand workplace deception is that too many studies assume an equivalence between individual amorality and lying. Although amoral liars exist, many people who lie perceive themselves as being decent people, and organizational environments help foster rationalizations for deceptive acts. Workplaces generate social pressures and situations that help people to overcome proscriptions against lying, just as everyday social niceties encourage "white lies" to help people preserve the peace in routine interactions with family and friends. We need to study those social pressures and situations rather than simply blame lying on "bad" people.

The sampling and equivalence limitations in the existing literature create several impediments to understanding deception as a common, yet complex, social behavior. Philosophical works do provide an introduction to the moral issues involved in deliberating whether lying is morally acceptable.[3] Sociologically relevant work, however, must examine real motivations for deceptions. Hypothetical examples are convenient but poor substitutes for researching real deception in that they do not capture the social contingencies that influence how people decide to act.

Studies of exchanges between a single liar and a single recipient of a lie also create blind spots. Many deceptions involve teams of people working together to tell lies in predictable circumstances. Brothers and sisters join forces to deceive parents; salespersons conspire to trick customers into paying more for a product; employees work together to conceal goofing off from their employers and customers. Deception is both an individual and a team activity. There are silent conspiracies apparent in the ways that people work together to lie and pretend not to notice lies. As the saying goes, "Love may be blind, but friends close their eyes." Scholars must pay attention to social context and the small group psychology involved in collective lying and reactions to lies. As children, for example, we hear pejorative terms such as "narc," "rat," and "tattletale" to describe people who expose lies and secrets. These terms are both warnings and insults.

To study actual situations in which there are clear stakes in calling someone a liar (such as with family and friends or at work) is very different from examining whether an experimental subject detects a lie. We must assess how people decide whether to expose, challenge, or ignore lies. Many people may detect lies but choose to appear fooled in order to avoid the consequences of accusing someone of lying.

Another blind spot occurs with infamous deceptions that are inappropriate cases for generalization. One well-known documented case of institutionally supported lying, for example, was the Allies' use of deception to conceal D-day invasion plans during World War II. The Allies built huge fake army encampments and used fraudulent documents to trick the German military. Studying D-day misinformation operations does identify effective techniques of perpetrating deception on a large scale. Yet D-day–related misinformation tactics are atypical. While scholars can analyze consequential deceptions in such an example, most people generally lack armies, an overwhelmingly powerful justifying wartime context, and hundreds of thousands of dollars to use to develop their deceptions. Diagnosed pathological liars and successful con artists are also popular case studies. They are interesting rarities, but they divert attention from studying routine liars in everyday circumstances.

Many case studies of deception also focus on criminal acts as the sample. While people do lie to commit crimes, criminal enterprises are just one subset of a range of deceptive acts. Hiding one's true feelings when asked about a colleague or "goofing off" are endemic workplace deceptions that are not usually crimes. For example, police officers may tell a victim's relatives that the death was painless, knowing the reverse to be true. Here deception is perceived as a kindness. Perceiving criminal acts as the only type of workplace deception that exists creates a blind spot for studying routine lies. The existing literature on deception can be summarized for limitations and blind spots (see table 1).

Table 1. Limitations and Blind Spots in the Deception Literature

Sampling Problems	The Equivalence Assumption
Examples of lies that are overly abstract	Assumes equivalence between individual
Examples of lies that are too individualistic	amorality and workplace deception
Examples of lies that are solely physiological	
Examples of lies involving exceptional circumstances and resources	
Examples of lies involving criminal behavior only	

Resulting Blind Spots in Understanding Deception

1. Abstract/hypothetical examples obscure concrete circumstances of real deceptions.
2. Individualistic examples of deception overlook collective/group acts of deception.
3. Physiological studies of deception do not expose any social motives for lying.
4. Analyzing exceptional or infamous deceptions is an unrealistic way to understand deception as a general and routine behavior.
5. Focusing on deception only as a criminal behavior creates blind spots in analyzing many common types of deception.
6. The equivalence assumption overlooks rationalizations and root social causes of deception.

To learn more about deception, we should sample deception in the workplace at a broad level and ask what deceptions are required as part of one's job. In his ethnography of police work, Manning (1977) identifies "normal lies," lies that are typical, rather than exceptional, in police work. Applying the "normal lies" perspective to more workplaces is a step in the right direction for correcting the blind spots in the literature.

Defining Deception

Scholars of lying generally agree in defining lies as "the willful delivery of false information" (Grover 1993a, 479).[4] This existing definition needs to be broadened to include a greater awareness of social context. The first problem is the definition's assumption of "willful delivery." There are multiple levels of awareness and involvement in perpetrating a lie. For example, if people who unknowingly communicate false information are not labeled deceptive (because there is no willful delivery of misinformation), then it is easy to overlook some orchestrated organizational deceptions, such as when institutional and individual actors use innocent agents of deception to mislead others. A classic example from the diplomatic world is when governments keep their diplomats in the dark about their country's actions. An ambassador from an accused country then appears more convincing when he or she denies any "false" accusations made against that country. Using innocent deceivers helps make deceptions more credible.

Sociologists must also broaden the sense of "delivery," "false," and "information" in the definition. "Delivery," for example, needs to include omission. Ekman (1985) asserts that knowing the true facts of a situation and not presenting them is deceptive, even though nothing may be stated to confirm or embellish an incorrect story. Being aware of deception but keeping quiet must count as "delivery," if we want to understand why some people stay silent and learn to "fail to notice" deception. A remedy for these definitional limitations is Erving Goffman's definition of a fabrication. Goffman (1974, 83–125) defines fabrications as "the intentional effort of one or more individuals to manage activity so that a party of one or more others will be induced to have a false belief about what it is that is going on."

Both Goffman and Georg Simmel have focused extensively on deception as an important subject for sociological study. Goffman emphasized that deceptive behavior had an integral and functional role in social interaction. He argued that people work hard to sustain the pretense that individuals, groups, and social settings are more ideal than they really are. Simmel (1950, 316) emphasized that lying is a severe threat to societies with complex and impersonal divisions of labor, although he did note that lies "also have sociologically quite positive significance for the formation of certain concrete relations." For both theorists, a deep irony of deception is clear: lies are capable of both severing and helping to maintain social relationships. Much sociological scholarship has focused on the "severing" potential of lies rather than their "maintaining" function, which is particularly important in the workplace.

Our modern life is based to a much larger extent than is usually realized upon the faith in the honesty of the other. Examples are our economy, which becomes more and more a credit economy, or our science, in which most scholars use innumerable results of other scientists, which they cannot examine. We base our gravest decisions on a complex system of conceptions, most of which presuppose the confidence that we will not be betrayed. Under modern conditions, the lie, therefore, becomes something much more devastating than it was earlier, something which questions the very foundation of our life. (Simmel 1950, 313)

In this well-known passage, Simmel argues that deception, in the form of broken trust, is devastating in an advanced society that depends on complex impersonal divisions of labor. Consider Enron's collapse, a contemporary example that confirms Simmel's point. Simmel's theoretical statement explains the logic behind scholarly work that examines deception as a threat. Researchers have sought to uncover what social control arrangements can best thwart deception and safeguard trust.

Transaction cost economics (Williamson 1975), Granovetter's (1985) "embeddedness" perspective, and Shapiro's work (1987a, 1987b, 1990) on the social control of impersonal trust—all examples from economic sociologists—emphasize the social arrangements that organizations use to safeguard the trust they place in economic partners. How can contractual arrangements best protect a group against the possibility of malfeasance and partners who combine "self-interest seeking with guile"? (See Williamson 1975.) Does being embedded in a network of familiar business partners help protect members against betrayal? These scholars view deception as a generic potential danger to control, while the nature and functions of mundane deceptions in organizations go unexplored.

Criminologists studying white-collar crime research how offenders lie to carry out their crimes. In doing so, they tackle deception as a strategic component of committing a crime. For example, price-fixing conspiracies require people to meet secretly to set prices (Punch 1996; Ross 1992). Employee theft requires knowing how to cultivate normal appearances and "sweeten" records to hide pilfering (Mars 1994). Insider trading can involve buying and selling stocks under false names to prevent the Securities and Exchange Commission from tracking suspicious transaction patterns (Punch 1996). Analyzing deceptive acts in this scholarly tradition is important for understanding how existing policing and social control arrangements are made vulnerable—for learning how criminals develop opportunities to commit crimes.

Of course, many deceptions incontestably cause harm and are criminal activities. Workers victimize employers by stealing, and companies exploit clients by misleading them. Such exploitations are harmful. But deceptive behaviors are multidimensional (again the sampling problem emerges), because deception involves more than subterfuge aimed at committing a crime. For example, going behind a supervisor's back to consult a better-informed co-worker about how to do a job is a common deception. This consulting can become deceptive when people want to keep supervisors from discovering their ignorance. Covert consulting also constitutes an underground administrative system that trains people in how to do their work. Understanding how deceptions victimize is critically important, but so is detailing the other functions that deceptions can have.

A Framework for Studying Workplace Deception

Goffman's investigation of deceptive behaviors provides a useful template for analyzing routine workplace deception. Goffman inventoried how people manipulate their physical actions, appearance, and speech to craft desirable impressions of themselves for others. According to Phillip Manning, Goffman studied how people produce credibility in social interaction: "Credibility is the quality of being believable, and this quality is integral to both trust and deception" (Manning 2000, 283).

Goffman (1983, 1) used the term "interaction order" to describe a "loose coupling between interactional practices and social structure." An interaction order describes how specific social contexts demand specific sets of social behaviors. Because given environments have definite expectations and social rules, there is order and predictable behavior in those settings. Goffman (1963, 5) argues that people care about preserving their social "faces" by trying to have a self-image made up of "approved social attributes." Social interaction calls for matching the right "face" and behaviors with the right context.

Deception enters the picture when people try to present themselves as meeting an ideal standard or performance that they do not really meet. Hence, marital partners may feign happiness to friends and relatives when they are unhappily married, and job applicants may list educational degrees on their resumes that they really don't have. Goffman (1959, 35) concludes, "When the individual presents himself before others, his performance will tend to incorporate and exemplify the officially accredited values of society, more so, in fact, than does his behavior as a whole." Lying, in practice, closes the distance between how people wish to appear to others and how they actually do.

The interaction order refers to the fact that people use deceptions in organized, predictable, and routine ways to meet expectations. Consider how different organizational contexts socially structure the need to act deceptively in order to meet predictable expectations. Service workers, for example, are not always happy to see you or overjoyed to serve you, yet they usually manage to deliver a smile when their managers are watching them.

Goffman's approach stresses that a need to lie exists in the routine expectations of social settings rather than just in the moral failings of individuals. Drawing on this perspective, I focus on social interactions at work and attempt to distinguish the dramaturgical expectations in workplaces that routinely call for lies. What structural features and predictable social expectations in the workplace make it sensible for people to lie there? I develop the notion of a dramaturgical infrastructure of work to emphasize the deep connections between impression management and the administration of work.

Deference to a hierarchical superior, abiding by rules, implementing managerial strategies, and working effectively with co-workers are in part judged by how well someone appears to conform to idealized attributes. People must appear credible, especially when they are secretly feeling or doing something other than what they are supposed to be doing. To understand how deception helps people navigate their workplaces means analyzing how organizations operate along a dramaturgical infrastructure. Activities such as following the rules, deference to supervisors, and meeting production quotas all can be simulated rather than actually accomplished. In practice many behaviors within organizations may be routinely and usefully corruptible dramaturgical accomplishments.

Goffman wrote little analytically about the independent variables that explain particular choices of impression management behaviors. He wrote more about the different impression management outcomes themselves.[5] However, in *Asylums,* he did examine how organizational structure affects people's behaviors. He offers a model of secondary adjustments and the underlife of organizations:

> The official doctrine according to which an institution is run may be so little honored in practice, and a semi-official perspective may be so firmly and fully established, that we must analyze secondary adjustments relative to this authorized-but-not-quite-official system. (1961, 193)

He defines secondary adjustments as "any set of habitual arrangements by which a member of an organization employs unauthorized means, or obtains unauthorized ends, or both, to get around the organization's assumptions as to what he should do and get and hence what he should be"

(Goffman 1961, 189). Secondary adjustments require unauthorized means to sustain the pretense of meeting an organization's assumptions about what an employee should be doing and to fool an outsider's sense of what organizational activities are really taking place.

Goffman (1961) argues that secondary adjustments recognize a hidden infrastructure within organizations—administrative and social processes that individuals manipulate and convert to their own ends. Within this infrastructure, carrying out duplicitous acts requires maintaining secrecy. That some secondary adjustments are also in an organization's interests is a public and legal problem that must be cloaked. Secondary adjustments are responses whose purpose is to thwart rules governing behavior, whether for individuals or organizations. How secondary adjustments are functional *and* cloaked is a legitimate subject for analysis, particularly for those interested in white-collar crime. Organizations take their own steps to increase discipline, and to legitimate selective worker practices and unofficially tolerate others. The social control of secondary adjustments is complex. This strategic minuet between worker and manager captures the complex dance between the organizational member seeking autonomy and the manager seeking control (Goffman 1961).

Goffman also distinguished between an individual's activities and the organizational landscapes in which secondary adjustments take place:

> An individual's use of secondary adjustment is inevitably a social-psychological matter, affording him gratifications that he might not otherwise obtain. But precisely what someone gets out of it is not the point—what is crucial is understanding not what the practice brings the practitioner, but what the character of the social relations are that its acquisition and maintenance require. This constitutes a structural, as opposed to a consummatory or social-psychological point of view. (Goffman 1962, 200–201)

Goffman was urging us not to miss the forest for the trees. We should focus on the individual's strategies of deception but also on the social relations and contents that create and sustain them. An individual's secondary adjustments in combination with the secondary adjustments of other organizational members make up the underlife of an organization. Goffman (1961, 199) metaphorically compares the organizational underlife to the role that an underworld has in a city.

In this book, I use the concept of dramaturgical infrastructure to describe the relationship between organizational structure and deceptive impression management. The idea is to connect the deceptive individual dramaturgy of working life (such as fake deference to superiors or secret gossiping about clients) to routine administrative processes and outcomes within organizations. A predictable set of expected appearances and social relations constitutes an infrastructure that is directly linked to working productively.

People try to look good at work and to appear to embody desirable social characteristics if they do not authentically have them. The expectations that workers want to meet are set by the workplace. A person's gender, race, assigned work, and place in the hierarchy all influence how they are expected to act at work. A person's external resources, such as money, allies, and experience, also can affect what sort of performances a person gives. Does someone know enough to fake an air of sophistication or access to superiors? Everyone's desire to embody social characteristics that are prized in the workplace culture structures how people work. People will act deceptively to meet these demands in the workplace.

Researching impression management means more than just describing how people act. What results stem from the actions? Impression manage-· ment is a powerful determinant of workplace activities and structural outcomes, more so than people conventionally acknowledge. Deception can play a crucial role in such organizational outcomes as determining who gets ahead, how well someone sells a product, and whether people get caught breaking the rules.

Organizational Sociology and Deception

The powerful role deception plays in workplace culture is hidden in plain sight and my aim is to bring it to the foreground. Organizational theorists have focused on various types of social interaction in the workplace. These types include emotional labor (Hochschild 1983; Leidner 1993), informal relations (Dalton 1959; Hughes 1984; Roethlisberger and Dickson 1939; Roy 1952), negotiated orders (Strauss et al. 1963), and strategies of pursuing upward mobility (Jackall 1988). In all of these studies, deceptive behaviors turn out to be a significant aspect of how people behave at work. For example, people act deceptively to win managerial conflicts (Morrill 1995) and to appear to be team players (Jackall 1988). However none of these studies highlights deception as a general organizational behavior, even though deception features importantly in their data and conclusions.

Consider Hodson's comprehensive research study *Dignity at Work* (2001), which makes use of data from dozens of ethnographies. In offering theoretical arguments about workers' attempts to cope with mismanagement and abuse, Hodson presents multiple examples of workers acting deceptively in difficult working environments. Their acts include sabotage, goldbricking, and surreptitious gossiping. Yet *Dignity at Work* never mentions these acts as deceptive activities. Its index does not even have an entry for deception or lying. Deception's importance as a variable in organizational analysis always is implicit but rarely assessed.

Scholars of the workplace should have a greater appreciation for how deceptive impression management influences organizational administration and structural outcomes. However, beyond criminal cases, there are few analyses that center specifically on deception as a noncriminal organizational activity.[6] This lacuna exists despite the numerous examples in organizational ethnographies in which authors describe deceptive behaviors that occur informally as part of work.[7]

Organizational sociologists have three frameworks for considering workplace deception. One tradition, which I label here as neo-Marxist, describes deceptive workers as people who lie because they seek autonomy and relief from mismanagement and abusive work environments. Here workers resist the affronts of the workplace through engaging in deceptive acts ranging from intentionally failing to meet production quotas to sabotage. Closely twined to this tradition is focusing on managers who act deceptively, usually by engaging in gross violations of law, to oppress workers, exploit consumers, and raise profits.

A second tradition, the criminology-deviance perspective, which sometimes coincides with neo-Marxist views of employers, emphasizes how problematic organizations and workers employ deception to carry out crimes such as insider trading, price-fixing, accounting frauds, and other exploitative transgressions. This literature is also reflected in work by economic sociologists, sociologists of law, and scholars of business ethics and examines forms of social control that potentially prevent these acts.

A third tradition, associated with the ethnographies that address the organizational culture of workplaces, describes deceptive behaviors only in the context of whatever organizational domain (co-worker conflict, emotional labor, negotiations, upward mobility, and service work) or specific profession (such as police work or real estate) that the researcher is studying.

These approaches are valuable but also incomplete. They neglect the study of deception as a basic aspect of daily work. The neo-Marxist school of thought perceives deception only as a tactic of resistance or exploitation. The criminologists and business ethicists see deception only in illegal or unethical activities. The organizational culturists avoid the narrow lenses of the other traditions, but they fail to offer any general theoretical explanations for why deception exists in so many workplaces. In this book, alternatively, I argue that acting deceptively is a routine form of administration, culture, and management in the workplace. I hope to establish the analysis of deceptive behavior as a crucial component of the study of how people work.

The Dramaturgical Infrastructure

There is a strategic partnership between structural demands for particular appearances and the deceptive impression management that a worker orchestrates to produce credible performances in response to those demands. Four domains of the workplace where deceptions occur can be charted as part of the dramaturgical infrastructure (table 2). These domains are neither exhaustive nor mutually exclusive. They represent my initial conceptual and theoretical foray into mapping out significant aspects of workplace deception.

The first domain, "authentication and credibility practices," emphasizes a microsociological level of analysis and delineates how deceptive techniques produce authentic-seeming appearances. The idea here is to capture the social architecture of deception and learn what tactics people use to construct convincing deceptions. For example, how do private detectives create successful fake identities in order to conduct undercover investigations? How does someone goof off while maintaining an appearance of working? Other relevant forms of deception here are "normal lies" that a professional carries out in official work, emotional labor that is insincere but that must appear credible, and attempts to cover up shirking and other clandestine activities.

The second domain, "subterranean education and shadow organizations," refers to the organizational backstage. This domain is most directly connected to Goffman's ideas of secondary adjustments and the organizational underlife and to the "negotiated order" tradition in organizational ethnography. Understanding how people fight, instruct others, exchange information, pursue better jobs, and break rules to complete work are all things that happen on the job. They are all part of subterranean education and shadow organization at work.

Table 2. Four Deceptive Aspects of Work and Dramaturgical Infrastructure

Authentication and Credibility Practices	**Subterranean Education and Shadow**
Work-related emotional labor	**Organizations**
Normal lies	Use of undisclosed allies and networks
Concealing shirking and rule breaking	Unofficial training
	Learning the flaws of the land
	Use of covert conflict management strategies
	Informal and hidden administration of tasks
Ethical Disengagement	**Managing Identity and Role Conflicts**
Overcoming individual ethical inhibitions	Coping with hierarchical "social rights"
Organizational and individual counterethics	Handling clashing membership obligations
Disowning individual and organizational	Doing "groupthink"
responsibility for ethically problematic action	Positive idealization of self-identity
	Civil inattention and self-deception

In the third domain, "managing identity and role conflicts," the main theme is how people use deception to confront and manage the role conflicts that are inherent in organizations. One such conflict occurs when supervisors ignore rule breaking by co-workers who are their friends rather than accept their responsibility to enforce the organization's rules. Workers also may project a more public cultural and ideological commitment to an organization than they feel privately. Individual and workplace interests diverge when burdensome or impossible goals are set. People may respond by using deception to complete or avoid these tasks. Workers also may project a more positive picture of their skills, creating and maintaining an exaggerated self-presentation. Workers sometimes lack the correct answers to work problems, satisfied customers, or the capacity to fulfill demanding expectations—deceptions help them to pretend otherwise.

The last dimension, "ethical disengagement," addresses how people overcome moral inhibitions against deception and unethical actions. This category references the moral reasoning that surrounds organizational deception. A crucial workplace phenomenon is that individuals and organizations attempt to disown any moral responsibility for acting deceptively. I identify rationalizations that individuals and organizations use in their mutual and sometimes competing efforts to disown engaging in deceptive behaviors. In part, this section is inspired by frustration with philosophically based abstract entreaties that people should just avoid lying because lying is wrong. People are not so naïve. Examining why moral inhibitions fail in concrete circumstances and what social influences can counter ethics is a valuable alternative.

An Overview

I begin this book with a case study of private detectives and deception, discussing how deception is part of their routine and official work. Then I examine the organizational resources, training, and skills that are required to perform deceptions, focusing on the organizational resources and individual skills that private detectives use to construct believable lies. I address how private detectives justify using deceptive techniques.

I then introduce a case study of unofficial deceptive behaviors. I focus on workplace deception as a system of subterranean education, that is, the covert acquisition and distribution of sensitive information needed to perform one's job. I examine how these deceptions enable workers to gather information that will help them learn how to meet required workplace appearances. I identify how people act deceptively to access and distribute gossip, overcome barriers to autonomy, and accomplish their work in hidden ways. I identify how difficult production quotas, bureaucratic inefficiency, anxiety regarding upward mobility, solidarity with peers, the desire to shirk, and resistance to authority all help explain the ubiquity of these clandestine deceptions. I also argue that everyday lying reduces workplace tension by allowing people to work around grievances without having to take official, risky, and open actions. Some of the clandestine deceptions associated with role conflict and managing hierarchical authority include helping to conceal covert sabotage, goofing off, and false deference.

I then examine the everyday ethics of workplace deception and the practical need to disengage one's personal ethics from perpetrating acts of deception that range from the trivial (feigning friendship with a co-worker) to the grave (committing crimes). I argue that workplace deceptions require organizations and workers to use tactics of "disowning" responsibility in order to carry out any potentially discrediting behavior. Workers tend to cite a "game ethics" and competition in arguing that workplace environments compel a person to deception; organizations in turn tend to blame amoral individuals for any lying.

In the conclusion I summarize previous chapters and identify the contributions that a deeper scholarly integration of deception can make to existing theories of the workplace. My research design and data collection methods are described in the appendix.

I

PRIVATE DETECTIVES AND
DECEPTION AS OFFICIAL WORK

Meet Jake Harlow. Still ruggedly handsome in his late thirties, his face is lined with world-weary experience. Jake Harlow is about six feet tall and has dark hair and a five o'clock shadow. His tiny two-room office is located in a decrepit downtown building. He is always late on the rent. An empty whisky bottle is in the drawer, and Jake has slept another night in the office. A new client arrives, a stunningly beautiful woman in a fur coat who will lead Jake into yet another two-fisted adventure.

Meet Anthony Catelli (a pseudonym, as are all names from my interviews). A Vietnam veteran and retired police officer, Anthony now works as a private detective. He is sober, middle-aged, avoids fistfights with low-rent henchmen and spends most of his day on the phone talking to clients, contacts, and giving marching orders to field investigators. He cannot look at the soles of your shoes and make Sherlock Holmes–type pronouncements about how you spent last summer playing tennis on red clay courts in Sardinia. On the other hand, he can tell you where your employee John Smith lives, how he spends money, whether he uses drugs, and whether he is stealing from you.

I met only one or two real Jake Harlows during this research, though I've seen plenty of them on TV and can read about them in countless mystery novels. I met many more Anthony (and Antonia) Catellis, but I have seen hardly any of them in the media. Real private detectives may be similar to their fictional counterparts in possessing investigative acumen and in exploring the dark side of human behavior. However, finding a noncustodial parent's location, peeing in an empty soda can to avoid leaving a surveillance, and checking whether warehouse workers are taking five-fingered discounts represent the nonglamorous routine work that real private detectives do. In this chapter I examine actual private detective work to explain why private detectives use deceptions.

What Private Detectives Do

Clients hire private detectives to uncover whether spouses are cheating on them, insured people are committing fraud, or employees are spying or stealing at work. They also hire them to scrutinize individuals with whom a client is contemplating starting a serious partnership. Examples include evaluating a romantic suitor's veracity, verifying a prospective employee's background, and certifying whether businesses and individuals that are seeking investments are portraying their finances honestly. People hire private detectives to locate missing children, bail jumpers, and stolen assets. They also serve subpoenas on uncooperative defendants and witnesses and investigate accidents.

Private detective work is adversarial because it requires conducting what Goffman (1974) calls "vital tests"—secret investigations of a person's loyalty and character. Targets of investigation who have acted inappropriately often conceal their transgressions and lie if they are confronted with accusations. Given this context, a private detective must expose a target's true activities against his or her will. Private detective work illustrates what I reference more generally as an *adversarial profession*, a class of jobs that work against and encounter resistance from "involuntary" targets of their labors. Other adversarial professions include auditors, collection agents, insurance investigators, investigative journalists, lawyers, police officers, and Equal Employment Opportunity Commission (EEOC) testers. Out of necessity, their work requires deception.

As background, social scientists have suggested that the importance of evaluating trustworthiness in modern societies has grown, leading to an increased use of private sector agents (Geddes 1989; Ghezzi 1983; Reichman 1987; Shapiro 1987a, 1987b). Private detectives are only one example of trust-examining entrepreneurs in the private sector that sell investigative skills as commodities to those organizations or individuals that can afford them (Schwartz 1968). The current security climate in the world is also increasing their numbers.

A private detective's most important challenge is to access *dirty data*—information "that is kept secret and whose revelation would be discrediting or costly in terms of various types of sanctioning (Marx 1990, 79)."[1] Dirty data occur in two forms: *deception cues*, which are "behaviors that reveal a lie" (Ekman 1985, 39), and *leakages,* which occur "when a liar mistakenly reveals the truth obscured by a lie" (Ekman 1985, 39). As qualified here, deception cues are indicators that lies exist, and leakages are signs exposing the secret information that lies attempt to hide. For example: Mr. Jones tells his wife that he has to work late at the office. A deception cue that exposes this lie is that repeated nighttime calls to his office go unanswered. A leakage indicator that uncovers the secret behind the lie is watching Mr. Jones enter a hotel room at night with someone other than his wife.

Private detectives have three general methodological approaches that they use to discover deception cues and leakages. The first methodology, *enactment*, involves using deceptive techniques to produce observable performances of dirty data to catch targets "in the act." Enactment includes documenting illicit liaisons and workplace theft and may require covert-participant observation such as undercover operations and unobtrusive surveillance. The second methodology is *reconstructing*, in which investigators use third parties to reconstruct past and present dirty data, addressing questions such as where stolen money or missing persons are. Reconstructing techniques include pretext interviews, confidential sources, paper records, and speaking with neighbors. The third approach is *surfacing*, in which private detectives gather evidence about whether dirty data exist. Surfacing goals include establishing whether a prospective employee's claims check out or whether an interrogation reveals that some workers are part of a theft ring. Private detectives may use confidential sources, pretexts, paper records, physical evidence (trash), "neighboring," and reactive surveillance during those fishing expeditions.[2]

The Three Investigative Approaches and Deceptive Techniques

Enactment

Enactment methods bring dirty data performances out into the open so that private detectives can observe and document them. *Unobtrusive* and *intervening* covert surveillance are the primary strategies for doing so. In unobtrusive surveillance, targets are unaware of being watched.

Conducting unobtrusive surveillance means recording events and activities as they occur, keeping the observer's presence hidden so that targets do not alter their actual behaviors. The goal is to record a person's naturally occurring behaviors without their knowledge. As one private detective explained: "We'll do surveillance work on an individual to see where he goes, who he is associating with, when he goes, what time he goes, and even to the point of videotaping; we'll run that type of thing, that kind of operation."[3] The aim is to examine normal routines and see whether people are doing what they are supposed to be doing (Harrison 1991; Fallis and Greenberg 1989; Rapp 1986).

Intervening covert surveillance requires both pretexts and undercover operations. A pretext is a fake identity or situation that a private detective concocts to acquire information and disguise who seeks that information and why. Examples range from pretending to be students conducting door-to-door surveys, called the "Trojan student" by Douglas (1976), to impersonating inspectors to enter stores. Private detectives manipulate familiar social situations to trick targets into enacting dirty data visibly. One operative, who posed as a customer at a grocery store, said:

> I had been working for them already, spot checking their employees, just going out and testing the integrity of their cash handlers. We'd go in and drop three dollars on the counter for a pack of cigarettes and walk away and another one of my agents would be standing there and seeing what occurred with the money.

An undercover operation involves the long-term maintenance of a pretext, such as posing as "just another co-worker" for weeks to observe employees surreptitiously.

Enactment strategies allow private detectives to observe dirty data directly. Electronic, photographic, and videotaped documentation enhance the evidentiary quality of what surveillance yields.[4]

Many targets assume that they can engage in incriminating activities safely because no one is checking up on them. Consider this surveillance:

> He was delivering items and the supervisor felt that he was stealing time from the company and that he was lying and confronted the employee. The employee got very hostile and the supervisor asked what we could do. So we did surveillance on him. When he was supposed to be working, he was playing basketball and doing other things. He was so darn confident; I mean he did anything he wanted. When we confronted him about his

work, he denied everything. He almost dropped when we showed him the pictures, and then what could he say. He could not believe this actually happened to him.

Private detectives also create situations in which targets believe that they can get away with discrediting actions without notice:

> He had a bad back, he couldn't work, he was collecting worker's comp and so forth and this company is paying him out money. They got a lead some-how that says this guy left to play volleyball. He was in a volleyball tour-nament. We found out where he was. We called his home on the pretense of saying, "We're with this certain shoe company." We're talking about the shoe sizes of his family. We found out the shoe size he wore. We went to the location of where he was suspected to be playing volleyball. The in-vestigator says, "I'm with this sport magazine. Do you mind if I take some pictures of you for these shoes?" We went to the vehicle and got the shoes. This guy's up there. We got him on videotape, he's hitting the ball, body slamming them, and we got him all on tape. When it's time to go to court, he comes in with his neck brace and his little walker and everything, and then he sees us in there and the prosecutor says, "We're just going to show you a tape," and he just got up and left when he knew he was caught.

Though private detectives and targets do not usually know one an-other, to avoid suspicion investigators take precautions to camouflage unobtrusive surveillance. They use disguises, tracking technology, and elaborate two- or three-person teams to conduct surveillance. Intervening covert surveillance is more difficult to conduct because in those situations private detectives construct, perform, and maintain false identities for a long duration in front of the target. Performing poorly in those situations threatens acquiring accurate information and is dangerous. I present the elaborate strategies that private detectives use to create convincing false identities and other deceptions in the next chapter.

Private detectives also operate many pretexts over the Internet and the phone. These deceptive pretexts do not need to be performed in physi-cal proximity to their targets. Some dirty data are easily available over the phone. Private detectives claim that people are very susceptible to phone pretexts:

> People are not careful enough about the information they give out. Sur-veys are horrible, telephone surveys. I can get your name, Social Security

number, income, just about anything from a survey on the phone and that is horrible, that is absolutely horrible.

Any of these items can identify deception if they reveal evidence that is counter to a target's claims.

Reconstructing

While enactment strategies prioritize catching people in the act, the investigative methodology of reconstruction asks "what happened?" Reconstruction techniques include physical evidence (trash), paper records, confidential sources, and "neighboring." Reconstructing strategies are effective because they try to limit a target's control over revealing personal, hidden information. Asking targets directly gives the targets control over whether to disclose information. Reconstruction strategies overcome this obstacle by accessing information through third parties. Reconstructing methods also use deception to camouflage that someone is trying to learn secrets.

Trash and crime and accident scene materials are all physical evidence that private detectives can use to reconstruct dirty data.[5] Trash is a particularly common form of physical evidence. As one private detective says, "Trash talks" (Fallis and Greenberg 1989, 100). Acquiring trash from a residence or business is called garbology. Roach clips, rolling papers, love letters, scribbles, client lists, empty drug containers, postmarks, birthday cards, canceled checks, bills, telephone records, and credit reports are all deception and leakage cues that are available in trash.

Credit card bills, for example, reveal spending patterns and location. Telephone records from a target's relatives can pinpoint a bail jumper's location. Consider how this private detective uses trash to reconstruct an embezzler's activities:

> We had an embezzler and we were trying to find out where the money might have gone. We'd pick up the garbage at four in the morning when the garbagemen came at five. They never had any garbage there. We would take it and dump it out on a concrete slab and go through it with rubber gloves, find documents, find bank account statements, find purchase orders and receipts, and we were able to put together a case to show that a woman had embezzled hundreds of thousands of dollars from her employer, and we also found out where some of the money was and what it had gone for. We recovered about thirteen fur coats, several cars, a lot of jewelry. A lot of the money we never found. But we did all that by going through the garbage.

Paper measures include archival data, official records, and personal items such as notes and diaries. An important caveat exists that people and organizations may falsify paper records to cloak secrets and throw people off the trail, which makes triangulating and using multiple methods to check out potential deceptions very important.

Private detectives can access records through trash, confidential sources, and legal searches. The Internet is a great boon in those searches. The Internet's anonymity also obscures inquiries. Trash and confidential sources provide information that written records cannot: such as physical evidence (roach clips or sexual materials in trash) and verbal corroboration concerning an individual's activities (for example, that person A was the leader of the theft ring).

Confidential sources often provide paper records and verbal information, which private detectives use to reconstruct dirty data, as well as deception or leakage cues that cannot be attained publicly. One informant defined confidential sources as

> anybody that has access to records that you wouldn't normally get. That's who good sources are. I had a guy who worked for the police department, who worked the computers. I could find out information. . . . I even had a guy in [a federal agency] who could find lots of information. I could get your income taxes for the last two years. It's all source information.

Private detectives also use confidential sources to learn about individual activities, social subcultures, and a range of informal information:

> Hell, I probably use them more as a sounding board than for anything else. I mean, I know a bookie. I've worked several cases where the guy was a gambler and either committed suicide or was killed. Well, I go talk to the bookie. What's the situation? How much debt does somebody have to get in before people really start leaning in on him? How do you gamble? I don't know anything about it. I go talk to the expert on it.

Confidential sources can range from bartenders to police officers to travel agents. Private detectives seek anyone with potentially useful information for reconstructing dirty data:

> I meet somebody and my first impression isn't "Gee, what's this guy going to do for me," but I'm always thinking that if I get a case in, say, the

meat industry, who do I know that's a butcher . . . or that's an architect; who do I know that's a doctor, who do I know that's an actor, who do I know that might be able to help me?

Confidential sources may be as deceptive as targets. Private detectives will check out third party claims whenever possible, verifying them with appropriate records or individuals. Private detectives know that they could be fooled if they rely exclusively on confidential sources who might lie for their own reasons.

Private detectives have a curious moral position in caring about validity. For researchers, validity and reliability are ethical and scientific concerns that establish research as professionally legitimate. Alternatively, issues of ethics, liability, and profit shape a private detective's concern for acquiring accurate information. Because many investigations do not end up in court, there are commercial incentives for unethical private detectives to emphasize the ambiguity of evidence to justify billing for additional investigators and work hours. Of course, many private detectives strive to communicate accurate and reliable information, both out of a sense of personal and professional ethics and to avoid potential lawsuits.

Accurate reconstruction of dirty data depends on an investigator's ability to interpret data correctly, particularly the accuracy of third parties regarding an investigated matter. A different problem occurs when observers are too inexperienced to assess information correctly. Though private detectives may qualify reconstruction statements from confidential sources as opinions, they still proffer them to clients, despite oft-stated cynicism about how sharp third parties really are. According to one private detective: "People . . . don't really study things. If you were to ask an individual to describe to you, you know, look out the window for ten minutes and describe to you what they've seen. You'd be surprised how much they miss." Consequently, investigators are often cautious about the truthfulness of those who supply them with information as the same private detective explains:

> The trick is to find the right neighbor. Every neighborhood has got the person who can't stand you and will tell outrageous lies about you just to try and get you burned. Every neighborhood has the productive neighbor who likes you and won't divulge any information or will slant it in the opposite direction, if they are talking. And every neighborhood, I assure you, has that one busybody who knows everything that's going on.

Surfacing

Surfacing strategies make use of paper records, confidential sources, pretext interviewing, physical evidence, neighboring, and unobtrusive or reactive surveillance. In surfacing efforts, private detectives scrutinize sources of information to check whether any hints of troubling behavior exist. In reconstructing efforts, private detectives try to learn what actually happened in a case. Private detectives use surfacing investigations as a fishing expedition when clients only suspect trouble. They attempt to assess whether dirty data exists, usually as a precaution.

A typical surfacing job involves checking out potential employees. To do so, private detectives triangulate multiple sources of information to see if any deception cues emerge:

> A lot of big companies are checking people's backgrounds to make sure they're hiring good quality people. So we check their criminal record, their driving record, and so forth to make sure that our client gets the best possible respectable employee. If they're good people, we'll tell them, "OK, this person has a clean criminal history; he has a clean credit history; he has a good driving history." There are neighborhood checks. We'll go out and ask some neighbors, "How's your neighbor? Has he ever been involved with the police? Do you know if he's involved with drinking, drugs, or whatever?"

To surface dirty data requires being able to recognize deception cues properly, as demonstrated below in a case in which investigators scrutinized credit reports:

> A credit report on an individual is pretty much what he's been doing with his life. For instance, if you have somebody that has a lot of credit cards and has a lot of money built up on credit cards, there are people like this, they take one credit card, pay off another credit card, and build up another—this kind of shows you that this person is not exactly stable. As to what he does for a living, pretty much you know that because of who you're dealing with, that'll tell you that he's living a little out of his means. If he's living out of his means that would tend to raise flags that maybe he is doing something that he shouldn't be doing. What you'll do is to see what their credit rating looks like. Why is an individual who, let's say is making sixty to sixty-five thousand dollars a year living in a half-million dollar home with no mortgage and no car payments? Well, he's paying all cash. Well, where's he getting the cash? He's getting it from somewhere. And it could give you an indication that maybe he is taking a kickback from an individual.

Surfacing strategies also access cues to deception through reactive surveillance. Reactive surveillance occurs when private detectives inspect subjects' nonverbal and verbal responses for deception cues—for revealing "expressions given off" (Goffman 1959). Another form of reactive surveillance, "hard shadowing," also takes place in personal protection and private security work. "Hard shadowing" refers to observing a target noticeably so that he or she is aware of being watched. The purpose of hard shadowing is to deter and intimidate targets. In some interrogation and interview settings, private detectives manipulate reactivity. They ask provocative questions to see whether subjects respond with telltale nonverbal and verbal signals. Nonverbal deception cues include covering of eyes, mouth, or ears at particular points; looking down; restless feet or hands; sweating; heavy breathing; and changes in facial color.

As one private detective explained:

> You can find out from body language. It gives you a good indication. Now if the person doesn't want to admit, you can tell he's lying, but you don't know what he's lying about. He may be just lying about a particular obsession and he sits there and says, "No, no, no." He's going to be hostile towards you; the way he's sitting is hostile toward you. Maybe he's put something in front of you. Maybe his arms are crossed. Maybe his hand's in front of his mouth all the time.

Looking for nonverbal cues indicating deceit coincides with attempts to solicit confessions. Clearly, people who are being interrogated may be motivated to offer false answers. Some verbal deception cues include evasive statements, denials of unvoiced accusations, querying about what would hypothetically happen to the person found guilty, changes in pitch, and impossible credibility circumstances.

Two common techniques are the memory test, in which the interviewee is asked to recall complex verifications of past behaviors, and the "phased assertion" (Douglas 1976), in which interviewers try to get targets to talk by pretending to know more than they actually do.[6] The first quote illustrates the memory test approach; the second, a nonverbal phased assertion approach:

> "Did you happen to know where that Walkman was? John Smith owns a Walkman, and . . . you didn't see it, huh? What were you doing there anyway?"
> "Going to the bathroom."

"Going to the bathroom, huh? It's funny because someone saw you stop by the desk. Oh, you were reading the paper? Which paper was that?"

I do it all the time, trying to have a conversation with the person and try to see the evidence he has at the same time. Does not make you guilty, but there's an inconsistency and you go on and on and on.

And:

You can sit there with a folder in front of them and just have a blank folder with blank papers. And they're looking at it, and you know the questions you're going to ask them, and they think you have all kinds of things on them. You can have videotape sitting there. Anything that could make them tell the truth.

Surfacing methods expose data that varies in terms of reliability. Some third parties, such as colleges, keep good records, so people who lie about completing their degrees, for example, are easily identified. But many third party sources are undependable for reasons ranging from poor record keeping to bias. Also, detectives can make errors interpreting subjects' verbal and nonverbal behaviors. The evidence that surfacing gathers is thus taken as leads, as pieces of information useful for directing investigations by suggesting what steps to take next (Sanders 1977). Private detectives can evaluate surfaced dirty data further by moving to enacting or reconstructing approaches.

Deceptive Role-Playing in Investigative Methods

Private detectives' deceptive role-playing generally takes two generic forms: pretexts and undercover operations. Pretexts are short-term fake identities that private detectives fabricate to camouflage themselves when they serve subpoenas or hide ongoing investigations. Investigators might disguise that they are watching a house by using vans marked with innocuous titles such as "ACME Repair" on the side. Someone might present herself as delivering a pizza in order to serve a subpoena to an uncooperative person. The goal is to fake a real situation convincingly enough for investigators to gain access to targets. In undercover operations, investigators may assume a character for a long time in order to observe targets secretly.

In *Strategic Interaction*, Goffman (1969) argues that deceptions between people involve five moves. The first move is unwitting moves, which actors make without any concern for fostering a particular impression in an observer's mind. The second are naïve moves, which occur when observers feel that a subject's actions are occurring naturally and are not responses to being watched. The last three moves are sets of control moves that individuals use to create specific impressions for observers, for example, uncovering, covering, and counter-uncovering moves. In the expression games that private detectives and their targets play, private detectives seek to construct credible identities that expose covering moves by targets while avoiding the target's counter-uncovering moves.

Verbal Pretexts

Private detectives use many deceptions that are solely verbal. Verbal pretexts may be delivered by phone: "I told the hotel manager that I was the individual who left and I needed a copy of my phone records for business purposes. The manager faxed me the phone records from the room." There is no physical deception incorporating visible props or movements. In verbal pretexts, private detectives simply tell a story to justify an information request. Private detectives use verbal pretexts to access financial records, personal information, and to examine a target's daily routine.

A private detective may pose as the person being investigated to a third party to elicit privileged information; or a private detective may pretend to be an innocuous third party who is an entitled or plausible recipient of the desired information. Common cover stories include the employer checking on a reference, the company checking a billing error, the businessperson verifying whether a check will clear, the genealogical service, the survey, the call from school, the contest organizer or radio station, *Who's Who*, the old college buddy, the old army friend, the customer disputing the telephone bill, the deliveryman, and the reporter.

The Facade Pretext

Private detectives use facade pretexts to camouflage surveillance activities. There are no verbal exchanges between investigators and targets. These pretexts incorporate physical props to provide effective simulations of everyday reality. Facade pretexts cloak surveillance by structuring a front stage that looks no different from what targets ordinarily see:

You might want to look like you're doing something on the street, although that's difficult if it's a suburb, because most people know what utilities are around. But I've used . . . different coats. You'll have your jacket on and you'll be around the house or the area with a jacket and you might, you know, leave an hour later with a trench coat, and believe it or not people think it's a different person.

Enacting these pretexts can involve a complex use of physical props:

> You can have one-man, two-man, three-man surveillance with their walkie-talkies, and they're driving and they'll be on one side of the street or they'll be in a different area. They'll make the turn and you could just do a leapfrog effect, dressing up, changing your clothes, changing your shirts, using fake mustaches, wigs, and so forth. Whatever you can do to change your identity when you're following somebody, because if they see you and see you again. . . . they're going to look in the mirror and see a guy with blonde hair in a blue car and then they look again and see a lady with red hair in a car.

Facade props are diverse. They range from uniforms to bird-watching equipment to vans with names of nonexistent companies. Private detectives also sometimes impersonate down-on-their-luck trash scavengers. Investigators use facade-only surveillance to collect garbage, in search of personal information and/or corporate secrets.

Facade pretexts also occur during personal protection (bodyguard) work. The normal stereotype of a bodyguard is of a gigantic, visibly muscled man who intimidates through his sheer size. This "hulking monster" image is omnipresent in the six foot ten behemoths seen on television protecting celebrities. However, these hulks are not the same as the bodyguards who protect corporate executives. When corporate executives hire personal protection specialists, they are more likely to hire a "sleeper" bodyguard. Sleepers are of average height and weight. They may be martial arts and firearms specialists, have emergency medical technician training, and be jacks-of-all-trades. Six foot ten bodyguards would stand out at corporate meetings and functions, diminishing their effectiveness. A chief executive officer's bodyguard, who was no taller than five foot nine, told me: "I can be more effective exactly because you will never notice me." The term "sleepers" is useful generally for portraying the advantages of private detectives' facade pretexts. There are also sleeper advantages for women, who in a sexist society are not perceived as investigative threats.

Interactive Pretexts and Undercover Operations

Short-term pretexts are one shot only and involve both physical and verbal performances. Private detectives perform them quickly. They reflect the game analytic properties that Harold Garfinkel sees as implicit in successful passing. These conditions are that "play" occurs in an encapsulated episode, that successes and failures can be identified clearly, and that there are common expectations in the game that govern acceptable performances (Garfinkel 1967, 140).

Consider the short-term pretext that one private detective uses to serve subpoenas:

> Well, one of the easiest things with women is to go out and buy a bouquet of flowers and knock on the door and say flowers for so-and-so, I need her to sign. They sign for it, and we say, "Well, you know, sorry, this isn't for you. This [subpoena] is for you," and walk away. . . . The delivery person route.

In this pretext the rules are clear and common knowledge. Delivery persons come to doors and ask for signatures, and the "rule" is normally that customers provide those signatures. The situation is encapsulated by getting targets to open the door and interact until the agent can hand them the subpoena and win the game. Success is incontrovertible—either the target is served or not.

Goffman's term "penetration" describes what long-term undercover operatives do. In his terms, an undercover operative is "an agent who is disloyal to a team that exploits legitimate (as opposed to clandestine) access to social settings in which the teams' strategic or dark secrets are unguarded or their discrediting conduct is observable" (Goffman 1974, 170). Their goal is to gain a position from which they can gather desirable information in secret.

Deceptive Exercises with Teammates

Pretexts and undercover operations differ in whether they are performed by teams or single participants. Team pretexts and undercover operations usually involve teams of performing actors, including backstage nonperforming teammates. The first type of team pretext, of performing actors, is common. Agencies use these teams for backup and to construct distractions: "For us to go into a building to serve a guy a subpoena is like planning an armored car robbery. I had one guy fall on the ground and the guard helps him and then an accomplice goes up the elevator."

Other examples of performance teams are sham romantic couples and repair crews. Team performers can be witting or unwitting. Witting team members are clients' paid informants, public law enforcement agents, and other investigators. Unwitting team members are people who are tricked into shoring up the credibility of an investigator's identity. For example:

> At a party if I know you have a friend and I see him talking to you, I may wander over and introduce myself. I know he's going to wander over to you, you're going to wander over here. Then he introduces me. You have no reason to believe I just met the person. He doesn't know anything about me, so chances are you're going to believe him and you're not going to be suspicious of me. My credibility has been established.

The second type of team, made up of solo performers and nonperforming backstage teammates, refers to team members who follow up on the leads that performers supply but who do not perform alongside them:

> We usually use undercover information as leads. The person works undercover and he finds something out. We'll usually try to cut that person out without ever identifying him. He knows the guy steals some things and he usually does it on Friday nights and takes it out to his car. We'll go stake out the car and photograph it or something like that. He knows that guys are out there smoking dope on lunch breaks. Maybe we'll get a van and photograph. We'll just use what he gives us as information. We'll try never to expose the undercover incident.

Undercover agents collect information for other investigators to follow up on. Agencies want to avoid undercover agents doing too much by themselves, which may endanger the investigation. Having separate agents do additional investigative work lessens the risks of discovery.

The third team is composed of performers and organization-level team members. The term "organizational team members" usually refers to the private detective agency and the company hiring the operative. Organization team members, such as the detective agency, verify phony addresses and claims of previous employment. They backstop verification efforts outside the immediate interaction.

Secrets and Performance Vulnerabilities

Private detectives' investigative techniques involve identifying and exploiting performance vulnerabilities. Performance vulnerabilities refer to the actions that targets take that provide opportunities for secrets to be exposed. Some examples of performance vulnerabilities include inevitable byproducts of dirty data activity (drug paraphernalia, mandatory paperwork such as income tax returns), gullibility (when a victim accepts claims at face value), carelessness (telling co-workers or relatives about affairs, being visibly intoxicated), and conscious choice (going to an observable dirty data activity site, falling for a ruse).

Private detectives' strategies integrate a practical knowledge of where to find these performance vulnerabilities in society (see table 3 for a list of places, persons, and things that private detectives use to access dirty data). There are important reasons to reflect on these sources. First, these potential secret repositories identify ways to discover lies at work, and they provide dirty data seekers with potential research sites. Second, knowing where to find dirty data is also a starting point for an in-depth understanding of dirty data as a distinct subject rather than solely as a corollary of other interests. A cursory examination of this table's information shows that private detectives investigate dirty data across complex webs of social affiliations. Dirty data are stored across varying intimacy levels and differ in having voluntary and involuntarily disclosed dimensions. Granovetter (1973) argues that weak social ties create bridges between acquaintances through which people can exchange useful information. Frequency of contact does not reveal how strongly or weakly tied people are. People may have close relations or more formal ones: What kinds of information are available? What is the social landscape or interpersonal networks in which different kinds of secrets reside?

Dirty data exist in predictable patterns. Some dirty data are hidden from familiars but not from outsiders. A co-worker may know about a target's drug use, gambling, or repeated visits to strip clubs long before family members do. Private detectives use the listed repositories to acquire different types of dirty data. They employ more than one source of information to avoid deceptive targets and because the more information gathering attempts, the higher their fees.

Private detectives think strategically about how to mine social relationships. They gather information from co-workers, friends, and bureaucratic entities rather than just from the subjects themselves. In this way, private

Table 3. Private Detectives' Secret Repositories*

Adviser	Background	Financial	Neighborhood	Official
Accountants	Alumni associations	Banks	Apartment managers	Court officers
Bankers	Children's schools	Credit bureaus	Bartenders	District attorneys
Clergy	Clubs	Credit cards	Doormen	FBI
Dentists	Competitors	Creditors	Friends	Fire department
Doctors	Correspondence schools	Debtors	Gardeners	Hospitals
Lawyers	Coworkers	Department stores	Hangouts	Mental hospitals
Professors/teachers	Current employer	Finance companies	Hotel clerks	Morgue/coroners
Realtors	Family	Oil companies	Janitors	Parole officers
Stock brokers	Former employer	Pawn shops	Landlords	Police
Veterinarians	Friends	Telephone	Maids	Public defenders
	Hobby clubs	Utilities	Markets	Welfare/social workers
	Magazines		Mechanics	Workers in public records
	Neighbors		Neighbors	
	Organizations		Paperboys	
	Past residences		Parking lot	
	Religious affiliation		Rent collectors	
	Schools		Restaurants	
	Union membership			

Records

Adoptions	County auditors	FAA	Misdemeanors	Probate
Better Business Bureaus	County courts	Federal information centers	Ministries	Property
Birth certificates	Credit bureaus	Federal records	Motor Vehicle	Register of deeds
Business licenses	Criminal	Felonies	National crime information centers	Registrar of voters
Chambers of commerce	Crisscross directories	Health department	Pensions	Sanitation department
City directories	Death	Juvenile records	Police records	Small claims court
Civil litigation	Divorces	Libraries	P.O. boxes	State controllers
Corrections	Department of Professional Regulation	Marriage applications	Post office forwarding	State courts
		Marriage licenses		Tax assessors

Table 3.

Records cont.	Licenses/Permits	Relatives/Friends	Travel	Utilities
Title insurance companies	Animal	Aunts/uncles	Airlines	Cable
Unemployment	Fishing	Boyfriend/girlfriend	Bus companies	Electricity
U.S. district courts	Guns	Brothers/sisters	Car rental agencies	Gas
U.S. postal inspectors	Hunting	Children	Hotels	Internet
Utilities	Machinery	Coworkers	Movers	Telephone
Welfare department	Vehicles	Fathers/mothers	Railroad Express companies	Water
		Step-parents	Ship companies	
		Friends		
		Grandparents		

* Some secret repositories overlap. Also, some sources cannot be legally accessed in some circumstances, although they can be obtained. This table is compiled from both work forms and informant responses.

detectives limit the amount of control that a subject has over the reach of her or his impression management.

Private detectives understand that acquaintances can know more dirty data than they choose to reveal. They also know that family members may be oblivious to another's dirty data, since it may be hidden to preserve the relationship. They know that neighbors may confirm suspicions of drinking that relatives will deny and that birth certificates can reveal undisclosed adoptions. There are abundant variations of unwitting and deliberate dirty data informants, from people unknowingly maneuvered into disclosing a neighbor's day work to Department of Motor Vehicles employees who routinely fulfill a third party's information requests. As one private detective noted:

> There's always a thread somewhere. The only time that there isn't is when someone methodically goes back and removes the traces so that they cannot be found. You can be found by any document. There are many clues—alumni, high school records, where they worked, friends, relatives. From any one of these areas you can get something, a date of birth, a Social Security number, and you can tie in those important clues to other clues. You look for every little thread.

To access these threads requires learning how to interpret important information. For example, private detectives must often obtain clues that reveal whether a prospective employee has a troubled past. This information is not accessed easily by asking the employees directly, but it is available institutionally in a "code":

> DETECTIVE: We'll either find out who their old supervisor was, talk to some of their other employees, talk to their supervisor, find out. . . . Personnel [doesn't] want to say that he was terminated because of this. You ask the question, "Is he eligible for rehire?" If they say no, you know he did something wrong. If they say yes, you know he's OK.
>
> D. S.: So there are codes like that, "eligible for rehire"?
>
> DETECTIVE: Right. If you talk to their supervisor, they're going to tell you information too. So again you have to analyze that and find out what's true and what's not true.

Private detectives use enacting, reconstructing, and surfacing efforts to locate dirty data. To do so, they engage in deceptive acts such as hidden surveillance, faked identities, bluffed knowledge, and surreptitious acquisition of documentary evidence. These deceptions are legal and are crucial to the routine work of private detectives as trust-examining entrepreneurs. A client's legitimate need to find out whether associates are breaching trust creates the market for deceptive techniques as a commodity. Having provided a broad overview of private detectives' investigative methodology, my analysis now shifts to how private detectives organize and successfully perform these work-related deceptions. How do they plan, develop, and implement believable deceptions?

2

BUILDING BELIEVABLE LIES

Private detectives lie to acquire information and to hide investigations. They use covert surveillance and perform long-term undercover operations that require deceptive role-playing. If their performances are not believable, their work fails, which raises the question: How do private detectives produce successful lies and pass muster as convincing performers? They must be good actors, develop fake credentials to support their role-playing, and be able to manage any challenges to their fictions. In this chapter I explore how they do so and what organizational resources help make their work-related deceptions more believable.

To examine how private detectives orchestrate their authenticity means learning more about what I call the social architecture of deception.[1] Few research studies have examined how people involved in noncriminal occupations consciously develop and choreograph believable lies. Fundamental sociological issues are inherent in thinking about how people make lies more believable. Goffman and Garfinkel have laid out the most concrete theoretical groundwork in sociology for describing how people pass themselves off as authentic in various social roles.

In "passing," deceivers manipulate taken-for-granted background expectations that people use to judge the everyday activities around them (Garfinkel 1967). According to Goffman (1963, 88) deceivers are "alive to aspects of social situations that other people treat as uncalculated and unattended." Mafiosi, drug users, or prostitutes behave naturally in their identities. Successful undercover operatives, to pass in their fictional roles convincingly, must learn how to detach and manipulate that same sense of authenticity that those real people have. They must effectively feign the experiences and behaviors that authentically characterize those identities and be skilled at acting. They must know what to wear, how to interact with others, what words go with what inflections, all of which are taken-for-granted aspects of specific types of people.

People follow specific steps to develop and perform convincing deceptions in their undercover identities and pretexts. I refer to steps in constructing believable lies as *authentication practices*.[2] Private detectives manipulate physical appearances, props, and normal expectations for behaviors to construct authentication practices. Private detective agencies support authentication practices by offering rehearsal and training venues, by matching employees and demographic characteristics that appear necessary to perform fake identities legitimately, by supplying operatives with appropriate props, and by backstopping agents' false biographical claims of prior social ties and employment.

Authentication practices must survive challenges. Authentication practices are evaluated in three different qualitative contexts that constitute a continuum of verification. First, there is a *performance-in-scene* level that occurs during interactions between an audience and a deceiver. Here agents try to perform a fake identity convincingly in front of someone so as not to give the ruse away. For example, does his or her southern accent sound authentic? The second level of verification is a *historical-contextual* one, in which detectives must support any claims that they have made about themselves that extend outside the immediate scene. For example, if the detective says that he or she lives in a trailer park, the agency must rent a trailer there to make that claim appear true, since it can be scrutinized. The third level is an *audience-exploitative* one, in which private detectives identify and exploit vulnerable characteristics in audiences to deter them from challenging a lie.

Deliberative and planned lies require control of social indicators that audiences use to decide whether a person or situation is authentic. Authentication practices manipulate these indicators, shedding light on how people can fool others and violate their trust. The deceptive interplay of private detectives and their targets reveal how "normal appearances" are staged and why audiences are so susceptible to fake performances.

Rehearsal and Practice

Rehearsing a performance in advance is important for appearing authentic (Jacobs 1992a). A private detective notes in agreement:

> Undercover operatives are like little actors and actresses. They have to know the job. If it's an executive position or a forklift they have to know what they're supposed to be doing. They have to have training for the forklift. We have a lot of college-educated operatives. We need to train them to make sure that the language they use is not college, that they are not using large words. Background is degraded. They have to know the requirements for their jobs. Basically, they have to know their roles and practice their roles.

People want to appear natural in their performances, so rehearsing provides an initial experiential basis for feeling comfortable in an undercover identity. In addition to refining any specific skills that an upcoming performance requires, rehearsing is also important for mastering the "character" of a given role, as one detective explained:

> We try to train them to adopt a certain attitude that will fit in with most of the people. When you look at the average employee thief or you look at the average employee drug dealer, it's not all that evil of a person. He's pretty much of a normal person, a little bit on the devious side. All those people display certain kinds of traits. They're goof-offs, they're just like people you knew growing up, that you went to school with. The kids that were always getting in trouble, the kids that would smart off their teacher. They're the same types. They're the ones that are smarting off their boss that don't give a damn. They'll take something that belongs to the company, drop it on the floor and kick it because they don't care if they break it . . . so our people cop that type of attitude, and then they just fit right in. It's not that hard.

In addition to rehearsing, there are instructional materials for learning how to perform deceptions more successfully. Some agencies use law enforcement manuals and videos to train investigators. Agencies also set up opportunities for agents to practice more technical aspects of performances in advance. For example: "On a Saturday or Sunday, I'll call our contact and say, 'I got five people. I need them trained on the forklift.' We go over there, they stay there two or three hours, learn how to operate the forklift and so forth." Private detective agencies also hire employees who have previous undercover work experience; thus they already come "rehearsed."

Third-Party Verification

An individual has a biography that exists outside of the immediate undercover or pretext role that he or she is playing. The person might be a mother or father, a former factory worker, an army veteran, a resident of a particular neighborhood, and so forth. If a target notices anything about an agent that seems discrediting, the agent's performance is compromised. Private detectives pay careful attention to the personal details that they claim when performing their pretexts or undercover operations, because they know that every biographical claim that they make extends another opportunity for someone to potentially blow their cover. Good liars need more than good memories—they have to supply evidence to make their faked tales "true."

As a first step, the client and agency help undercover agents develop and rehearse identities and specific biographical details. They choose details that are difficult for targets to verify:

> We have to make up background. We don't tell people where they live; they can't tell people where they live, and we don't like having people invite them over to their house for that reason. They can say, "I live with my sister or I live with my parents or . . ." We really have to get into that situation when it would happen. We like to do everything off, away from the people's vicinity. "We just came back from overseas," "We came from another state."

The next step an agency takes is to provide third-party verification. When an investigator claims to have particular affiliations or habits, these fake identities often connect them to a range of organizations, props, and people. Do you hunt? Where do you go? Did you work at that factory? When? Where did you do your prison time? Any stated habits or affiliations, whether fake or genuine, can invite unwelcome scrutiny. Agents have to withstand people testing their claims.

Third-party verification operates outside the immediate physical interactions that agents have with targets. The detective agency is always the agent's tacit teammate in helping manage any attempts targets might make to check out their stories. For example, an agency may have a host employer corroborate and create a fake work history for the undercover agent. The private detective agency also takes other steps to reinforce the identity claims that performers make: "We have to make everything verifiable. If we have to rent a room out at the YMCA because somebody said they do that, that doesn't mean they'll live there but we'll rent a room out."

Agencies may operate "pretense lines." Pretense lines are phone numbers for fictional companies that agencies create for the express purpose of enabling operatives to claim a work history there. Private detectives backstop this cover by listing the false company's telephone number with the phone company in case someone checks to see whether the company is listed:

> We have to put together a good background; that's why we have our pretense lines here. When people call up, we know who's out there, so fine, so we answer the phone "ABC Company" or whatever it may be. . . . You could call information and you could say, "We want the telephone number for ABC Company," and it comes to us, so we go all the way through to the telephone company for our pretense lines also.

Detective agencies and the undercover operative's organizational client both help agents establish credibility. Manufacturing external credibility is a crucial tool in organizing deception because people view evidence as more convincing when that evidence appears beyond the operative's control. Team members help cement an "authenticity" that performers cannot manufacture by themselves. Passing is not just a matter of an individual's skills but also of his or her ability to draw on external resources that make their performances appear more convincing.

Realistic Demographics

Private detectives must cater effectively to existing sexual, racial, and physical expectations and stereotypes to pass convincingly in undercover roles. Strategically using operatives of a specific race, ethnicity, and sex to achieve credibility is a widely acknowledged requirement in confidence games and undercover operations (Blum 1972; B. Jacobs 1992a, 1992b, 1993; Marx 1988). Private detectives are aware of ethnic and sexual stereotypes, and they exploit them to appear authentic in their roles. For example, private detectives argue that some undercover jobs require black or Hispanic operatives because whites would be "too out of place."[3] People use stereotypes to order the world simplistically; private detectives know that playing to those expectations helps ensure that undercover operatives pass successfully.

The need for realistic demographics encourages organizations to recruit minorities to pose in minority-dominant settings or to hire females for "female" settings. An organization, for example, will place a female operative in a secretarial position and a male operative on a loading dock. Agencies also support efforts by agents to exploit stereotypes. More than one female investigator told me that gender stereotypes help them deceive more effectively:

> You know, I hate to say this but I think I have an advantage because I am a woman. No one expects a woman to be doing a surveillance. If a man is sitting on the street in a car, people get suspicious and call the cops, they get worried. But a woman's OK. . . . Women aren't as threatening.

Contingency Pretexts

Private detectives also supplement deceptions to outflank suspicious observers and targets that challenge their credibility. When confrontations occur, private detectives use "contingency" pretexts:

> Once I was on a long surveillance and I was watching a house for a long time. A woman came and tapped on the windshield and asked me what I was doing. I said that I was meeting a girlfriend to look at a house and I was enjoying the area so much that I was passing some time waiting for my girlfriend. The woman said OK, she was worried because she was going to be leaving and her young kids were at home. I said that she didn't have to worry. I say all kinds of things.

Another investigator noted, "You should have a plausible story in case you're stopped and it could be anything. You know, you could be an inspector, you could be looking for property, an accountant, anything."

Private detectives use contingency pretexts spontaneously, to fit the specific circumstances of a surprise challenge to their performance. Private detectives can rehearse contingencies for possible challenges, but the chance is always there of encountering unpredictable ones. Contingency pretexts should appear wholly credible, as this contingency pretext does:

This was a shampoo manufacturer and they were infringing by producing shampoo, putting it in similar bottles, and then selling them to large retail outlets. It's a lot of money. So I went to the store and it was closed. Next door there are two other stores. And I looked through the window and I saw the product so I was photographing the area, in particular, the stores. This man came up behind and goes, "What the hell are you doing?" Me, I go, "And who are you?" He goes, "It's my store next door." I told him I was an attorney and I was looking for property and there was an empty store there, a vacant store. So he even took me in to the realtor, which was next door. I went next door and I even toured the store where the product was. He had no reason to believe I wasn't an attorney or I wasn't whoever I said I was. . . . As long as you don't panic, you don't run, you could get around it.

Contingency pretexts can cool people down, but they also run the risk of creating a new claim that a target can scrutinize. If an investigator is to stay undercover for a long time, he or she must be careful when selecting contingency pretexts. In short-term pretexts, the detective only needs a contingency pretext that is good enough to last for that one encounter.

Identity Tags

Identity tags are "officially recognized seals that bond an individual to his biography" (Goffman 1969, 22). They connect an actor to a claimed identity or affiliation; for example, there are official tags such as passports, driver's licenses, and birth certificates. Unofficial identity tags are informal, such as proper apparel, business cards, a letterhead, accents, and physical markings.

The fraudulent use of official identity tags such as passports and birth certificates is an important legal concern (Marx 1988, 1990; Rule 1983). Until recently, people could create new identities by requesting a deceased infant's birth certificate and using that name to apply for secondary official documentation such as driver's licenses (Lapin 1989; Marx 1990). Technological innovations now make it easier to create tags, including using the Internet for "how to" lessons and to locate helpful resources.

Deceptive identity tags are not necessarily illegal or even problematic. Business cards and letterhead are legal if they are made for fictional companies. It is legally problematic, but not unheard of, to use a target's own official identity tags against them. For example, a private detective might contact a bank to access someone's account balance. To do so, they provide the correct account or Social Security number to appear to be the account holder.

Identity tags are props. The organization around the agent also can supply identity tags. For example, careful attention is paid to accurately impersonating delivery people, so the correct physical facade helps authenticate the delivery "identity":

> Both of my individuals that do process serving have uniforms that look like UPS; they have uniforms that look like Federal Express. We don't do the mailman uniforms because there might be some problems there. . . . A brown uniform, a brown ball cap. I actually even have a brown van. Not the big panel van but a brown van. The other guy has a white van. We actually try and go out with vans and boxes. We just come in with a big box and you have a clipboard with a signature sheet on it and underneath the signature sheet is the process service.

Besides purchasing appropriate props, private detective agencies also manufacture their own useful identity tags. They purchase identity card manufacturing machines like the ones used to make university identification cards, and they use computers to create business cards for fake companies:

> You can always produce ID. With the computer systems now, you could produce some really nice identification cards very quickly or business cards. Business cards are very easily produced. In fact, I think I have one here that I used not too long ago [opens his wallet and shows me a fake business card]. These were produced on a computer, and I didn't like them, so I redid them, but basically you could put anything you want on there. Somebody asks you for a business card, you can give them a business card right away, without having it printed. Just do it on a computer program with a good laser printer and you have any identification you want.

Calculated Unintentionality

Deceivers need to manage a distinction between expressions given and expressions given off (Goffman 1959). Expressions given are intentional. Expressions given off are physical signs that people display involuntarily in social interactions, such as sweating or trembling. Private detectives know that odd physical behavior and reactions are discrediting, so they try to disguise these signs. Just knowing that involuntary signs can give someone away is an advantage:

> If you start getting nervous about something, they'll detect it and once they detect it, they'll find other ways to test you. You have to be credible and you have to be able to handle something, and even though you may be sweating and dying inside, you just cannot project it.

Private detectives always try to come across so that the impressions they give off appear natural. One illustration is the rule of always using your real first name when you go undercover:

> The easiest thing in the world to do is to tell the truth because you can remember the facts. You know your real name, you know your real address, you know your real personal history. It's the created one that gets you into trouble. I never used anything other than my real first name. Therefore, I'd always react to it and therefore if anybody called me wanting to talk to the real Fred instead of the fictional Bill, it wouldn't be unnatural for me to respond to them. I'd hate to be introduced as, let's say, Charles, have someone who knew me outside say Fred and me react to it. And you will react to your name. Even if it's just a slight flinch, you will react.

Private detectives have a repertoire of faked expressions. They include remembering not to put your hands in front of your face when you lie, using a steady voice and looking directly at people when you lie to them. Rehearsing also teaches agents to avoid giving off physical cues that might discredit their passing.

Authentication Practices that Exploit Audience Characteristics

Seduction

Goffman (1969, 37) defines seduction as "maneuvering a definition of the situation such that the subject is led to believe that the observer is to be treated as something of a teammate to whom strategic information can be voluntarily trusted." Seduction occurs when performers intentionally commit illegal or unethical acts in front of targets to gain their trust. For example, as one private investigator commented, "Depending on the situation, I'll encourage the operative to steal in front of other employees to gain their confidence."

Private detectives achieve credibility in this instance through discrediting themselves. Targets believe that undercover operatives will not commit crimes that could taint future legal testimony. A further motive for committing discrediting acts is the hope that appearing as a disreputable character will sway "troublemakers" to seek the agent's participation in ongoing illicit activities. At the very least, the hope is that targets will have a false sense of security about their activities remaining secret, since they now "have something" on the agent.

Seduction also occurs via flattery. One private detective said that "the reason they end up trusting you is because you're a damn good salesman, because you have something to contribute to what they want—admiration, respect, hero worship works real well." Flattery helps authenticate undercover operatives and diverts attention from their deceptions.

Harmlessness

Private detectives state that appearing harmless helps avoid challenges and aids information gathering:

> Meeting people in person, if you come off as harmless, if you develop a pretext that makes you a harmless individual, most of the time it will work. . . . If you seem harmless, you get a ton of information.

One form of harmlessness in pretexts and undercover operations is using "stocked characters" (Goffman 1971). Stocked characters are people who work as janitors, delivery persons, or waitresses, who, "properly uniformed and certified, are allowed to cut across the schedules of ordinary people and in exchange for accepting something like non-person treatment, they are allowed the run of private places" (307–8). Agencies place undercover operatives in jobs where targets will consider them harmless, and also where they can move around in the work site:

> A lot of times we have guys who are janitors. That gives them more the mobility to get into the place, to meet a lot of people. . . . They think, "Janitors, oh yeah, they really don't know too much." Then, they speak to them a lot more.

Stocked characters also have some access to the backstage. Keeping your mouth shut and just listening helps operatives not give themselves away:

The investigators . . . when you're in there . . . you have to keep your mouth shut, because that tells them something right there, first of all. The less you say the better off you are. If you don't say anything to anyone about yourself, the less lies you have to tell, the easier it is to maintain your cover. It's pretty easy to slip out of cover and make a mistake, so you just don't say anything. And secondly you come off as a more trusting person. If you're a guy that's always talking, smart talking, even if they don't think that you're an investigator, they think that he's got a flannel mouth, you're liable to say something. You want to be the type of person that no matter what anybody says it just doesn't bother you. "I killed six people over the weekend." "That's nice." Not "Jesus Christ! Six people, how'd you do it? Did you stab them? Did you shoot them?" I was telling my people that one of the best things you can say to somebody is "No shit." If I tell you something, say "No shit." It's kind of like a come-on, tell me more, but not like I'm too interested.

In direct contradiction to harmlessness, some private detectives argue that stressing targets, particularly in verbal-only pretexts, is also an efficient authentication practice:

When you do a pretext, particularly telephone, what you wanna do is stress the person out. The more things he can tell you. . . . A friend of mine uses "voter registration board" or something like that. Well, there isn't. . . . And he tells you, "So, I'm with the board of elections. Listen, we sent you questionnaires three months ago and they haven't been answered. Are you aware that not responding to this questionnaire is contempt of court and you can be held liable?" Well, right away your mind is racing. "Well, I never received it." "You never received it? Well, confirm your address for me please." So you give me your address. I've got your address. "How about your Social Security number? OK, we can try to do this over the phone. Either that or you can come downtown." "No, no, I'll do it now." "OK." And then I'll ask you maybe ten different questions. And you'll give me just about anything I want to know, because right now you're stressed, you're afraid that first of all you might get charged with something, second of all you might have to come down. I knew a guy who said that he was with the tax audit board of the United States or something like that. And they'll say, "Well, David, according to our records here you owe us. . . ." Or, "You have a secondary income of eighteen thousand nine hundred and fifty-three dollars that you're not reporting tax on." You go, "What?" Right away you go boom [claps hands]. You're flipped. And they'll say, "OK, maybe our computers are screwed up. Let's try to do this by the phone. If not, if you prefer, come down to the Federal Building downtown. Bring your tax records for the last six years." Well, what are you going to do? You're going to do it on the phone. And then they'll ask you questions, whatever they want.

Other ways in which private detectives apply stress include telling a target that his or her bills are unpaid or carrying around blank subpoena forms and threatening to subpoena targets if they do not provide information. Private detectives state that stress works because targets become too distracted to focus on challenging them. Operatives then offer a quick release from stress by asserting, for example, "I can give you a break if you tell me over the phone." To get out of the situation quickly, the target provides the information and eliminates the stress. The target's goal becomes not to challenge but to placate.

Harmlessness and stress are authentication practices that work through diversion (B. Jacobs 1992a, 1992b, 1993). Harmlessness and stress strategies divert attention because targets become too complacent or too panicked to think straight. Good liars, like magicians, understand the value in distracting people's attention so that they do not figure out tricks.

Obliviousness

I was surprised to hear private detectives say repeatedly that many targets are oblivious to any possibility that they are being investigated. The distinguishing characteristic of oblivious targets is that they have been engaged in their activities for a long time and have not attracted any prior notice, so they feel home free:

> People are very confident after a while. In the beginning, they're very cautious. You know, the guy will be looking over his shoulder, but after a while, he's very confident and he feels that this doesn't happen.

Oblivious targets take things for granted and just go along with the show of normalcy that private detectives enact. Situations appear normal, so targets do not suspect anything out of the ordinary, especially from routine characters. All that targets are asked to do is play along with stocked characters, which they do because they are oblivious to any potential dangers:

> Yeah, I have flowers for Mrs. Jones. Now I'm standing there in casual attire, I'm carrying a florist box of flowers with a big red bow around it and a little gift card on it. In fact I bought them myself and [that] I don't know the woman from Adam is beside the point. I have flowers for Mrs. So-and-So. I didn't say that I was a flower delivery guy. You assumed I was. All I've said is I've got these for her, I'd like to give them to her—where is she? You said that she's over there.

Private detectives assert that many targets in domestic cases are oblivious:

> Number one, they don't believe anybody knows what's going on. Most of the time, when people are cheating, they're in what I call a lust phase and they are pretty much oblivious to the whole world. They see what they want to see and they're looking at the world through rosy-colored glasses and they're relatively easy to follow. I can't even begin to imagine how many cases I've worked on ever since I've been in the business. . . . I spent a week in Acapulco, practically living with this man, and he didn't know it, and that turns out to be the general truth.

Private detectives also consciously exploit protective practices (Goffman 1959). Protective practices occur when people disregard any discrepancies in another actor's behavior or image. People prefer a perceptually ordered and routine world, one where no incongruous events exist that cannot be easily explained (Pollner 1983; Garfinkel 1967; Heritage 1984). People do not want to appear crazy, even when confronting cues that suggest that something "crazy" is happening, like they are being followed. People also use protective practices to avoid confrontations. For example, when a target confronts a private detective whom he or she suspects is following them, the private detective may start out by saying that the target is crazy:

> Even if you came up to me and said, "What are you looking at?" I'd tell you, "What, are you nuts? We're not looking at you. Who are you?" Chances are you're not going to say anything to me; you're going to walk away because you're not going to believe I'm actually watching you. A lot has to do with television. The guy looks in his rearview mirror and he goes, "We're being followed." Well, that's not reality.

People with no initial reasons to suspect surveillance will hesitate to publicly accuse the ACME work crew parked out front of spying on them, since everyone knows that only "crazy, paranoid people" would make such accusations. Thus private detectives credential themselves by transforming protective practices into defensive ones.

Associates of targets (such as neighbors or co-workers) are also oblivious and thus might proffer relevant information. When confronted with a plausible pretext that does not sound harmful to a target, they will provide information without voicing suspicion about the requester's authenticity:

> I tell the neighbors that I'm with a parcel delivery company, I'm trying to find this guy who got a package here, it's smelling, I don't know if it's important stuff in there. "Where are you?" says the guy. "I'm in the office in the [city two hours away], I don't know how the fuck this thing got here, but do you know this guy? If not, then I'm going to get rid of it." "Well, he works days, he comes out nighttime." So then we know that the guy is working on a comp case, while receiving workers compensation. See a lot of them are working in the meantime.

Street Smarts

The most ambiguous authentication practice is street smarts. Some private detectives think being streetwise is teachable, while others say that this credibility comes only from having real experience in the portrayed role. "Experience-only" advocates argue that operatives who come from the streets and have worked in the kinds of jobs and areas where the undercover work is located perform the most realistically:

> There are some people that couldn't stand being in some dive bar on the South Side because it's just not something they're used to. They're very uncomfortable with it, and they're uncomfortable with the language and the manner of dress and the kind of cars you ride in and just how people interact with each other on certain social levels. They have no idea of how to act in a situation. You may get challenged by somebody. I mean, he may call you every name in the book and you're scared to death. You don't realize that he's just bullshitting with you. . . . . Being street smart is the ability to know what's going on around you and how to act under any given circumstances. It's really knowing how the city operates, knowing how people operate in the city. You're either street smart or you're not, and the only way to become street smart is to live in the city on the streets, existing and surviving under difficult circumstances.

Their argument is that these performers can display minute details and attitudes that people learning the role for the first time could not know, even if well trained.

The alternative view rejects that operatives have to come from the school of hard knocks in order to role-play convincingly. They view rehearsal and studying as providing enough background to enable an operative to pass convincingly. Put in sociological terms, streetwise people argue that credibility comes from having authentic "cultural capital" linked to that role. Other private detectives believe that if you can identify appropriate cultural capital, then you can perform that cultural capital as if you come by it naturally. When targets believe that cultural capital cannot be faked and a detective fakes being streetwise successfully, the deceiver is bolstered (ironically) by the target's view that such a role "cannot be faked."

Human Chameleons and Social Camouflage

One private detective described successful undercover operators as "human chameleons." But too much can be made of the individual liar's skill and too little of the social context that helps camouflage and sustain deceptions. A chameleon is physiologically able to blend into natural environments in order to deceive predators. A successful liar is a human chameleon who manipulates social environments into strategic camouflage.

Authentication practices work when performers put on a skillful performance and audiences lack the initiative to test performers. The private detective's craft lies in successfully mimicking authentic appearances. How to make a fake ID that looks good, getting the brown delivery uniform, knowing that hotel guests sometimes call back for copies of their bill—the art of the lie is knowing what people think will be plausible enough and then corroborating those assumptions in a skillful performance. But this artful enterprise also depends heavily on audiences choosing to be lulled by the appearance of plausibility. This reciprocal relationship is at the heart of understanding how lies are made believable. Successful deception is the product of knowing what buttons will misdirect an audience so that one can take advantage of their tendency to indulge self-fulfilling prophecies, to be complacent, and to take things for granted. The authentication practices of private detectives embed deception into the naturally occurring features of the world. By detaching and corrupting those signs, liars bewitch people by using their own familiarity with the world.

Goffman noted this danger of being taken in, of assuming that the appearance of legitimacy equals legitimacy:

> The more closely the impostor's performance approximates to the real thing, the more intensely we may be threatened, for a competent performance by someone who proves to be an impostor may weaken in our minds the moral connection between legitimate authorization to play a part and the capacity to play it. (1959, 18)

In this regard, passing successfully is threatening to society. For example, a person who fakes their way into Harvard should theoretically, according to legitimating criteria, not outperform students who had the actual credentials to be accepted. If an impostor passes convincingly as an authentic performer, then her or his success imperils the justifications underlying the elitism, privilege, and legitimacy of different social roles and statuses.[4]

Even categories such as gender, which appear to be a wholly natural status, are vulnerable to passing. Garfinkel (1967) analyzes how "Agnes" (a biological male) manipulated characteristics of gender in order to pass convincingly as a woman while he awaited a sex-change operation. Successful dramaturgy shows that one does not have to be legitimately entitled to play a role in order to perform that role successfully.

When fakers can play legitimate roles convincingly, relationships of trust are threatened. People who want to violate trust have to appear as if they are complying with all the indicators of credibility that will make someone appraise the situation as trustworthy. By researching how people use authentication practices to make their lies believable, we come closer to identifying what techniques of passing people can use to violate trust.

Authentication practices can differ depending on the existing relationship between a deceiver and the recipient of the deceit. People who know each other have more information with which to assess the likelihood of deception—they also may, because of relational dependencies, have less ability to openly recognize being deceived. An employee, for example, may know enough to figure out that the boss is lying, but being less powerful than the boss may not be able to challenge the lie. What makes the lie convincing— that is, treated as true whether people believe it to be so or not—is the powerlessness of the audience and not the liar's prowess. But between relative strangers, who have impersonal relations with each other, the dynamics of constructing convincing lies are different. Private detectives have the advantage of not having to overcome familiarity; on the other hand, they also have to be successful in mimicking "what everyone knows" about how delivery people look and so forth. Private detectives construct lies that cause the instincts of targets to be misled, leading people to be entrapped by their own faith in familiarity as a criterion of honesty.

A lie must be performed soundly to be believable, and crafting those performances well is an intricate art. But the relationship between the performance of the lie and tendencies of audiences cannot be overlooked.

In delineating the authentication practices that private detectives use, I identified several individual and organizational resources that are used to develop and employ work-related deceptions, and some characteristics of audiences that are exploited to sustain those deceptions. I also described a continuum of verification that is implicit in the actions that private detectives take to craft convincing deceptions.

Their authentication practices demonstrate four sociological dimensions of constructing deceptions. First, successful lying depends on consciously applied dramaturgical skills. Second, audiences have vulnerable social predispositions in their assumptions about what is legitimate and plausible in the world. Third, the criteria that people use to discern authenticity are malleable and exploitable social constructions. Fourth, there is an implicit stratification in making deceptions appear credible. When people can use institutional and organizational resources to support their individual deceptions, they have a better chance of faking authenticity convincingly.

3

JUSTIFYING WORK-RELATED DECEPTIONS

Everett Hughes (1984, 342) identified "the arrangements and devices by which men made their work tolerable, or even glorious to themselves and others," as a core issue for study in the workplace. Researchers, particularly symbolic interactionists, responded to this call by investigating how workers develop "dignifying rationalizations" to mitigate the shameful implications of having to do "dirty work," such as physically disgusting or morally degrading tasks (see, for examples, Davis 1984; Klockars 1984; Hughes 1984). In this chapter I adopt and extend this approach by examining how professionals account for the use of noncriminal, work-related deceptions.[1] I focus on how professionals exonerate controversial types of work and workplaces, a different issue than how individuals in controversial roles make themselves feel better about what they do.

Scott and Lyman (1968, 46) define an account as "a linguistic device employed whenever an action is subjected to valuative inquiry." Accounts are excuses and justifications that reconcile untoward actions and social expectations. A rich literature exists on how people use accounts to excuse and justify criminal behaviors.[2]

Studying how people account for criminal behaviors is important. Yet criminal offenders are a small subset of the pool of individuals who use accounts. How do workers legitimate using legal but controversial work-related deceptions?

States license private detectives, who must comply with ethical codes and complete educational and experiential requirements in order to be licensed. To preserve their legitimacy and fend off critics and rivals, all professions must demonstrate that the means and ends of their work reflect prevailing cultural values (Abbott 1988). Given the social stigma attached to lying, private detectives have to make the use of work-related deceptions appear legitimate. Although scholars have studied the legitimating strategies that police officers and undercover operatives use to explain their work-related deceptions,[3] little work exists on the strategies, ethical resolutions, and "working personalities" (Skolnick 1975) of private detectives, their private sector counterparts in social control. The growing employment of private agents of social control in North America warrants further investigation of the work-related deceptions and accounts that private detectives employ.[4]

Little research exists on how organizations or groups use accounts differently than individuals do, such as when a person accounts for such simple deviant acts in their personal life as telling an off-color joke or being drunk. Nichols (1990, 133) identifies the neglect of the collective and group use of accounts as an "elementary omission" in scholarship on accounts. Professional groups differ from individuals in the way they construct and use accounts, because their work comes with broader aims, power, and a wide range of stakeholders. A sharper analytic focus is needed to discern the distinctive qualities of offering accounts within a professional context.

An important difference exists between the individual and the organized group when it comes to lying. How people account for their behavior privately may be dramatically at odds with how they account for morally controversial behavior that is a part of "doing their jobs" (see also Jackall 1988). I argue that workplaces provide repertoires of excuses to carry out deceptions that help sustain them as normal work. Emphasizing the amoral individual results in paying less attention to how deception functions as a collective workplace activity. When acting deceptively is part of fulfilling one's everyday work obligations, rationalizations for lying are a structural necessity. Providing these rationalizations is not mere charity directed at a worker's well being. Preserving the right to practice morally controversial behaviors demands that practitioners can justify their work.

In this chapter, I identify specific accounts for work-related deceptions and how a professional affiliation makes those accounts more powerful; professionals can draw on cultural and structural resources that are not available to individuals in their private lives. These cultural and structural resources include the economic and demographic characteristics of employers, practitioners, clients, and targets; state licensing; the profession's social repute; asymmetries in specialized knowledge between practitioners and laypersons; case and client selectivity; and favorable occupational metaphors and rhetorics of expertise, neutrality, training, and professionalism. Our task is not to speculate about the morality of individuals who lie but to identify aspects of work organizations that allow people to sustain lying through ethical disengagement. I conclude by considering how accounts help preserve the ability to engage in controversial work practices such as lying.

I classify private detectives' accounts into analytic categories of *means-ends justifications*, *technical-legal justifications*, and *ethic-of-neutrality justifications*. These accounts transfer blame for engaging in deception to targets of investigations (they deserve it), existing laws (if deceptive investigative techniques are legal then they are permissible), and to clients (deceptions are at their behest). Akin to a legal precedent, a successful account also functions to justify lying in multiple professional circumstances. Successful accounts for work-related deceptions help disassociate practitioners from being blamed for adversarial work while institutionalizing a profession's jurisdiction to practice morally contestable tasks.

Previous Research on Accounts

Scott and Lyman (1968) describe accounts as falling into two categories—excuses or justifications. People who use excuses acknowledge committing a negatively viewed act but reject personal responsibility for their actions. Everyday examples of excuses include "It was an accident" or "I did it, but I was drunk." People who use justifications acknowledge committing a discreditable act but claim that extenuating circumstances legitimated that behavior. Everyday examples of justifications include "I was following orders" or "Those people had it coming to them."

At their core, accounts represent an individual's attempts to transfer responsibility for discrediting actions to other people or pressures, such as alcohol, scapegoats, or a superior's orders. All accounts reflect an attempt to negotiate the level of stigma or punishment that is attached to an individual's troubling action. Accounts in general are "stories and narratives" that represent ways that people organize their own images and that of others in the social world (Orbuch 1997). These stories help to explain behaviors in a positive light. Harre, Clark, and DeCarlo (1985) argue that in producing accounts, actors demonstrate their knowledge of ideal ways of acting and idealized reasons for doing what they have done. Individuals offer accounts to preserve a positive image (Orbuch 1997).

How do professionals use accounts to positively characterize occupational identity? Although scholars have identified new accounts and conducted empirically focused analyses of how people account for specific actions, this body of work identifies neither organizational contributions to accounts nor how professionals in the private sector use accounts to legitimate legal but controversial "dirty work."[5]

Recent scholarly reviews of research on accounts stress paying attention to how different groups use accounts (Hunter 1992; Nichols 1990; Orbuch 1997; Young 1997). More emphasis is needed on the different contexts in which people and groups offer accounts. A key theoretical attribute to examine with professionals in mind is how accounts possess a cumulative power. This cumulative power refers to the capacity a particular account has to legitimate or excuse repeatedly engaging in a behavior. For example, if someone knows that saying "Boys will be boys" will usually lead an audience to tolerate a boy's aggression, that particular account assumes a cumulative power. Citing this account then allows boys to act more aggressively because the account perpetually excuses or justifies that action.

Cumulativeness is important in deception because knowing that an account works over time means that the power exists to exonerate repeated incidents of potentially discreditable behavior. Accounts do more than rehabilitate individual reputations. They preserve the capacity to engage in discrediting behaviors by successfully mitigating norms against those behaviors. The social resources available to organizations and professions make a powerful contribution to the cumulative potential of accounts.

Rationales for Deception

Popular culture is replete with imagery of private detectives as deductive geniuses and adventurous heroes. However, there are also negative portrayals of private detectives. They have been depicted historically as agent provocateurs, union busters, frame-up experts, violent servants of big business, and wiretappers—as one respondent put it, "as somebody who'll do anything for a buck." Private detective agencies such as Pinkerton and Burns were particularly vilified for using deception and violence to help destroy unions and break strikes, particularly from the 1890s through the 1930s. Such work was condemned harshly by congressmen and unions, for example, "His business is the conscious and deliberate exercise of deceit and treachery. He is a constant menace not only to the existence of unions, but to the security and livelihood of every fellow employee at whose side he works" (House Committee on Education and Labor 1939, 80). Public and legal criticism that deceptive techniques attack individual privacy, along with negative historical portrayals, motivate private detectives to account for their work-related deceptions.

The deceptive methodologies of undercover operations, undisclosed surveillance, and false pretexts that private detectives use in their work raise ethical questions. Plaintiffs have cited private detectives' deceptive methodology in multiple lawsuits that accuse private detectives of violations of privacy, trespass, document theft, and entrapment (see Geddes 1989).

In response, private detectives employ three types of accounts. In means-ends justifications, private detectives portray work-related deceptions as instruments of justice against criminal threats. In technical-legal justifications they argue that when a particular deceptive method is legal, there is no moral issue involved in using that deception. Ethics-of-neutrality justifications portray deception as a morally neutral professional tool, with any moral judgments about the motives for using deception as a separate issue that pertains to the clients that initiate the work. I discuss these accounts in detail below, emphasizing how each one draws on different aspects of occupational structure, types of clients, prior work experience, and training.

Means-Ends Justifications

Private detectives have a pragmatic reason to lie in their work—they need to investigate people who are themselves acting deceptively. This pragmatic basis underlies the moral rhetoric that some private detectives use to account for deceptions, which is that the ends of uncovering dangerous and deceptive people justify using deception against them. As an undercover investigator interviewed by Gary Marx put it, "If you want to catch a rat, then you have to go into the sewer" (Marx 1987, 83).

Klockars (1985, 55) identified a "Dirty Harry" problem that police officers must address: "To what extent does the morally good end warrant or justify an ethically, politically, or legally dangerous means for its achievement?" The "Dirty Harry" problem for private detectives involves differentiating themselves morally from targets, since both "are in the sewer" when using deception. An "end justifies the means" philosophy portrays work-related deceptions as instruments of justice that defend against criminal threats. When private detectives compare themselves to police officers, they engage in what Fine (1996) identified as "professional analogizing."

To uncover criminals is personally and professionally rewarding, as one private detective notes during a discussion of insurance investigations:

> One thing that really satisfies me is when in insurance cases I get all the information on someone who turns out to be defrauding the insurance company and showing the insurance company the evidence. I get a lot of satisfaction from showing fraud. And I'll tell you why: because my insurance rates are too high, and they're the reason why—the defrauders.

A male private detective conducting undercover operations in blue-collar workplaces comments on morality in undercover operations:

> It didn't bother me when I did it. I go in there and I'm looking. Hey, those people are dealing drugs on the workforce. You have people working cranes; you have people working on big machines. If they're there under the influence of any type of drugs or alcohol, you know they shouldn't be there. You know, you're out there for the safety of the people.

In this framing, targets under investigation are committing serious transgressions (such as adultery, drug dealing, insurance fraud, stealing, and trademark infringement) that must be exposed and punished.

Private detective work is organized in two ways that promote means-ends accounts. First, some private detectives only select cases that involve criminal targets (rather than noncriminal targets such as adulterers). By selecting only those cases, private detectives can view themselves as representatives of justice. One private detective, after leaving an agency that worked on adultery investigations, comments on his new job:

> Here we specialize in surety recovery work, bail theft investigation, and prevention. I am much more satisfied and comfortable in doing that kind of work. These are people that have been charged with a crime, a serious crime in most instances, and have fled from lawful prosecution.

Litigation history also supports some means-ends justifications.[6] For example, when people accept offers of employment, request loans, file claims with insurers, apply for jobs and for admission to educational institutions, they must agree to contractual arrangements that allow a degree of intrusion on their privacy (Reiss 1987). This conceding of individual privacy is attributable to a perception that organizations have the legal right to investigate the truthfulness of claims.

In *Forster v. Manchester* the plaintiff argued that a private detective had conducted unobtrusive surveillance on her that invaded her privacy and constituted harassment. The court ruled against that plaintiff, concluding: "There is social utility in investigations because it is in the best interests of society that personal injury claims be valid and that fraudulent claims be exposed" (La Marca 1986, 604). *Forster v. Manchester* and similar verdicts demonstrate that private detectives can draw on legally and morally accepted social precedents in order to inspect trust compliance using deceptive techniques.

Private detectives who use means-ends justifications also argue that private detectives are just like police officers. Before becoming licensed, many private detectives have backgrounds in public law enforcement, and many police officers also moonlight by working for private detective agencies (Cunningham and Taylor 1985). Invoking equivalence between police officers and private detectives is an attempt to justify deceptions by connecting private detectives with the legitimacy that police officers have in fighting crime for the greater public good.

Private detectives use their extensive connections and ongoing relationships with police officers to access information (Cunningham and Taylor 1985). An occupational structure that draws on retired law enforcement officers as personnel encourages the ethos of ends justifying the means, as a retired police detective, who now runs his own private detective agency, explains:

> We don't do that type of work here [working on behalf of criminal defendants], and the reason is because we are all policemen; we have a lot of retired police officers that work for us. We won't conflict with the investigation going on by the local police. It's hard for my people to be neutral on a criminal offense.

An additional structural reason why the "quasi-public law enforcement" comparison that private detectives use is effective is because private detectives are sometimes employed to carry out work that public law enforcement agents perform. Such work includes conducting investigations into internal thefts under $25,000, out-of-state retrieval of bail jumpers, physical security, missing persons, and murder investigations.

Clients hire private detectives for these cases for several reasons. Sometimes public law enforcement agencies lack the resources or desire to work on certain cases, such as internal thefts under $25,000. Sometimes clients are dissatisfied with public law enforcement's efforts on a particular case and think that private-sector agents will provide better results, because they can work exclusively on their case. Clients also may believe that private detectives offer more discretion than police officers, which is important when clients want to keep their problems to themselves. For example, one private detective comments: "If I'm in, let's say, one of the companies that is escorting money, I might not want the rest of the community to know that an employee of mine took $50,000 of my money, because then what's my credibility?" Other clients simply want to avoid legal obligations that arise from working with public law enforcement.

There are important issues in substituting private inquiry for public law enforcement investigations. An instructor comments during in-house training:

> You have to be reasonably careful, especially in cases that are going to go to court, because you don't want to do anything to jeopardize the case. In cases that are never going to court, it really doesn't matter too much on what you're doing, because mainly it's for the benefit of your client and it's not going to be used for anything but for their common knowledge, so you don't have to be concerned.

What this private detective glosses over is the potential harmful impact of unreported results. Employing a private investigator gives a client greater discretionary power over what becomes public knowledge. In many cases, the clients can decide how to act on the results of investigations, and they do not have to make those decisions public.

A means-ends justification also involves making moral differentiations among types of cases. Some cases warrant applying deceptive and other adversarial techniques and others do not. In making those distinctions, practitioners use case selectivity and only choose cases with criminal targets for employing deceptive techniques. Cases that do not involve criminal targets may be cast aside as morally inappropriate—as "emotional" and less professional work.

For example, private detectives with a public law enforcement background have a pronounced disdain for working "domestics," a slang term for investigating suspected infidelity. "Domestics" involve no criminal offense and have potentially devastating emotional impacts on clients. Case selectivity in avoiding "domestics" dodges a "dirty work" label while subtly affixing that label on competitors who accept those cases. Consider this private detective's comments about working domestics:

> It is tedious. It is a lot of hours staring at doorways, sitting in automobiles. Being cold, being uncomfortable, staying up till bad hours. And it's not very rewarding personally in a situation where someone is going to end up getting hurt, someone is going to experience anguish, someone is going to be emotionally hurt. I've had people scream; I've had people cry; I've had people go into rages. There isn't a whole lot that's positive about it. I prefer not to do it. Fortunately, the agency I'm working with now does not seek that kind of work. Those who do it and specialize in it are very good at it apparently and apparently it's very profitable for them, but there's a lot more going out there that I'd rather be doing.

Case selectivity in avoiding domestics illustrates a status distinction among private detectives. Abbott (1981) argues that a practitioner's degree of removal from emotional, disorderly, and "nonprofessional" work helps determine their professional status. Private detectives who use a case selectivity approach disdain domestics as less professional work associated with less prestigious practitioners.

Private detectives are also criticized for being perceived as "mercenary" if they work on behalf of criminal defendants:

> I was trying to solve a murder case on one particular assignment and on another particular assignment I was trying to get a guy off on an armed robbery beef. I'm the prosecuting team one day, and on the defense team the other day. I'm with the cops one day, and I mean they're friends of mine. It's like, "Where are you now?" Because I mean guys who are friends of mine are in bars. You know they're going, "Are you on a good assignment now, or are you on a bad assignment now?" And that's why people don't trust private eyes. It's not who pays you more; it's who pays you first.

Other private detectives echo this point in recalling being called "whores" and "people who will do anything for money."

Screening client character in noncriminal cases helps repel this unfavorable mercenary image.[7] Client selectivity again becomes a form of case selectivity. Many private detectives turn down missing person cases for clients who give off disturbing signs. A detective specializing in missing person investigations explains:

> You check out the individual. Why does he want to find this person? Why did the person run away? In the background you might find he's looking for his wife, and he's an abuser. You start talking to friends and "Hell, yeah, this man beats the hell out of his wife." You look up police records and you look up hospital records and you find out this guy has been beating up his wife and he's probably going to beat her up again. I will listen to somebody, but I don't take it for total truth what they tell me.

Using case selectivity supports an account for work-related deceptions that deceptive methods are applied where they are deserved. An ironic aspect of using case and client selectivity is that this argument denigrates the general profession by implication; the account draws its strength from implicitly criticizing peers. A private detective makes this point by stating simply, "In this business, you have people that would do things as long as you pay the money. They have absolutely no questions of doing anything for you."

Technical-Legal Justifications

Some private detectives reject means-ends justifications and argue for a more "objective" defense of their work. They avoid an explicitly moralizing defense that a target's misdeeds justify work-related deception. Many private detectives use deceptions to investigate noncriminal behaviors, such as lying to get unlisted phone numbers, a goal that is less amenable to claims of working in the interests of justice. Such investigators adopt an account that anything legal goes and anything illegal does not. Legal techniques are acceptable practices and require no moral justification. Laws governing the profession form the standard for assessing the morality of work. If a form of deception is legal, then whether it is moral or not is moot.

One private detective, discussing how he wears an intentionally misleading fake delivery outfit during some investigations, offers an illustration of a technical-legal justification:

> DETECTIVE: Wearing a uniform is not illegal. I'm not misrepresenting myself. There is no restriction on someone owning a uniform. It's not a violation of law to wear it. Now, if I'm walking through your building in it and you say, "Who are you? What are you doing here?" And I say, "I'm with UPS," now I've broken the law. Now, I've misrepresented myself.

D. S.: But you can wear the uniform as long as you make no claim to be that?

DETECTIVE: As long as I do not misrepresent myself, as long as I don't pose as something other than what I am.

Note the irony here in how the law's technical character is obeyed while the law's intent is subverted.

Substantial profits tempt, but potential sanctions still prevent many from taking illegal actions. Moral issues are less powerful than a rational choice, a risk-reward consideration of employing illegal work-related deceptions. A private detective explains:

I will do my best to avoid breaking the law. I may get right to the edge of it, but I try to stay away from that. It's not so much morally, it's my fear of being locked up. Other than that, I will do almost anything and everything I can to get the job done.

Another investigator speaks to this calculus in discussing why he turns down legally risky assignments:

I've had people who want to get somebody's tax records. I've looked around: Can you do it? Is there anybody out there that's selling this kind of information? Obviously, it's got to be a governmental employee. But then you start looking into the fines and penalties and everything involved. You can go away for a long time for accessing that information. Is my client going to pay my legal bills? Is he going to take care of my family while I'm gone? Nah. OK, maybe I could make ten grand on this. What are your implications further down the road? It ain't worth it to me. A short-term gain is fine, but eventually you're going to get busted. I know that, I'm in the business. I bust people all the time. You're going to get caught, and it just isn't worth the effort.

A twist on the technical-legal justification is that some private detectives believe that if targets are dumb enough to make compromising information available, then they are idiots who deserve what they get. Private detectives often express disbelief at what people were willing to tell them over the phone and at the discrediting actions that they took in plain public view. One private detective expressed shock at the incriminating materials that targets throw away:

In one instance, we literally ended up with a credit report on someone. They had requested a copy of their credit report and then discarded it in the trash. . . . Just threw it in the garbage and it went out on the curb and we're going through the dumpster and "Well, look at this." And considering it was one of these situations where it was a divorce case, the husband was pleading. . . . The wife wanted certain things and certain amounts of money and property, and he was saying, "I don't have that kind of money." He was hiding assets, and of course here along with his credit report is also a bank statement, which in part lists a couple of accounts which he's denying exist. And he knows that there are people looking into this because it's being contested and it's a long drawn out, very bloody divorce. He knows that people are looking, and he throws this out full in the trash. It never occurred to him that somebody might pick up his garbage and go through it.

There were many variations on this theme, including embezzlers who kept incriminating receipts in their work desks; cheaters who visibly made love in public parks; persons claiming debilitating injuries who were videotaped lugging heavy objects; and the topper—a man who threatened to blow up his workplace who left his threatening message with his name on the facility's answering machine. Tales of "idiots" are staple war stories for detectives. However, in a subtler vein, blaming a target for providing discrediting information is an approach similar to Scott and Lyman's (1968) "denial of victim account," which is a strategy of shifting blame to victims. Here attention is shifted from private detectives' deceptive conduct in acquiring information (covert surveillance or undercover work) on to targets who fail to protect their vital secrets particularly well.

Private detectives cite this view specifically to justify performing pretexts. One private detective defined pretexts as "I got a reason that you give them that would induce them to tell you." The subject's falling for the ruse minimizes the private detective's sense of moral culpability in acquiring the information. As one licensed apprentice concluded, "If I start asking you questions and you don't ask me why I want to know and who the hell am I, I haven't done anything wrong."

Ethic-of-Neutrality Justifications
Formal professional knowledge and claims of thorough training support the contention that deceptive investigative techniques should only be applied neutrally. A "neutral extension of techniques" refers to a working ideology among private detectives that they must be objective, dispassionate, and impartial in applying deceptive investigative techniques.

Private detectives continually proclaim neutrality: "We are not out to get anybody, we're impartial," "We're not judge and jury," "We don't manufacture evidence, we just observe what occurs naturally." Detachment is a consistent theme of professionalism—people should have no personal interest in a given case that might influence an outcome (Hughes 1984, 378). Claims of neutrality encourage using deceptive techniques because objective applications of such techniques are held to produce accurate and honest reporting. Thus, neutrality ideally assures that subjects who behave faultlessly will be declared so, as long as investigative techniques are applied and reported neutrally. No innocents suffer, and only the guilty are punished.

A philosophy of neutral extensions of techniques allows private detectives a welcome discretion. Neutrality permits them to identify for themselves what constitutes fairness in applying investigative methods. Training and agency-specific criteria also affect that labeling. Private detectives also profit from the structural advantage that they have to define their work. They know exactly how far one can bend the truth to accord with professional standards.

The following private detective's statement is typical in its emphasis on the importance of working neutrally:

> We are there to find the truth, not to make a case. Any investigator who goes in trying to make a case … "I got hired to find something wrong, therefore, there has to be something wrong." No, you didn't get hired to find something wrong. You got hired to find out *if* something is wrong. Therefore, if you go back to them and say, "There's nothing wrong. We couldn't find anything," you've done your job just as well as if you caught twenty thousand thieves. You've done your job. Anyone who approaches it any other way shouldn't be in the business. Rule number one is do no harm. You're there because you're trying to prevent harm or stop injury, whether it's financial injury or physical injury. Therefore, you're damn sure that the people that you are pursuing are the individuals involved. I consider myself just as successful when I categorically prove that this individual is not involved and is innocent of any allegations brought against him as I am when I prove he is involved and he is guilty of those allegations. I'm interested in what the facts are, what the truth of the matter is.

A tension emerges between justifying investigative work as a means to attain noble ends and furthering a client's potentially less-than-noble ends. Neutrality, if properly invoked, dissolves this tension and ideally allows both abstract good and a client's ends to be met at no undeserved cost to subjects.

Private detectives may feel pressured to avoid compiling objective results if those results run counter to a client's benefit. Private detectives are
in business to make money. Unscrupulous detectives increase their profits
by manufacturing false reasons to persuade a client to continue sponsor-
ing an investigation, such as by exaggerating the amount of documentation that they need to establish spousal infidelity. The longer the private
detective works the investigation, the more billable hours there are. Private detectives also may be sympathetic to some targets and wish to avoid
pursuing actions that harm them. They also receive "just find out, I don't
care how" pressure from clients.

Any such "subjective investigations" are labeled unprofessional and
unethical (Cassidy-Ervin 1989; Connel 1989). Private detectives who manufacture false information are considered highly immoral by other private
detectives:

> A private detective who doesn't give a damn who he hurts—because we
> can do serious injury to an innocent party if we are not ethical, if we don't
> play by the rules, and if we don't consciously work at being legal, lawful,
> ethical and fair—an unethical detective is someone who wants to make a
> case rather than find the truth. An unethical detective is someone who goes
> in with a preconceived idea of what he's going to find out and makes the
> facts fit. That's unethical.

Of course finding the truth can crush people—there is a neat justification hidden here. Subjectivity is also labeled dangerous for business, while
neutrality is praised as a means to gain professional credibility. In-house
training reveals a constant stress on maintaining professional neutrality:

> STUDENT 1: What if we're working for the plaintiff and we find something
> that just blows his whole claim right to hell?
>
> TEACHER: Important.
>
> STUDENT 1: Our obligation is to discover not just evidence that might nec-
> essarily prove our point of view but all of the evidence, right? The shad-
> ing part is the . . .
>
> STUDENT 2: The lawyer is going to do the lying, right?
>
> TEACHER: Our responsibility is to discover the facts, the truth of the matter,
> not to make a case. We take it all and we give it, positive, negative—we
> give it all to our client and say, "This is what we have found. Now whether
> this is to your benefit or to your detriment, you will have to make that
> determination but these are the facts." . . . If we do find something that

weakens his case, it is very important that our client counsel knows that so that he may take another tack.

STUDENT 3: He may drop the case.

TEACHER: He may drop it. He has a responsibility. And given the way court law is going, attorneys will pay a penalty for bringing frivolous litigation. That is just the moral and right thing to do. Otherwise, then it destroys our credibility as an investigator. One of the things we want to be able to establish out there on the street, and this is in order to generate the cooperation of witnesses, is you are neutral. Yeah, you're working for this particular lawyer, but you are a reporter. Somebody works for somebody.

Liability, a very real concern for private detectives, strengthens the assumption of neutrality. Steadfast legal and neutral extensions of techniques avoid lawsuits and other dangers.

Investigators also will demonstrate symbolic distance from clients by citing anecdotes of clients' "cold-bloodedness." For example:

> We're called in to obtain all the medical history and documentation that we can to establish whether or not a person has an undeclared or misrepresented preexisting condition which precipitated their death within their contestable period. There are certain riders in policies. I had a case I worked on. A woman was killed as a result of an auto accident, a roll-over. She stormed out and was killed. She [had] recently applied for a policy, but the policy has a smoker rider in it. So, I'm up there investigating, interviewing the beneficiary, which is her husband, asking questions, did she smoke or not? The guy is kind of freaked out, "Why are you asking this kind of stuff? My wife died in an auto accident." "Yes, yes, I know." These are very touchy and sensitive cases, and I've had people break down and cry on them. The idea is that the woman was found to be a smoker during that contestable period. Do you know they don't have to pay off the full death benefit? They'll refund the premiums paid to date. They're cold-blooded; they don't care.

This cold-bloodedness label helps private detectives put more distance between themselves and clients, which supplements their sense of neutrality. Private detectives remain neutral and ethically unscathed because they associate assignments' "dirtiness" with clients, despite their being the tools of accomplishing that dirtiness. Disavowing a client's motivation is a way to transfer responsibility for anything disreputable about the case to clients.

Professionalism is also appealed to as the guardian of neutrality. The responses private detectives gave when asked for examples of unethical behaviors support this view (see table 4). Private detectives reported ethical violations tied to indicators of professionalism rather than to categories of generic moral violation, such as "private detectives shouldn't lie." The behaviors identified as violations threaten the professional competence claim of private detectives and, by extension, the perception that private detectives conduct dispassionate and professional investigations. What is further noteworthy about these violations is that no methodological applications are viewed as ethically problematic in themselves other than explicitly illegal actions such as trespassing and wiretapping.

Private detectives' accounts differ from an individual's accounts because, as professionals, they can use institutionalized credentials, such as licenses, to make themselves appear neutral. To be licensed, private detectives must meet training and apprenticeship requirements, which along with work experience provide specialized knowledge that enables them to claim a neutral professional use of deceptive techniques. Their ability to find "truth" and to work neutrally also borrows from popular images of private detectives' "artist" and "craftsman" skills, another example of the

Table 4. Self-Reported Unethical Behaviors for Private Detectives[*]

- Charging time that no one worked (false billing)
- Manufacturing fraudulent evidence
- Wiretapping, planting bugs
- Taking advantage of mentally incompetent clients
- Selling confidential information to other sides during an investigation
- Exorbitant profit mongering
- Providing information that could result in grievous harm to others (e.g., giving someone's location to someone who is a threat)[**]
- Defamation of others (e.g., telling others that someone is committing a crime when this fact is not established)
- Obtaining information illegally
- Practicing without a license
- Using untrained employees
- Providing unlisted telephone numbers to clients
- Trespassing
- Offering services that a private detective is not qualified to perform

[*] These behaviors are labeled unethical by the private detectives themselves. Self-reports are not descriptions of the sampled private detectives' own actions. The initial interview question, which I then followed up, asked private detectives to identify what they consider unethical actions. Their responses would usually include a disclaimer, such as "I would never do this, but some guys . . ."

I have listed all unethical behaviors that I heard respondents mention. I did not collect information about respondents' perceptions of the frequency of each behavior or their comparative rankings of each behavior's severity. In addition to these behaviors, the state licensing board disciplines several violations that private detectives themselves do not report as unethical behaviors. These include violations such as failing to register operatives with regulatory officials and not paying licensing fees.

[**] Many investigations have negative repercussions for their targets. The identified adulterer, fraudulent claimant, and employee thief are punished as a result of investigations. What this respondent alludes to are situations such as a private detective finding someone for a client and later learning that the located person had a protection order against the detective's client.

difference in specialized ability and knowledge between laypersons and professional practitioners.

Abbott (1988, 61) argues that professionals will continue to associate themselves with outdated images of their profession if those images are appealing to the public, even if the old image offers an inaccurate portrayal of actual activities. Abbott's observation suggests that professionals can wield "ceremonial myths" about their profession as legitimating defenses. Blumstein et al. (1974, 565) conclude: "It cannot be overstated that people respond to our symbolic restructuring of our deeds, much more than to the deeds themselves." Their observation suggests that ceremonial occupational myths play a crucial role in legitimating professional accounts, and, in doing so, in obscuring actual behaviors.

Overall, claims of neutrality portray deceptive techniques as tools that professionals can use properly, which makes the reason why someone wants to apply those tools the forum for moral judgment. The actual objective method itself is exempted from judgment. Neutrality thus enables professionals to portray themselves as conduits of actions dictated by the morality (or cold-bloodedness) of others. Thus, traits of other social actors, such as clients' cold-bloodedness, targets' crimes, or peers who are "unprofessional," can be held responsible for any contestable actions, while the techniques associated with adversarial labors remain neutral.

Reputation Laundering

Private detectives do not identify dirty work as a stable category. There are disparities between laypersons and practitioners, and among practitioners themselves, regarding what work should be defined as "dirty." The interviews and observations presented here communicate some of this divergence. For example, some say that catching criminals justifies acting deceptively; others perceive tasks as either legal or illegal, with a deception being an irrelevant moral consideration. Still others see moral assessments of their work as being evaluated appropriately at the level of the clients; after all, the clients' agendas sponsor the use of deception. What is common to all private detectives is their knowledge that negative images do exist of their work and the ways in which deception is used in it. They necessarily have responses to this, some of which they provided in our discussions of the traits that characterize ethical and unethical private detectives.

Accounts of work-related deceptions advantage practitioners over unwilling targets of work-related deceptions. They also help obscure any potential harm resulting from employing work-related deceptions. The structural nature of professional work particularly heightens the target's disadvantages. While many occupations have a two-way exchange between practitioner and client, for example, dentist-patient or teacher-student, professions that operate adversarially have a three-way interaction, in which two sides ally against another. One client pays the practitioner and the other "client" is the involuntary target of the professional's adversarial "customer service." As a consequence, occupational accounts often consist of statements about why it is OK to do some particular procedure to a target, as long as techniques are applied appropriately. In this sense, traditional targets of adversarial labor can be viewed only as "deserving the dirty work that they get" (Hughes 1984).

Contemporary society is confronted with the dilemma of protecting privacy in an age of ever-increasing capacity to invade privacy.[8] Marx (1990, 532) summarizes one perspective on preserving personal privacy as "the only people who worry about privacy are those who have something to hide." This perspective, which is embedded in most private detectives' occupational accounts, can justify intruding on privacy, a specific disadvantage for targets.

Some private detectives seek criminal targets to strengthen accounts for adversarial work. This "vilification" requirement is important because accounts do more than assign blame. They are cumulative stories that extend beyond the borders of an individual case where they are applied. A dangerous self-fulfilling prophecy results from applying accounts, in which targets are perceived mainly as suspect individuals. Occupational-level accounts thus may help justify images of targets that perpetuate adversarial professional behaviors.

In the case of private detective work, there is little doubt in private detectives' and targets' minds that investigative deceptions can yield harsh consequences. Targets stand to lose jobs, marriages, financial resources, and personal freedom. They may well have brought those consequences on themselves. Investigations using deceptions, however, also clearly help advance those consequences.

Potential harm also exists in a corollary danger of using deceptive techniques in investigations, which is that they can generate unintended information. For example, a legitimating rationale of assigning an undercover agent is to discover whether people are stealing. Those agents must submit daily reports of everything they observe. These reports may describe activities that are unrelated to suspected theft, such as people who criticize management or who are rude to co-workers, their drinking or sexual habits outside work, or, historically, workers' union activities (which are now illegal to report). Undercover operatives also state that the information they report can benefit workers through identifying people who are working harder than their supervisors realize and by exposing cases of discrimination and sexual harassment.

Any examination of the professional context for offering accounts must consider the larger implications accounts have for clarifying the relationship between professional structure, deception, and "dirty work." Analysts of "dirty work" traditionally study the "manner in which the socially deviant do the necessary but unacknowledged dirty work for 'the good people' whose respectability must keep them above such things" (Davis 1984). Seen from this perspective, private detectives are private-sector agents of social control who engage in work-related deceptions for "benevolent" clients. If such an agent commits objectionable acts, the client can attribute free will and discretion to that agent and hope to avoid any moral taint derived from the practitioner's actions.

Private detectives act as "adversarial" proxies for clients, a substitution that enhances the ability of clients to protect their images. Private detectives can also account for those work-related deceptions by reallocating responsibility for "dirty work" to targets, clients, or the law. A "dirty work" label is initiated at the top, passed to the client and then to targets, a process I refer to as "reputation laundering." For professionals, account-giving involves laundering labels across laws, consumers of services, and targets of work. The result is that these accounts mitigate a professional's sense of personal liability for engaging in morally controversial, work-related deceptions.

The cultural and structural features of professions, such as clients, training, licensing, asymmetries of expertise and prior work experience, expose a different dimension of accounts, namely their potential affinity for being anchored within organizational contexts. Individuals do use accounts when their deviant behaviors threaten to sully their personal reputations. The key for further research at the level of both data and theory is to study accounts at the level of the institutions, groups, and actors that have a stake in the success of particular accounts. Identifying and distinguishing which particular organizational and professional resources are more important than others in crafting these collective accounts is an important direction for further research. Accounts are socially structured opportunities to preserve or lose legitimacy for given behaviors. Because there are stakes in losing or gaining legitimacy for using deception as official work, accounts have to be considered in terms of how organized contexts, such as professional life, offer specific resources to reinforce them.

4

THE SHADOW WORLD
OF UNOFFICIAL DECEPTION

$\mathbf{S}$o far I have addressed how private detectives construct, rationalize, and implement deceptions as legitimate work. My second case study focuses on informal and unofficial deceptions in the workplace. The terms "informal" and "unofficial" refer to clandestine deceptions in the workplace, such as goofing off and subverting rules. These informal deceptions constitute an unofficial means of navigating the social relationships and tasks that are part of everyday work.

Private detectives consciously plan and implement official deceptions such as undercover operations as part of their legitimate organizational work on a client's behalf. Managers, operatives, and clients are consciously aware of and partner those actions. Unofficial deceptions, alternatively, exist in the broader workplace underworld. In running a business enterprise, managers do not officially condone clandestine deceptions such as lying to customers. Yet when observers look behind the scenes, they sometimes find that many managers "wink and nod" at employees who mislead customers. The Sears auto repair scandals, for example, revealed a widespread in-house policy in which employees were encouraged to deceive customers into paying for overpriced and unnecessary car repairs.[1]

I now shift from analyzing the official deceptions in the organizational "foreground" to investigating unofficial deceptions in the organizational "underworld." Informal deceptions can constitute the real mechanisms for doing official work, but they are not acknowledged officially. The data that I present in the upcoming chapters is more open-ended and probing.

Influenced by Goffman, I describe routine forms of deceptive impression management in the workplace. Goffman conceptualized recognizable social practices that were previously unnamed and thus less recognizably available to researchers. I hope to identify similar subtle deceptive behaviors in workplace culture.

In upcoming chapters, I also directly connect aspects of the dramaturgical infrastructure to distinct types of informal workplace deception. For example, I describe how new workers and supervisors act deceptively during their training. I identify what expectations motivate those deceptions and how they constitute an underlying system of subterranean education in the workplace. In this chapter, I introduce some broad analytic themes for exploring informal deception: administrative functionality, social contradiction, subtle collective implementation, and qualitative complexity.

Melville Dalton's *Men Who Manage*

Melville Dalton's *Men Who Manage* (1959) is an exemplar for research on informal workplace deception. Dalton, a successful business executive prior to pursuing graduate study in sociology, drew on his extensive work history in the business world to inform his scholarly research on managers. In *Men Who Manage*, he identified everyday workplace deceptions at the managerial and lower levels in two production facilities and, in additional research, among saleswomen at a department store. The deceptions he exposed included "sweetened" records to cover up workplace injuries and safety violations, covert discrimination against workers, conspiracies to manipulate production quotas, conversion of company resources to personal ends, the rejection of innovative ideas and efficient practices because their originators were disliked, hidden collusion between union representatives and managers, and the cultivation of secret informers among lower-level workers. His book details how consequential these types of deceptions were for understanding how work was really conducted.

For example, Dalton noticed that hidden incentives formed an important part of recruitment and compensation. Managers recruited and retained sought-after workers with rewards such as shortened workweeks by punching their timecards in their absence. Managers also received perks such as shop workers using company resources to make goods for them and repair appliances in their homes. Dalton saw these deceptions as ways to unofficially structure incentives to accomplish organizational goals.

He also noticed that the organizational chart identifying formal hierarchical lines of authority never squared with the actual people other workers sought for advice in crisis situations. A contradiction existed between hierarchical positions on the organizational chart and the actual influence that someone had despite their official ranking.

This observation influenced Dalton to ask what traits characterized people holding high levels of informal authority. He identified these traits as being able to work around the rules; being perceived as someone who exercises leadership in challenging projects; avoiding being the butt of jokes; cultivating a reputation for resourcefulness during emergencies; having powerful contacts and ties; good looks; a "desirable" ethnicity, race, or gender; and contacts in the community.

Dalton's work offers an initial basis for considering how important unofficial deceptions are in managing workplaces. He saw that deceptions had *administrative functionality* in helping people complete important administrative tasks such as recruiting, production, retention, and decision making. Administrative functionality refers to the administrative functions that deceptions perform over and above individual goals that may initially motivate them.

As an example, in chapter 5, I consider how deception occurs in training new workers. New workers may lie during their probationary periods to appear to be "quick learners," though they are much more confused than they find prudent to admit. Some supervisors do their utmost to avoid the obligation of training new workers, subtly discouraging new workers from asking questions that would "waste" a supervisor's time. These two individual interests—in new workers not appearing "slow" and supervisors saving time and energy—have an administrative functionality of producing altered training systems and production outcomes for new workers, who end up learning somewhat "off the books." These informal deceptions raise the question of how people learn on the job when official routes of doing so are not followed.

The administrative functionality of many deceptions also raises an issue that Dalton did not address: ethical disengagement. How do people feel about turning to deceptive mechanisms for accomplishing their work? How do they perceive moral accountability for routine informal deceptions—if they even see them as a troubling issue? If organizations benefit from deceptions, what internal mechanisms of administration help mitigate responsibility for resorting to them? These mechanisms may be different from the ones that people who carry out official deceptions use.

Dalton argued that informal deceptions help resolve underlying social contradictions in the workplace: "Rules are not sacred guides but are working tools to be dropped, revised, ignored as required in striking successive balances between company goals on the one side and their personal ends and the claims of supporters on the other" (1959, 247). Here, in an early precursor of transcending the amoral individual deceiver model, Dalton stated that deceptions help people appear to conform to rules even though they are actually "dropping, revising or ignoring them" to meet the desires of workers and company goals. A contradiction here is that members of organizations may believe that they have to break the organization's rules to serve either their own individual interests or the organization's.[2]

Lies help conceal these social contradictions. Our behavior is not supposed to contradict ideals, yet workplaces often impose contradictions on workers, who then have to resolve them for themselves. Workers have to adhere to rules that contradict their practical workplace interests. For example, washing one's hands every time one is supposed to in a restaurant kitchen would slow down work. In the training example, people are supposed to appear to learn quickly on the job regardless of how difficult tasks are or how well they have been trained.

Dalton also noticed that adept workers and managers acted deceptively by manipulating rules to attain their own goals, which did not always overlap with those of their employer. Peers saw workers who could navigate outside the expectations of rules as being "strong"; managers and workers who wouldn't circumvent rules even if necessary were considered "weak." Informally, weak leaders always capitulated to rules and strong leaders got things done despite them. This perception does not square with bureaucratic ideals. Deception is at the heart of a social contradiction between the administrative need to follow rules and being seen as a weak leader for doing so.

"Role strain" (Grover 1993a, 1993b) illustrates a social contradiction between conflicting individual and organizational obligations. A police officer's partner, mindful of the "thin blue line," fails to notice that probable cause did not exist when his partner made an arrest. What are different types of role strain, beyond not betraying one's co-workers? The range of potential situations of role strain needs to be explored more fully. Just how many social contradictions can workers encounter and deal with using deception?

For example, one informal rule is to avoid "bothering" your supervisor with questions, yet you are supposed to ask questions in order to do your job competently. These social contradictions place individual workers in situations where formal and informal norms about worker behavior conflict. Workers want to avoid appearing to be "someone who needs handholding." The way out of this dilemma is to act deceptively, such as in the former case, by pretending to know what you are doing in front of the supervisor until you can eventually find a way to get an answer to your questions elsewhere.

There are also contradictions between teams of workers, in crafting false appearances of being on the same page, liking one another, not being sexist or racist, being cooperative rather than competitive, and so forth. In all of these combinations, individuals or collusive teams can put forth deceptive appearances, and the resulting deceptions may very much be in the organization's interest. Covering up discrimination, appearing to comply with a client's expectations, hiding dislike for other workers, and managers obscuring their own incompetence—these cover-ups may be damaging in the long run, but in the short run they help keep organizations afloat. These deceptions are all the product of routine expectations for appearances in the workplace.

Organizations ritualize appropriate deference and demeanor with bosses or clients. Asked why he withheld his complaints about his boss, one respondent remarked, "Like B. B. King says, 'The boss may not be right, but he's never wrong.'" People may dislike workers whom they must respect officially and resent certain roles and tasks they must perform. Faking deference and demeanor is deceptive and serves as a routine aspect of organizational infrastructure. What you are expected to do, you do or hide not doing; what you are expected to feel, you feel or hide not feeling.

Oftentimes workers must perform tasks when they lack information, enthusiasm, training, or autonomy to do their work as ideally as the task requires. Resolving such infrastructural problems can require adopting a range of legitimate and illegitimate solutions. You can ask questions to learn how to do your job and/or try to fake your way through a task. The distribution of information, autonomy, and training in an organization are also routine administrative aspects that operate in part on a dramaturgical infrastructure. Sometimes knowing how to look as if you know what you are talking about is more important than knowing what you are talking about. People who can avoid examinations of their competency can hide their inadequacies in the organizational underworld.

Organizations also employ informal criteria for determining someone's advancement, which requires candidates to cultivate proper appearances for higher-ups and important colleagues (Jackall 1988; Morrill 1995). This informal world is rife with deceptive possibilities such as misrepresenting one's educational attainments or one's dedication to the company. What is pertinent, as Jackall (1988) notes, is not simply identifying what lies people tell, but articulating (and, for some, changing) the organizational structure that sustains having to tell those lies. Jackall identifies a "bureaucratic ethic" that encourages workers to adopt rational, means-ends criteria over more subjective moral criteria to judge the appropriateness of their own and organizational actions. How do people learn to see means and ends, instead of rights and wrongs, in the workplace? The presence of specific types of social contradictions provides a fertile breeding ground for informal deceptions. The dramaturgical infrastructure concept is helpful here because it identifies specific social situations and administrative routines in organizations that call for some workers to adopt deceptive strategies.

The Subtle Collective Implementation of Informal Deception

Informal deception is an individual action, but it is also a cooperative enterprise in a workplace. Exploring deception as a cooperative and functional behavior requires expanding a view of lying beyond perceiving lying only as an aggressive, mean-spirited activity by an individual. People lie collusively to avoid work or for self-protection, such as to avoid an unpleasant colleague. Managers and workers can form a collaborative team to create a required false appearance to appease a client. They can create the appearance of being in compliance with various laws. There are required appearances of diligence and deference, of delivery dates, and appropriate production. In such situations, informal deceptions are covert and cannot be acknowledged publicly.

Informal deceptions can also occur with the hidden blessings of management. Examples include collectively organized informal schemes, like the ones Dalton noticed of illicit conspiracies between a union and management, overlooking safety violations that helped enhance productivity, and processing timecards for absent employees. Organized informal and collective deceptions illustrate "how things really get done around here" and have administrative purposes that have not been adequately studied.

The term *vranyo* in Russian describes the subtle collective participation people can have in deception. Vranyo occurs when one person lies to another, the second person recognizes that the first person is lying, and neither of them acknowledges that any lie was spoken. For example, someone states (knowing otherwise) that he will meet monthly production goals. An audience hears this claim and knows it to be false. No one acknowledges the lie publicly. That participation, of knowing a lie and saying nothing, is a form of nonenforcement that can give a lie continued life because it was not exposed.

When expectations do not square with available evidence, participants must decide whether to gloss over discrepancies out of self-preservation or point them out and risk punishment. When a co-worker claims to work incredibly hard but is lying and an observer knows that colleague is lying but does not expose the lie—that is vranyo. In subsequent chapters, workers demonstrate a strong inclination to vranyo. Vranyo occurs routinely in meetings when people pretend to agree with interpretations of events in public though they all disagree in private.

The Complexities of Informal Deceptive Behavior

I asked each person I interviewed to define deception in his or her own words. A generic summary of their responses is that individuals act deceptively when they knowingly provide an inaccurate impression to an audience. For example:

"Oh, I guess I'd probably say that deception would be leading someone in one direction while you were trying to do something else or not telling the entire story."

"You're purposely trying to mislead or . . . or misdirect someone else, by something you're doing, whether or not it's hiding part of the truth or actually deceiving."

"Presenting an appearance of yourself or circumstances which is useful to you but which you know to be untrue."

"I would define it as trying to make somebody think something in a different way than it actually is."

"It's someone manipulating you to believe something that's not true."

"Deception would be cases where you intentionally convey an impression of something that's not accurate."

Some respondents also emphasized a view that deceptive acts are always negative. For example:

> I would define deception as doing something which is negative or doing something bad and then trying to hide it or cover it over, either through actions or some words.

This negative-only view resonates with a perception that deception is primarily a malevolent activity. Of course, many deceptions do have malicious ends. Almost everyone I interviewed or observed agreed that hiding knowledge is deceptive when done for antisocial purposes such as stealing or fraud, and all respondents defined deception as a form of misrepresentation. At the same time, many people did not view some behaviors as deceptive, even if a generic definition of deception could define them that way. For example, informants sometimes concealed negative opinions of co-workers or misrepresented themselves on résumés. Yet they did not think that concealing such information from others was deceptive, although on reflection some respondents later agreed that the act was deceptive. Consider this exchange:

> EMPLOYEE: There's [names a co-worker] in the hall. You walk by and say [he then puts on a fake "friendly" voice], "Hey, how are you doing?" [His tone of voice changes] That bitch!—You know, I mean, I do that all the time.
>
> D. S.: Why didn't you call that "deception" earlier?
>
> EMPLOYEE: Yeah . . . I would.
>
> D. S.: But it wasn't something that came to mind?
>
> EMPLOYEE: You can also call it being civil.

Concealing that you dislike someone by acting friendly is common at work as well as in other social situations, and it is also a deceptive misrepresentation of one's feelings. Résumé "fiddling" occurs, for example, when people list skills on their résumé (for example, experience with a specific computer program) that they barely have. Résumé fiddling was, according to one person, "telling the most optimistic version of the truth."

People can provide others with misleading information in a workplace without always having a nefarious motive. Selectively defining what is deceptive shows that people use motives for misrepresentation to assess whether something is actually a *deceptive* misrepresentation. People prefer to label "deception" by assessing someone's motives, rather than their actions. Using the motive and ends of an act rather than the act of deception itself is a neat trick, because doing so allows people to engage in deceptions without the bitter aftertaste of identifying themselves as liars.

I routinely asked people to describe behaviors that illustrated the "deceptiveness" of acts in accordance with their definitions for deception. However, I identified some behaviors as deceptive, even over an informant's initial objections. I did so when I thought behaviors, regardless of motive, were meant to encourage others to believe something that the person knew was false. It is important to focus on both these nuances in order to appreciate the qualitative complexity of workplace deception.

In upcoming chapters I illustrate more fully the four broad properties of informal deceptions that I have identified here and that are found in table 5. Deceptions may take the form of subterranean education and shadow administration or of cultivating social currency in the workplace. I also discuss in more depth how people and organizations attempt to disengage from a sense of ethical liability for both everyday and egregious lying. I address some of the impacts of deception on organizations and how a greater appreciation of deception can enrich the contributions of important organizational theories.

Table 5. Four Broad Properties of Informal Deceptions

---

1. Informal deceptions have *administrative functionality.*
   Example: Dalton (1959) on informal authority, covert compensation and hidden recruitment incentives

2. Informal deceptions resolve *social contradictions* between:
   A) Individual interests and organizational ones
   B) Organizational rules and organizational interests
   C) Conflicting interests of workers, co-workers, and managers
   D) Workers and stakeholders outside the organization
   Example: Types of "role strain"

3. Informal deceptions often represent a subtle *collective implementation* and are not just the work of a "few bad apples."
   Example:. *Vranyo*

4. Informal deceptions are *qualitatively complex phenomena.*
   Example: People having different prevailing definitions of what counts as "deception"

5

SUBTERRANEAN EDUCATION AND TRAINING

During a colloquium on this book's arguments, an economist described his view of how people learn to deal with deceptive coworkers. He said that people will realize over time which co-workers say "A" and mean "A" and which co-workers sometimes say "A" but mean "B." After repeated observations to learn who really does what they say they will, workers can then deal with liars in a predictable and rational way.

I agree that repeated observations help people predict who lies and how to deal with them. However, uncertainty, complexity, and social content are left out of this A and B explanation. If we assume that we can distinguish between scam artists and straight shooters, a number of "what shall I do about it" problems still remain. For example, can I ever confront a liar without facing dire consequences? Suppose that liar is my boss? If I am concerned about my job security, is it best to ignore that the boss is lying?

In this chapter, I examine how people act deceptively in the workplace to acquire and act on accurate information. Decision makers cannot always get accurate information. Managers have no psychic powers that verify a business partner's trustworthiness. Self-interested individuals will paint rosier pictures than exist, which aggravates the uncertainty of deciding what to believe.

Organizations can never avoid some degree of uncertainty in planning their actions. The principal-agent problem, transaction cost economics, "embeddedness," and bounded rationality are some theoretical approaches in organizational theory that address how the limited availability of accurate information can impact organizational decision making. These approaches identify numerous organizational-level solutions, which can range from implementing detailed contracts to govern employee-employer relationships to installing surveillance cameras to watch workers.

Workplaces regulate the control and distribution of privileged information according to a person's level in the hierarchy, a gatekeeper's discretion, and penalties in employment contracts, such as facing dismissal for revealing proprietary information. Information is a resource associated with a position's "need to know." Divisions of labor create very different pools of specialized knowledge among workers. There are also lower-level employees who gain privileged information by processing that information for higher-ups. Official systems for distributing information are a starting point. However, there is also the individual level to consider. Further research is needed to consider what covert streams of actions individual self-interested workers use to acquire and exchange information that organizational controls miss.

Individual workers try to offer organizationally desirable presentations of self in response to whatever workplace appearances are required. They may want to look like a "quick learner," a "bending over backward mentor," or an "in the loop up-and-comer." At the same time, people have to figure out what is really going on around them, since they are stuck in the midst of many competing strategic actors like themselves. Managers may portray an organization's situation as better than it is or promise rewards that do not exist. Are these managerial claims true? A co-worker may claim expertise at a task but be incompetent. Can you learn this fact before you trust this co-worker or subordinate with the task? What information from managers, co-workers, and subordinates can be deemed reliable? Superiors have the hierarchical advantage that subordinates are not supposed to question them, while subordinates lack that protection. The resulting problem, then, is how do people access and act on accurate information when they sense that they cannot openly contravene an official but inaccurate version of events?

There are countless struggles on the person-to-person level among workers who are striving to acquire and conceal accurate information about events and people at work. The economist's rational framework collapses under the weight of these complex struggles. People feel a need to keep discrediting information secret at certain times and not others. They must determine when to trust others and decide how to act on sensitive information, all the while avoiding reprisals for missteps in gathering or using information. Intimidating managers, subordinates who do not feel free to voice critical opinions, the aware and upwardly mobile, busybodies, stool pigeons, and backstabbers: these workplace characters all have major roles in the drama of everyday work.

Workers become involved in covert networks for exchanging information in the workplace to solve the problem of uncertainty over both learning and acting on accurate information. People create alliances with co-workers, trusting some with particular levels of confidentiality and trusting others with less. I refer to these covert exchanges as *systems of subterranean education,* whose goal is to selectively distribute information about ongoing workplace practices with an eye to self-interested knowledge and performance. Subterranean education is a key part of the workplace underworld and of the shadow administration of work.

Subterranean education is not simply an overly complicated synonym for gossip, although much gossip is the lifeblood of subterranean education. Hodson (1991) argues that gossip among workers is a means of social control, bragging, increasing solidarity, information exchange, and character assassination. Because of workplace monitoring, and to exclude some from participation, people exchange important information underground as gossip. Subterranean education recognizes this function of gossip. Yet subterranean education does more in constituting several other shadow administrative functions, such as being a system of training and mentoring, covert lobbying, buck-passing, retaliation, and tension reduction; a system for collective monitoring; and a means of enhancing production and trust among co-workers. Subterranean education includes gossip and is a dependable forum for doing an organization's legitimate work clandestinely.

The deceptive qualities of subterranean education come from exchanging accurate information in an underground and secretive manner and acting as if this informal exchange system does not exist since it contravenes established systems for exchanging information. Informants believed that they heard more honest information in subterranean systems than they did during official discussions. To address the functions and systems of subterranean education as a deceptive arena in workplace culture, I begin with the training process. It is the first place where information about how to perform one's work is covertly exchanged.

Training Partners

At an ideal level, the training of new workers should be straightforward. Experienced employees partner up with new hires and familiarize them with work procedures. Stages of training are clear and connect to practical aspects of doing the job. Comprehensive and detailed instruction manuals exist. Trainers are active mentors who answer questions dutifully and patiently, and trainees are enthusiastic, asking questions and working hard. The new employees soon advance to performing work competently and independently.

As opposed to this ideal, new workers and interns described inherent deceptions during this process. New workers and trainers both sought hidden advantages and shortcuts throughout the training process. Interns and entry-level workers, for example, routinely lied about how quickly they understood new information and instructions, which meant they couldn't ask too many questions. As one novice banker puts it:

> I was very nervous about doing a good job right out of the blocks, and I didn't want there to be any question about my abilities. And I thought asking too many questions would cast some doubt over my abilities.

Informants repeatedly said that they did not ask follow-up questions about instructions that they didn't understand, even when their new supervisors asked if they had questions. They wanted to avoid appearing too stupid to understand instructions the first time and to keep their ignorance hidden from supervisors, as this finance intern made clear: "I don't want him to think I'm stupid. Instructions are like a test to see how quick you get things, and I don't want to look bad."

Workers feel pressure to have something like "instant experience," as if they can immediately do their new job quickly with no hand-holding. The need to look as if you know what you are doing is particularly aggravated when people stated in interviews and on résumés that they knew how to perform the job. People desire to avoid appearing "slow" to avoid embarrassment and a perceived cost to their careers.

Some mentors choose not to perform an instructional role. Though such supervisors may say, "You should come to me with any questions," new workers learn that asking them questions will produce an unenthusiastic response. Training, as one informant stated, "was a task where he was like I don't want to be bothered with it." Subjects described supervisors as "raising their eyebrows," "rolling their eyes," or "sighing in resignation" if approached with questions. For example:

> Sometimes he answered my questions. But the way he did it, the briskness with which he did it, I mean the unfeeling, almost annoyed . . . really

sent me the message, he doesn't want to answer my questions. He doesn't really care right now. It's his agenda not to teach me.

These actions constitute a shadow administrative practice of *unacknowledged discouraging*. Unacknowledged discouraging occurs when someone dissuades an action or question without openly making an explicitly discouraging statement. If a supervisor offered an explicitly discouraging statement out loud, that supervisor would be publicly responsible for discouraging the person. Unacknowledged discouraging allows supervisors to dismiss the obligation to work with trainees without being culpable for avoiding that work. It also provides a means of making subordinates accountable if they end up making a mistake, just through the simple device of being able to state, "If you had a question, why didn't you just ask?" As an intern at an investment firm observed, "A lot of the attitude is 'figure it out.' But then again, if it goes wrong, then you're always asked why didn't you ask?"

There are different styles of unacknowledged discouraging. In addition to eye rolling, briskness, and sighing, respondents also took note of whether supervisors had a history of lashing out at subordinates. If supervisors had a reputation of responding harshly to people, respondents would avoid asking them questions:

D. S.: Why did you feel like you couldn't say you didn't know how to do it?

EMPLOYEE: I think that it was a couple of things. First of all, the guy that assigned it, at times he could be very difficult to work with.

D. S.: By that you mean?

EMPLOYEE: Just in that I had seen him, he had never said anything to me or reacted very negatively toward me and I had gotten along with him fine—but I also saw that if you somehow got on his bad side or he got ticked off with you or irritated with you, he could just treat you like crap for the rest of the day and throughout.

A supervisor displaying a bad temper may knowingly (or unknowingly) intimidate others so that they don't ask questions or initiate interaction. This intimidation has a lingering reputational effect that continues to impact the organizational culture. As an example in college culture, consider professors (usually tenured) who initiate their first class with fire and brimstone statements about how tough the course, exams, readings, and paper assignments will be. These fiery descriptions are intended to drive students from the class and to lower the professor's workload. The professor may turn out to be a lot easier than promised.[1]

Some respondents also believed that supervisors gave vague instructions to pass the buck for any subsequent problems. An advertising executive describes how this buck-passing strategy operates:

> EXECUTIVE: He doesn't necessarily point the finger at me, but he'll use his generalizations again, to say "Well, my instructions were not carried out," when people know that it's me that's supposed to be doing the carrying out, or maybe me and a couple of other people.
>
> D. S.: And he doesn't go back and say, "My instructions weren't clear in the first place"?
>
> EXECUTIVE: Oh, no, never.

Vague instructions also enable supervisors to avoid committing time and effort to instruction. Those instructions lead subordinates to consult other workers for help.

Several respondents also had mentors who gave instructions to do work that the mentors themselves did not know how to do, which suggests that perhaps some of the "quick learners" who moved up the ladder never learned the work along the way. Supervisors can hide displaying inadequate knowledge when their subordinates do not know any better, and subordinates are unlikely to expose them except discreetly. Supervisors can diffuse any vulnerability stemming from not knowing what they are doing by having subordinates do work that they do not know how to do. Learning how to do the work can be someone else's problem, not the manager's. Subordinates then are accountable for knowing the task. In this sense, supervisors pass on discrediting forms of ignorance and complicated tasks to subordinate workers, making learning how to do the work their problem. Subordinates are stuck, unable to acknowledge this form of buck-passing except to peers at a close hierarchical level. To reveal supervisory ignorance is unwise, as this junior executive remarks:

> EXECUTIVE: If this person that assigned this project to me didn't know how to do it, at least they were good at really just putting on a sort of facade that they knew all these things. I would say that was the case with this person.
>
> D. S.: Would it occur to you to say something along the lines of your superior doesn't really know what he's doing?

EXECUTIVE: No, no. Similarly, it wouldn't occur to most people at least to go to someone else above this—if he had a supervisor above your supervisor—and say something. Because I think the other person would be, have the attitude of, I don't care—get the hell out of my office.

Supervisors also used opportunities to answer questions to "showboat." In those circumstances, some supervisors offered overly sophisticated answers that subordinates could not really use. If they asked for clarification, they would get useless self-aggrandizing answers:

A few times I asked the people above me if they could help me. The fellow intern that was with me was making faces because he just couldn't believe the arcaneness of what this guy was telling me. He knew the information so well, and this guy was very pompous and arrogant. He just liked to hear himself talk, and he just talked about it in a way that made it sound very, very complicated and made him sound very knowledgeable. . . . He wanted to make himself look better in my eyes, I think, and that was at the expense of really good information. He could have acted more as a teacher, instead of as some higher-up.

Sometimes supervisors never even bother to ask whether subordinates need instruction. A new hire noted:

They wouldn't stop to think that, you know, hey, how's this guy going to know how to do this? Where's he going to get the information? They sort of assume that maybe I'd go to someone right above me and find out. I mean they sort of typically assumed that I would go to other people besides them, leave them alone, and just get the job done. They'd just think that I'd get it done without me going to them for help.

Covert Strategies for Learning a Job

The combination of wanting to look like a fast learner and minimal mentorship causes new workers to develop alternative information-seeking strategies. They must find people to provide them with information who will not complain about their requesting help. They often seek information from people close to them in the organizational hierarchy:

I'd probably go to the higher person once or twice, tops. And of course,
I'd go to the person below and maybe underneath the person below. And

the lowest person I'd go to, I'd feel more comfortable going to more and more, because they were a level close to myself, and I'd feel less threatened by them.

These slightly higher than a new worker or a lower-level worker (though still lower-level) colleagues, who end up helping may take advantage of their position. Blau (1963) analyzed "consultation with colleagues," and noted that people will instruct others in exchange for the respect of being asked and an acknowledgment that "students" are obligated to "teachers" afterward for future favors. After instructing on technical questions, teachers would ingratiate themselves so that they could expropriate future labor from their students. An intern describes this microsociological system of eventually co-opting later work:

> INTERN: They'd just butter me up a little bit, talk to me, ask me questions about school, talk to me about my school and things like that. The purpose there was just that they'd butter me up and just befriended me and allied with me so that maybe I'd have a hard time turning them down. Pretty soon they'd sort of spring some little assignments that they'd want to push down on me. So if I knew them well, I'd have a problem saying no to them. So that happened on occasion, too.
>
> D. S.: So people would strategize instructions in a way that would save you for the future?
>
> INTERN: Exactly, yeah, just as I'd, in a sense, "use people," people would use me and get to know me so that maybe I could work on their projects and help them out.

These deceptions are part of an administrative subsystem of subterranean education that is oriented around teaching new workers how to approach learning their work. This covert system has larger consequences, such as providing a default system of training to save higher-ups from unexpected questions and having to exert effort training people.

The system also anchors accountability in subordinates. New workers avoid demonstrating their ignorance and develop other ways to learn how to work. The more experienced workers help in exchange for reputation benefits and for chits to exchange for later labor from learners. All of these functions are also underground ones; the unacknowledged deferring of work by superiors and the hidden work of training subordinates is not recognized officially. The moment of first learning the job can involve covert consulting strategies, extracting favors, and avoiding mentoring work and accountability. A larger system of subterranean education is evident in how people negotiate these first informal steps of gaining work information.

Subterranean Education and Vague Information

An additional problem that subterranean education solves is when available information about work conditions is vague. Workers gossip informally to gather a more accurate impression of ongoing events. Sometimes this gossip constitutes an informal educational and training system, a "streetwise MBA" in how work is really done in the company and what supervisory proclivities there are. The importance of "knowing what isn't so" is crucial for navigating organizational culture. Access to that education is a source of upward mobility and survival. Denying access to networks of informal gossip may punish informal rule breakers.

One type of underground mentoring and training is offering warnings. Experienced workers alert other workers to be wary of particular superiors, as this junior marketing executive commented:

> EXECUTIVE: He's an intermediary between our project manager and the president. He flat-out asked me, "How are things going?" "Oh, peachy keen. Great!" And he actually said to me, "You know, you don't have to lie; tell me what's going on." But there's no way, because I don't trust him enough, in the decisions he has power to make, to tell him anything.
>
> D. S.: So why wouldn't you trust somebody in that case?
>
> EXECUTIVE: Well I'd been warned about it. I was warned by another person on a different account.

Training transcends teaching someone technical operations. Subterranean education also involves distributing information about pariahs, helpful persons, and underground policies:

> Gossip is very important, I think, because it helps you navigate around the office. It helps you know who to avoid and who to gravitate to, so a lot of that information is very important—maybe even more so than the information that you're using to do your job.

One typical warning identified "office landmines." An "office landmine" is an individual who explodes at the slightest provocation, into public displays of unreasonable and uncomfortable anger at subordinates. For example:

> Everyone knew—when I say everyone, I mean people at my level and people higher than myself knew that if you asked this person anything he would jump off the handle and be very defensive and aggressive.

Having to deal with office landmines meant learning to adopt deceptive strategies of deference, as this banking intern did:

> I'd blatantly kiss his ass. Just be like, so-and-so, I was wondering if I might be able to interrupt you for a minute, and almost be like a whimpering little idiot, because that way, he wouldn't go into his defensive mode nearly as easily.

Part of having an ear to the wall is also noting who is doing well or who is in trouble. There are sometimes specific individuals who are "lightning rods" for criticism. A lightning rod is a "complaint magnet" and scapegoat who is always singled out for criticism, even if other workers commit similar errors. An intern at a nonprofit shared this tale:

> I mean, she got mad at him for some stuff that he thought she shouldn't get mad about. And she never got mad at us, and she would tell us that . . . I mean the interns, we were very good friends and we all got along really well. And we would joke about it. . . . She would just tell us stuff about like, what was going on in her life and a lot of stuff about the office. And he didn't hear any of it, and we would end up telling him. And also she would—and maybe this was kind of an outgrowth of it—kind of complain about him to me. She would talk about him. . . . And he knew it, so she was definitely down on the male intern.

Lightning rods in the office are functional for building solidarity. Workers may rally around blaming those individuals. Individually, people also use such information to privately look over their shoulders and see how they are doing comparatively.

It is also important to hear about bad supervisors. Respondents stated that experienced workers spread negative information about problematic supervisors to "make sure that we didn't get too much into, you know, thinking this guy was a great guy. You know to make sure that we knew where everyone stood, and that we knew the real story on it." They alerted co-workers about what attitudes to take toward particular superiors, with

their warnings helping at a strategic level to establish a consensus of opinion about particular people. In this sense, several functions of subterranean education are clear, including establishing trust and solidarity and
acting against enemies and rivals.

Deciding to share denigrating information with others is risky. What if
you share an insult about a co-worker with someone who betrays that disclosure? Workers worry about risks and issues of trust in sharing secrets:

> I said I think it's ridiculous that she doesn't trust her staff enough,
> to think that she can't give us a day. You know, like what were we going
> to be doing today? We didn't have anything pressing for her to check up
> on us to make sure that this had gone out, or this had come in, or what-
> ever. And I thought it was absurd that she called. And so we kind of had
> this quick, sort of heated like—blah! And we all got it out. And then I
> realized that another colleague was there, who hasn't been a person I've
> ever talked to about my feelings about my boss. Shit! You know, I didn't
> need for her to know that. And, well, like, is she going to say something
> to my boss?

Identifying whom to trust leads to information-sharing strategies and to
being wary about distributing information. Workers want to relieve stress
through gossip, but they also worry about becoming the next target of
group derision:

> I mean, at the same time you're making these comments about people, dif-
> ferent people, if you leave to get a drink, you know, you may very well be
> the butt of the next joke.

Interviewees uniformly believed that cultivating the right impression is
crucial. For example:

> D. S.: What's reputation generally, though? You know, when you say
> people want to cultivate their reputations, what are you talking about,
> exactly? What is reputation?
>
> EMPLOYEE: That you're a good worker, or an asshole that shirks responsi-
> bility all the time, or . . . you want to be known as somebody who works
> hard, keeps your nose clean, and gets along with everyone. Everyone
> wants to be known that way. No one—very few people—are that way.
>
> D. S.: So the problem is to get as close as you can to being that.
>
> EMPLOYEE: Sure, and if you're not, make them think that you are.

There are rules about what a person can say and to whom. In the case below, a finance executive and I discuss his version of what the rules are:

D. S.: OK, Tom will say Dick is a terrible worker . . .

EXECUTIVE: Right. It's just . . .

D. S.: It's not a big stab [referring to the interviewee's preceding comment about a "stab in the back"].

EXECUTIVE: It's not, it's not as big. I mean, obviously these people aren't going to be the ones who are affecting you as much.

D. S.: So the difference is, if he goes to the boss, and Tom says to Sally the boss, Dick can't do any jobs . . .

EXECUTIVE: That would be a faux pas. Right there, that would be like a big social faux pas. You don't do that. That's like tattling; I didn't see a whole lot of that there.

D. S.: OK, so if it goes up a level . . .

EXECUTIVE: There's like a self-imposed limit. There's like a line that you don't want to cross. If you start complaining to your superiors about somebody you work with, I would think that that line would be crossed. I didn't see a whole lot of that. I didn't see anyone.

D. S.: So up-the-level ratting is the big thing?

EXECUTIVE: Yeah.

D. S.: And straight-across . . .

EXECUTIVE: Right, straight-across level is . . . very, very small . . . more like a dagger than a butcher knife.

D. S.: OK, why don't we go to "machete?"

EXECUTIVE: Machete would be going, talking to a senior vice president that the person's who's next to you, say five, six levels down, is incompetent. That would be a faux pas. Because the senior vice president could act on that. Whereas, if you're telling a friend of yours in the same level as you that so-and-so . . .

D. S.: It might be jockeying for position, but it's not doing anything so evil.

EXECUTIVE: Right, exactly.

D. S.: So straight-peer is kind of like a safety pin in the back.

EXECUTIVE: At the same time, it's not a whole lot but it could affect . . .

D. S.: It'd still be enough to kind of make you a little wary, is that what you mean?

EXECUTIVE: Right, right, I would say so. Definitely prepares you a little bit. If you're interacting with people you can't cross any lines, because then you'd be seen as an outcast. So you have to stay within the lines. You gotta know where the boundaries are and not cross them, because if you do then people are going to perceive you as a loser.

Once co-workers trust each another enough to share discrediting and risky information, they form strong bonds. These bonds enable people to work more efficiently and sympathetically with one other, because they now will trust each other with secrets. Trust is also supported by the mutual sense that people have to stick together given extant working conditions that are, at times, unfair to them.

A management consultant illustrates these collusions, such as the deceptive lobbying discussed below. Such conspiracies can only transpire among trusting colleagues:

> CONSULTANT: You could say that you've helped out on a project when you didn't and your groups of friends will collude for you. Let's say a certain person wants to get involved on a certain client account . . . . Here is an example I can think of: One of the analysts wanted to get on this client account because they wanted to work for the client, with the hopes that they would get an appointment contract so when the head consultant is looking to hand out the project to someone, and people knew how much you wanted it, they'd say, "Oh yeah, he's been so busy helping out so much with us, helping us with your project, he knows a lot about this project." Another consultant didn't want to be on this client, didn't like being with this client, but had done it before, said, so and so helped on the project and knows a lot about the client. . . . And it's collusion—a lie—but the person did get what they want. But let's say that "Brad" [an ostracized and disliked peer] wanted to work with this company. They wouldn't help him out like that. So that's, I mean that kind of deception, to help out a friend, deceiving bosses, help them to get what they want.
>
> D. S.: Are these kinds of things talked about routinely?
>
> CONSULTANT: In terms of deceiving the boss, I mean very routinely. Yeah, I mean there's just constant hanging up the phone, making themselves look busy, putting on a facade of productivity in a sense. . . . They were always trying to help each other out, lying to the boss about what was going on. Like, oh yeah, we had that meeting today to talk about the account, when they didn't have a meeting. That stuff.

Working together in these conspiracies requires solidarity and trust built in part from sharing gossip and secret information. A similar hierarchical position also helps in that solidarity accrues from knowing that someone else is in the same boat. Deception here can have some standardization. People at equal levels of the hierarchy confront similar deceptions by supervisors and have similar cause to engage in deceptions in response. They share in an awareness of resenting hierarchical abuses, hearing broken promises, and receiving stingy mentorship. This common "exposure position" improves trust and solidarity, which is reflected in and strengthened by collectively participating in deceptive activity. A routine aspect of the dramaturgical infrastructure is sharing a common exposure position—you are either labor or management.

People's sense of affinity with those around them affects their ability to absorb information and contribute to subterranean education. As new workers enter organizations and professions, they must identify what informal membership standards their peers have for collegiality. Is one to eat lunch with colleagues or to be aloof? Is there discretion in choosing the amount of interaction one has, or is too much fraternization problematic? Membership in informal groupings within work organizations can be official and/or moral. One can be an officially employed member of an organization. A subtler type of membership is a communal and moral membership, in which workers must decide their degree of conformity to the onsite cultural norms of their new peers. Do you go out drinking on Friday evening? Play on the organization's softball team? Participate in small talk? Or do you adopt a straight-laced demeanor, communicating with others only when the job requires it, putting in your time but not your sociability?

Moral people are supposed to tell the truth. This imperative conflicts with practical reality. As people become socialized, they grow to understand and identify circumstances in which valued others, such as family and friends, will expect them to lie and cover up for them. We all can identify situations in which refusing to lie excludes people from being full members of groups. Simple evidence for this claim are the readily familiar pejorative terms for people who do not lie when other people want them to, such as being "tactless," "a tattletale," "a puritan," "a troublemaker," "naïve," "disloyal," or "insensitive" (Hunt and Manning 1991). These terms all imply that failing to lie for others will sever social bonds.

The expectation that co-workers will engage in collective cover-ups is an aspect of moral membership in an organizational and professional community that encourages deception. Workers in organizations are teammates, and as such they are pressured to conceal discrediting information about their team. Secrecy is also a structurally enforced feature of bureaucratic administration. Max Weber noted, "Every bureaucracy seeks to increase the superiority of the professionally informed by keeping their knowledge and intentions secret. Bureaucratic administration always tends to be an administration of 'secret sessions'; in so far as it can, it hides its knowledge and action from criticism" (1958, 233). Granovetter (1985) argues that "moral content" comes from repeated interactions between partners in a given workplace. Teammates accrue guilty knowledge, which helps forge trust between "guilty" people through a mutually beneficial decision to not reveal discrediting information to outsiders. Such collusion is a basis of worker solidarity (an especially well-documented example is in the case of police officers—see Manning 1977 and Van Maanen 1983). Attaining "moral membership at work" means meeting whatever criteria are involved in being willing to keep a group's secrets.

Tension Reduction

Exchanging information also is a way for people to blow off steam, as this political consultant related:

CONSULTANT: People blowing off steam, that's the basic thing. Or sometimes it's retaliating because people feel used.

D. S.: And "retaliating" means? Give me an example.

CONSULTANT: Well, people get worked hard. The hours are long, demands are high. And so sometimes people look for, just sort of to feel better about their own situation, you know? This guy treats me poorly, but I have the last laugh because he's completely screwing up the project he's working on. He just lost a big account. What does he know?

This sort of subterranean education about poor performance reduces tension by allowing workers to press grievances and to publicize observations that they are not "allowed" to have because of a lower hierarchical status. Subordinates cannot criticize higher-ups openly so they distribute degrading knowledge covertly and can feel better for doing so.

Peers also notice and resolve troubling excesses by co-workers without necessarily exposing the transgression involved. For example, a management consultant told me of an incident in which she and her assistant thought that a co-worker's constant requests for help were a means of getting them to do his work. She and her co-worker retaliated by doing an extremely poor job on the tasks that he gave them. Since the co-worker transgressed by asking them to do his work, he could not criticize them in public for doing the work badly. Their retaliation was a self-limiting and successful form of internal sabotage.

People lower down the hierarchy have limited ability to have a meaningful opinion and investment in ongoing activities that are publicly above their station. As one informant put it, there are "social rights" in an office—in terms of what one can say and to whom one can say things. People lower down in the hierarchy have limited social rights but reasons to wish for them.

Workers must ignore evidence when available information does not square with what a supervisor represents as true. It is a requirement to publicly ignore "unacknowledged discouraging," to appear to have more skill than one really does, to defer to annoying clients, and to pretend not to see a supervisor making mistakes. These demands, when at odds with one's true impressions, can produce an emotional dissonance (Hochschild 1983) between feigned and felt emotions.

Subterranean exchange of information dissipates this stress by allowing workers to offer punishable opinions with lower risk. Blowing off steam also allows workers to function effectively. For example, subordinates can bypass supervisors who are poor teachers, while showing an appropriate deference, because they can learn covertly from more experienced colleagues. Getting an education outside the formal expected system permits more efficient operations in other ways. The trust that comes from sharing information covertly also enables people to work more efficiently as a team on legitimate work. In other contexts, it also improves morale and alleviates tensions that build up from perceived grievances.

Gossiping can also allow dangerous knowledge to be kept quiet. People can get the moral satisfaction of identifying wrongdoing to colleagues while not blowing the whistle to any external sources. Thus, in an ironic way, gossip, a form of sharing covert knowledge, is also a means for keeping secrets local while defusing some of the energy that might otherwise lead a secret to be exposed publicly. As one informant put it, "Informal griping lets you kind of vent some of these frustrations . . . but not necessarily stick your ass out too far."

Some subterranean education, perhaps gossip, is also a vehicle for influentially weak workers to express strong investment and interest in their organization. Where some might focus on gossip, for example, as an outlet for rebelling against authority or for sabotaging rivals, gossip is also sometimes an involuntary substitute for authority, constituting vicarious backseat driving by wannabe decision makers. Organizational hierarchies can put most workers at a great distance from having any real decision-making influence or power in an organization. Subterranean education is a primary means for bridging a gap between the desire for involvement in organizational decision making and the reality of irrelevancy. Workers who complain in private are like irate but powerless sports fans who call in to radio talk shows to say what they would do if they managed the local sports team.

When a worker sees bad decisions or strategies pursued, saying so and posing alternative courses of action can be exercises of actual commitment to trying to see the right things done. However, because they are out of the loop of power, such workers are stuck as backseat drivers whose commitment and vision lie fallow. A world of managers who do not return phone calls, mistreat clients, offer problematic ideas, and deal with subordinates badly represents a reality that some workers would like to change simply so they can do a better job at work. Their only recourse is to create a vision of doing so and share it with others, without necessarily being able to put that vision into action.

Subterranean education can also have dysfunctional consequences for organizations. Systems of subterranean education distribute information that can promote conflict or is flat-out wrong. Backbiting criticism of superiors and co-workers is disloyal and may lead to inefficiency. Subterranean education can also foster greater solidarity among workers than managers might want, particularly if managers cannot keep problematic information secret.

The Underground Exchange of Disparaging Information

How do people covertly exchange disparaging information? Subordinates fear that criticizing their boss openly risks retaliation. This view logically prevents them from testing whether their superiors actually are vindictive, as this entry-level worker explains:

> The ideal manager would be someone that could take criticism, reflect on it, and then deal with it or try to change it. I don't think that's realistic,

though. A lot of people in general, and especially managers or people who are higher up, have these more-inflated egos than your average person. So when you say something critical of that person, they're definitely— especially if you're lower down, because they're going to be like, who the hell is that person to say that? —they're just going to ignore it. They're just gonna push it to the wayside, probably just get angry with you. Obviously, that's not always the case, but I think in my experience that would have been the case, that if you'd say anything like that, there would have been that reaction.

Hence subordinates hide true opinions about organizational activities and others in the organization from superiors and only voice them covertly. These negative opinions that are risky to express, along with negative opinions of co-workers and any other data that produce unpleasant confrontations with peers or superiors, emerge underground.

Using the example of initial training, we can conceive of organizations as having two rivers of information. One flows on the surface, from which people drink openly. The other river flows underground, and people have to drill for it and tap it before they can drink from it. In chapter 6, I identify some categories of derogatory views that people distribute underground in those hidden waters.

6

DECEPTION AS SOCIAL CURRENCY

An image is composed of desirable characteristics that people or organizations wish to communicate about themselves for public consumption. Impression management is the study of how individuals and organizations use props and behaviors to communicate an image. What is most important sociologically about image and impression management is their value as a form of *social currency*. Successfully cultivating particular impressions for others has rewards. The key is to know what a particular image means in a given context. Impressions that are valued at work are the coin of the realm in workplace culture. It is in this sense that I discuss impression management and deception as a form of social currency.

As an example, think of Pierre Bourdieu's currently in vogue concept of "cultural capital," which (loosely considered) is a set of affinities, knowledge, and cultural dispositions associated with a particular social class, such as being exposed to institutions of "high culture" and having a college education. Sociologists can deliberate over what ought to be included as a form of cultural capital or examine different ways that someone exhibits that capital. But the bottom line analytically is learning which cultural capital associated with a given social class has more power to produce successful social outcomes. It is important to appreciate cultural capital as a valued form of social currency.

James Coleman's concept of "social capital" examines the importance of an individual's placement within valuable social networks, focusing on how establishing good connections with people is immensely useful for social mobility. People try to place themselves advantageously within social networks. In doing so, people want to mine the social currency embedded in knowing the right people.

In this chapter I examine the social currency that comes from cultivating particular desirable appearances in the workplace. It is hackneyed and obvious that people wish to cultivate good appearances in order to pursue a desirable position in the workplace. Workers also have to figure out how the system works. How does someone identify what performances are best? At first glance, one does not know which individuals are really making the mistakes, who is only posing as a hard worker, and whose individual hard work is going unrecognized. Although there is nothing new in stating that employees have a front stage and a backstage in the workplace, exploring how problematic it can be in the workplace to tell one from the other is underemphasized, as is how people communicate such information once they uncover it.

Goffman (1959, 32–33) notes that "those who have the time and talent to perform a task well may not . . . have the time and talent to make it apparent that they are performing well." Similarly, those who lack the time or talent to perform well may have the time and talent to make it look like they can perform a task well. Deception occurs here in the impression management people employ in efforts to be associated with desirable characteristics when the underlying reality is different.

Workers must associate or disassociate themselves with an array of meaningful "social credits" in the workplace. They must seek credits for successes, for being a team player, for being a hard worker, and for appearing to defer. Simultaneously, they must avoid receiving undesirable credit for failed tasks, mistakes, and personal shortcomings. They must decide what social credit to grant to their co-workers, such as determining how hard different people are really working. If goofing off, people must also manage to still receive credit for working when they are not doing any work. Workers also engage in credit wars where they try to deny co-workers credit for accomplishments that they wish to take for themselves.

In short, workplaces have social desirability biases running rampant. In the organizational underlife, all sorts of subtleties of appearance exist. I argue here that appreciation is a form of social currency among superiors and subordinates. When superiors fail to appreciate their subordinates properly, the result is resentment and covert retaliation. Mistakes, in another example, come to take on two dimensions—committing them and then manipulating responsibility for them when they occur. People's deceptions reveal some of the social credits they seek at work and how they manipulate appearances to obtain them.

Hierarchy also dictates how people can fight for credit. Manipulating one's image is anchored in the fact that superiors and subordinates have different amounts of power. Hierarchical resentments can feed deception and also provide roadblocks for lower-level workers in obtaining promotions or receiving credit themselves, leading to efforts to use deceptions to topple the standing of higher-ups. Rude actions by higher-ups subtly diminish their authority with underlings, producing deceptive retaliations. Bosses also have more weapons and legitimacy at their disposal to garner useful credits while distributing negative ones to underlings.

Social credit is a nonfinancial form of local workplace capital. Seeking social credits makes workers behave as alchemists; they are always trying to transform the ephemeral attribute of reputation into real gold. In *Moral Mazes*, Robert Jackall (1988) illustrates how managers try to meet a "team player" image that is necessary to ascend the corporate ladder. The social credits involved in those attempts require more than mouthing aphorisms from Dale Carnegie—one has to work hard to gain mentors and avoid being blamed for problems. If the axiom is true that success has a thousand parents but failure is an orphan, it is incumbent on prospective "parents" to deny a rival's claim of parentage. Consider this example from a consultant being denied credit for success:

> The guy I work with brought in a big account. And I know he brought in the big account because I was with—I remember talking to him. One day, he pointed out an article and said, "This looks like a firm we should be in touch with" and then he did get in touch with them, developed the relationship. It turned out to be a good client for him. And I talked to two other people in the firm who claimed that they brought in the client, even though they had nothing to do with it. At some point, maybe they had a phone call with somebody. But they liked denigrating this guy I worked with. And one good way for them to do it was to say that his big client was actually something he had nothing to do with. I talked to two completely different people in the firm, who both claim that they brought it in. And I know they didn't.

People also attempt to deny credit for status. Organizational titles identify and bestow an apparent credit of having a certain status and caliber of work duties. A title can also deceive. An administrative assistant, for example, might do extremely skilled work but have a title connoting lower status than the work being performed merits. Conversely, a person with a lofty title might do less skilled work than the title implies. Part of the problem is that companies assign many low-status titles (but not always corresponding work) in order to pay people lower salaries. People want to understand how much respect should be attached to particular titles—what social credit does a title actually have? For example:

> She was a "project director," so she was sort of like in charge of all these committees, making sure that all these committees met and all that kind of thing, and keeping everything together for all these places. I did go to a few meetings with her. And it was like she was a nobody at these meetings. She took notes. That was her job. And so it sounds really important, "project director," but essentially this means you're a secretary.

Informants informally criticized the larger organization and individual co-workers all the time. Organization-level criticisms include allegations that favoritism is the true basis for a promotion, that decisions are made irrationally and involve self-dealing, and that managers misrepresent how well organizational operations are going. The array of derogatory information spread about individual co-workers is almost too infinite to categorize. A nonexhaustive list includes criticizing a coworker's competence, appearance, and demeanor; racial, ethnic, religious, or gender stereotypes associated with a co-worker; the amount of work they are or are not doing; and whether a co-worker is too deferential or ambitious to be trusted.

My phrase "learning the flaws of the land" speaks to workplace socialization. Learning derogatory information about one's work environment is an acclimating, important form of workplace wisdom. Learning derogatory information is not only important for feeling "in the loop" and knowing the "real" story (an indication of status), people also feel they increase their chances with better, streetwise knowledge of actual workplace conditions.

Whatever a worker truly thinks about co-workers and the larger organization, the last place it will be aired is in open formal events such as meetings. As a consequence, administrative occasions, such as meetings and reviews, are uncommon venues for honest opinions about touchy subjects. People are onstage and too vulnerable. However, participants are expected to present information publicly regarding the meeting's substance, even if that information reflects poorly on themselves or others. This ideal picture of a meeting's requirements glosses over the reality that individuals have contradictory interests and connections to discussed issues. This is role conflict.

People handle role conflict by acting deceptively and never revealing their own problems in meetings. A real estate manager told me that there were morale problems in the branch office he managed, but at regional meetings he said nothing. In his words, "The attitude in the office might be shit, but I'm not going to stand up and say that." A worker in an environmental nonprofit organization described his colleagues presenting rosier pictures of their projects than was warranted at the organization's annual meeting:

> Every year, all the country program staff and all the headquarters staff get together to talk about the next year's goals and plans for the organization. It's intended to be a review, a critical review, of what we really need to do in order to meet the main goals of the organization, which is to conserve . . . and to protect. . . . So that being the general goal, conservation of ecosystems, you would think that the way to get there in the strategic planning session would be for everyone to take a step back from what they have been doing and say whether or not it's been successful and if what they're planning to do is actually attacking the problem and proposing solutions that have a good chance of working. What ends up happening is that either the people who present those programs kind of present a very rosy picture of what they're doing and justify everything they're planning on doing without having any critical evaluation of it, or they just keep to a bare minimum and discourage discussion, critical discussion, of what they're doing, just so they can kind of get through the whole process and go on and do what they're going to do anyhow. That's probably the clearest consistent example of deception.

I then asked this respondent to elaborate further on how presenters gave rosy pictures and avoided identifying or discussing problems:

> She was asked to present, very clearly, what all the threats were to that area and the proposed and the potential interventions—meaning the type of programs, policy work, scientific research, education, etcetera. And to critically evaluate what she's doing and whether or not they were going in the right direction. She proceeded to give an incredibly beautiful slide show of the area, using up all of her time and more before they could get to questions and answers. And so that by the time she finished this really spectacular slide show and the president tried to open up the discussion to that critical review of threats and potential projects, there really wasn't any time, and we already had been running late, because other people had been doing the same thing. We ended up kind of saying, OK, well, we'll take a look at your proposed plan and get back to you with comments, and time to move on to, you know, to the other program.

Having meetings where issues are discussed publicly, away from trusted insiders, discourages honesty. People understand that stating a weakness in a meeting extends an invitation to other participants to criticize you and possibly blame their own problems on you. Why make the mistake of cutting yourself and bleeding, so that the sharks around the table can smell blood and rip you into pieces? The pressure to not display negative information publicly reflects an informal and well-known administrative rule that honesty is punished. To admit failures is to court curtailed resources, embarrassment, and failure to advance. An advertising account executive noted:

> I think they see it [the truth] as a threat. They're going to open up and honestly say, "What we've been doing . . . has just not worked, we haven't had any successes, so we're going to take this new tactic in the future, or we'd like to get some discussion going, about what we should do." The perception is, if they do that, they're dead.

Since people hide discrediting information, whether in meetings or elsewhere, workers make covert efforts to obtain accurate information about what is really going on. They have to learn the flaws of the land that others conceal. One type of concealed discrediting information that workers noted is that managers distributed false information about turnover. An intern described a discussion of turnover with her colleagues:

> INTERN: I asked him in my interview what the turnover was like, and he told me that "hardly anybody leaves."
>
> COLLEAGUE 1: "I'd say it's more like 100 percent."
>
> INTERN: "What he told me was just a big old lie. And I think that he is leaving too."
>
> COLLEAGUE 1: "Yeah, I think you're right."
>
> COLLEAGUE 2: "See, when I first got here, four people had just quit, and ever since then it's been boom, boom, boom, some people quitting all the time. It's so funny. It just goes around and around."

Managers also lie about the consequences of employee turnover. For example, one entry-level finance services worker learned that managers lie about the losses incurred when a high-level manager departs:

> Brock [the divisional president] told me about this guy from [the division] who recently went to [a competitor], that we were able to retain close to 90 percent of his business and contacts. I go to [Fred, my manager,] who tells me: "Oh, you mean [name]." I said: "Yeah, that guy." Fred says: "Yeah, I was there. Anytime Brock gives you a number like that you have to divide it by two and that still is probably too much. So we're probably really looking at 45 percent or less."

Excessive turnover exposes organizational problems that managers want to avoid discussing. Turnover can reflect workers really having a case against existing work conditions. Turnover also is a cumulative result of broken promises, such as undisclosed ceilings for promotions. Hiding organizational problems indicates that organizations and individuals both fear being punished for honesty. How honest revelations get punished also organizes everyday social interaction into clear borders of what can and cannot be noticed or commented on openly at work.

Another common discovered flaw of the land is the situation in which an employer broke promises they made when signing up new employees. This bait-and-switch deception runs two ways, as many informants revealed that they lied when they were looking for work. Informants freely criticized bait and switches by their employers but did not reflect as disdainfully on their own such schemes.

One broken promise described occurred when employers lied about what work new hires would perform, including how that work would grant them access to organizational higher-ups. Organizations know that new hires are keen to get experience that will increase their potential upward mobility. One entry-level finance worker stated that he was told that he'd "have high-level contact with high-level managers." He subsequently learned that this "contact" meant that "they'll take you to lunch once a year, you know, something like that."

Employers also often promised more rewarding work than employees ended up doing. For example:

> I was hired by a senior vice president with the pretense that I could learn so much about the industry from her, she's got the experience. . . . The opportunity sounded so great and . . . it ended up being completely different when I got there. I was just sort of—file, file, file; fax this; answer that phone. It was more secretarial work.

Some employers acknowledged that there was drudge work here and there but that "everyone pitched in to do it." Once people signed on, they soon noticed this promise was broken, as this nonprofit employee noted:

> At some point I said, "Well, maybe Betty or Frieda [higher-ups] will help stuff [envelopes] when they get in." Susan looked at Judy and said, "Did you hear what she said? She said maybe Betty and Frieda would help stuff." Judy laughed and said, "Yeah, right, Betty and Frieda will help stuff. They don't stuff envelopes." When I interviewed here Betty told

me that when we have mailings the whole office stops working and everyone helps. I have never seen either of them help. When we had the huge . . . mailing, Betty sat on the phone the whole time and neither of them helped.

New workers enact their own deceptions when seeking work. One deception is presenting more qualifications or interest in long-term employment than one really has:

I like to work on a contractor basis. So the temp-to-perm came up. And I really had no intention of ever becoming an employee, even when I was hired. But that was one of the questions: Are you willing to consider temp-to-perm? And sure, I'm good enough, if they pay me $200,000 a year, I'll become an employee. But that's obviously not the case. And I said no. But when they hired me, I said, "Sure, I'll consider it." Which I meant, but I didn't intend to do it.

Some interviewees also embellish their virtues:

Certainly I might try to fake it a little bit when I'm asking a question. Like, I don't know about the design process at all, but I'll ask a question that has to do with it. And I'll throw in the word "palette," because I know that that's important, and I know what it means, but I don't know what the rest of that means, in context, of the work that they do. So there is a certain amount, I guess, of fakery.

Existing workers sometimes knew people interviewing for an entry-level position. In such cases they sometimes juxtaposed their prior knowledge of a person against the claims that the person made in interviews:

EMPLOYEE: You sit outside of an interview room, and you know the person in there, and they're saying things...

D. S.: Like?

EMPLOYEE: Oh . . . embellishments of work experience.

D. S.: What do you think they exaggerate about it?

EMPLOYEE: Maybe having more responsibility than they had. Because at lunch, the day before, we'd both be saying we're peons.

Workers and employers made rare events sound common, because, hypothetically, a rare event could occur more often, even though that is unlikely. Consider this account of why failing to qualify work experience on a résumé is not deceptive:

> D. S.: You had a job where you did a credit analysis twice.... Say, a hundred and fifty times you did data entry. And when you say, "duties: detailed credit analysis."
>
> EMPLOYEE: That's fine. That's not even embellishment. That's the truth. It's just not the whole truth.

The person is not lying about the credit analysis experience because single instances when it did occur make the statement accurate.[1] Workers in advertising, market research, and political consulting firms also report employers using bait and switch to solicit new clients:

> EMPLOYEE: We'll say, you know, we had extensive experience in X, Y, and Z, when the truth be told, there was probably one survey, eight years ago, or something like that.
>
> D. S.: Who's doing that kind of stuff? Who's pitching that way?
>
> EMPLOYEE: All of us.

Hiding Irrational Bases for Decision Making

Some informants thought that employers made irrational decisions about hiring, promotion, and other business practices. Favoritism loomed behind some organizational decisions—someone is promoted unfairly; work tasks and supervisory treatment are allocated unfairly; everything is based on a higher-up's unjustifiable discretion.

Exchanging tales of favoritism serves many purposes, including learning covert information, airing grievances, and tightening bonds with similarly peeved colleagues. Doing so is also a way that people keep track of what rewards others receive—as such, hearing favoritism tales is a means for workers to collectively monitor the workplace for inequality.

Workers scrutinize managers and ongoing administrative promotional practices to glean information about criteria for advancement. Sometimes among higher-level informants this scrutiny is a means to calculate their individual opportunities against a baseline of ongoing promotions. If a promotion is grounded in a type of "unfair" favoritism that diminishes one's chances, the effect is devastating. Here a mid-level female manager recounts the impact a promotion based on male bonding had on women in her organization:

Couple of years ago, there was this guy who's been in charge of the . . . program. He started out here as an intern, very young, total politico, very good at schmoozing. And the president, particularly, ends up having his favorite folks and his favorite areas that he focuses on. Doesn't mean that he doesn't think anything else is important, but that's all that he really pays attention to. It was very obvious that he has, or had and still has, a very tight, slap-on-the-back boy relationship with this young fellow. And that of course spilled over into relationships with the CEO. So this person was made a vice president, without a master's degree. And there was just a huge reaction amongst women in the organization, of just incredible cynicism. Not necessarily reflecting the capacity of the person to do their job, who was promoted. But reflecting, well, this is what you gotta do, you got to go out and basically be a big swingin' dick, as we call it, and do the boy thing, in order to get anywhere in the organization. . . . That really affected particularly lower-level women, because they're the ones that are just out in the workplace and they're trying to see what's going on. And then there are women sort of at my level who are pretty vocal, and they're pretty capable of actually going out and talking to people. And I don't think that they really realized what a shock . . . what that effect had on the organization, particularly when there were women who had worked here for a long time and had contributed amazingly to the organization and had the respect of everyone.

Favoritism stories also alleged sexual attraction as an engine of promotion, and these stories crossed gender lines. A female informant described a promotional decision, in her belief, based on a romantic relationship between a female supervisor and a male subordinate:

EMPLOYEE: This guy, just out of school—I don't know, somehow I guess he was sort of the suck-up type. So, the boss, my boss really liked him. And I heard a story at one point; they had gone on some company boat trip, just a company sort of thing, just for the division. It was a drinking sort of thing—these women friends, my boss and her friend, were kissing this guy. Like he had lipstick all over his face. And not like three months later he got a promotion to being in a special group that got a raise and everything. And I was pretty amazed that he had gotten this, because it was in an area that he had never done anything with at all. There was a woman who had been in that area for twenty years, who didn't get the specialist position when this new guy, who just came out of no place, that doesn't know anything about 401(k)s.

D. S.: So this was something kind of like contact or affiliation over competence . . .

EMPLOYEE: Definitely.

D. S.: I mean is it really that simple, or is that too white hat, too black hat?

EMPLOYEE: No. I would definitely say I almost believed that they may have been having an affair or something . . .

D. S.: Was that over any kind of actual experience? Like the guy just did not have the expertise to be doing this kind of work?

EMPLOYEE: Definitely not. He may have had potential to learn it fast or something like that. But definitely I would say, there were other people that sort of had their position [meaning more experience].

Favoritism stories may or may not be true. They are difficult to verify, and certainly relevant parties can deny them, if they even get to hear the allegations. Of course, the stories are derogatory; they imply that an unfair variable explains another worker's success, often alleging discrimination, lasciviousness, and nepotism. In *Complex Organizations*, Perrow (1986) analyzes such particularism in hiring within bureaucratic organizations. He argues that if a prospective hire offers cultural traits that make them a particularly effective employee, such as being a member of an important association or having useful local contacts, those discretionary qualities make hiring that employee a better option than hiring based on training or experience. This argument is in sync with Kanter's (1977) earlier explanations, in which men tend to hire men who resemble their own social and demographic traits, because existing workers are more likely to trust and feel comfortable with people who are like themselves, and so they reproduce themselves. These hiring patterns are criticized on two counts in subterranean education.

First, women and minorities believe that this form of reproduction excludes them and ignores meritocratic criteria, which, if they had been observed, might have helped them advance. Alternatively, in cases where minority candidates move forward, the direction of the favoritism tale reverses, with others claiming affirmative action favoritism. Consider this reported conversation:

"I know Martha wants Michael to be the next president, but I also know that Louisa really wants to be president bad." Sharon said, "Yeah, but Bill really doesn't like her. I think they might just leave Andrea as president again even though she is not great, because she is a woman and also a minority, so it looks good."

Second, favoritism tales in promotion and hiring are inevitable when people with similar backgrounds and credentials compete. If the competing group is composed only of white males that come from roughly equivalent schools and share the same cultural capital, a preference for one over another candidate requires explanation. In such cases, there are claims of nepotism, favoring a particular fraternity or intervention by powerful mentors and other third parties. One respondent noted, "When résumés are passed about or talked about, Greek houses always come up. I am shocked."

Allegations of favoritism over merit also are useful to press adversarial ends. One real estate manager described another manager's sex discrimination:

> MANAGER: A major sales producer is being recruited. Most managers want to hire her, but a major decision maker doesn't. He doesn't want to hire her because he doesn't think she's pretty enough.
>
> D. S.: How can he reject her without stating exactly why?
>
> MANAGER: He'll mask it . . . not cut her a good deal.

The manager who told me this story does not favor discrimination—his primary purpose in telling this story was to malign the "major decision maker" in the tale, not to protest sex discrimination. His end was adversarial, not remedial. The manager's account also describes the camouflaging of irrational decisions. Here the higher-up will offer a small salary to induce the recruit to reject a job offer. A lowball offer camouflages discriminatory intent.

Subterranean Education as Diluted Whistle-Blowing

An important issue in favoritism tales is that people are aware of discrimination, but rather than blow the whistle on discrimination to the press, higher-ups, or internal watchdogs, they blow the whistle to colleagues. Blowing the whistle to colleagues may prevent guilty knowledge from ever being exposed outside the organization, where perhaps real deterrent actions could be taken. Condemnation is attained at a safer cost and contained internally. The pressures to create a remedy are mitigated by stating the "wrongness" of an action to co-workers. Doing so castigates an enemy without initiating external social control. Internal condemnation can displace remedial justice because the teller exhausts moral indignation without initiating an outside disclosure. Guilty knowledge is shared and diffused; subterranean education becomes a means of blowing off steam but not of truly blowing a whistle. In telling the tale, the worker may hope to transfer an obligation for action to the listener, or more likely will look at the act of exposing the behavior internally as fulfilling the obligation to "do something" morally.

However, an upwelling of derogatory information, as it spreads among workers, may lead to retaliatory or remedial action. The ripple turns into a wave. Spreading derogatory information in this way, like political "leaks," may in some cases be a means of building covert support so that when an advocate goes public with the information, a constituency for change has been built. Identifying what factors enable internal whistle-blowing to turn into internal change is a worthwhile pursuit.

Favoritism in Shaping the Direction of Work

Favoritism in shaping the direction of work references statements that "favorites" of higher-ups prosper by coming to earn more money and being able to do more interesting work, while nonfavorites suffer. The derogatory content is in stating that managerial decisions are discretionary and based on successful flattery. This type of favoritism tale was endemic among people employed in nonprofit organizations. My explanation for the abundance of such tales of favoritism among informants from nonprofits is that they have greater individual discretion in determining work than their for-profit counterparts do. Perhaps profit-making organizations also are larger and produce more fixed services; nonprofit organizations are typically smaller and produce more abstract and variable products that are open to discretion.

Favoritism in nonprofits sometimes takes the form of diverting resources to the "pet" causes of higher-level workers. There are two variations on pet causes. One kind is a funding initiative to which a higher-up wants to donate more resources than already allocated. The other type of favoritism is deciding subjectively to favor some clients over others. The first cause is strictly budgetary, the second is personal, but both involve deception.

In the first case, causes are favored in several fashions. The general pattern is to shift resources to one cause over and above what are supposed to be equal allocations among causes. Money for a favored program may be siphoned off secretly:

I think that what the person who signed the checks, the executive director, his whole action was deceptive for the funders. They represented that they have all these type of programs that were working great—here is what the children's program is doing. And they were using what the children's program was doing and pretending like they wholeheartedly supported it, in order to get these huge funds, because that's where the money is, in children's programs. And then they would actually use those funds for their own programs, for the literacy training, for the jobs program.

In this case, money was siphoned off to fund different causes than the one represented. All informants at nonprofits observed money from one donation or grant diverted to a different initiative. Sometimes this diversion was written into the plan of the donation or grant, so that donors knew that their money might be distributed elsewhere. But informants also gave accounts of money being redirected in undisclosed and perhaps not condoned ways. One community organizer noted:

Somewhere in the neighborhood of $10,000 was supposed to be used on video equipment, tapes, whatever, to be used to make educational films and documentaries on the problems. No money was spent or allocated for that. No equipment was purchased. And the explanation was that all the other programs required so much more time and resources, so that we couldn't do that.

Informants never believe that people took any money to line their own pockets; they just wanted to support favored causes. Switching money to other causes sometimes led nonprofit workers to hoard monies, hide funding sources, and fight over resources. This switching is clearly a form of shadow administration that employs deception. For example, some informants described bait-and-switch schemes in which money was sought for project A, when that money would actually go to project B or into a general fund from which all projects drew.[2] An environmental fund-raiser explained:

I think there's also misrepresentation to people who give money that they think they're giving money to a specific project, when in fact it's going into a general fund. That had happened to some donors I've seen, and it infuriates me. I've been involved in pitching a proposal, saying, "We're going to use your money to do this work," and then when it gets to the door, it's swiped up by the general fund.

Another informant described deceptions between employees about leads on potential sources of funding:

> Just people withholding, or not sharing, information about upcoming projects and leads, or donors, with other people, so that somebody says, "Hey, I heard you got a good lead on, you know, some money for doing the same kind of work that we've been interested in doing." And people have said, "Well, you know, nothing's said, it's really, I don't know what's happening yet." So, when it comes to donors and getting cash, there's an incredible amount of deception, until the money's actually in the door. And even when it's in the door, there's a hoarding of that, as a sugar daddy, for that program. And that goes straight up to the top. The president actually hoards a certain set number of foundations and organizations that give money as his own pet sources. Nobody can touch them, and everybody knows that it's up to him.

These deceptions also occur between organizations:

> These other groups in our coalitions . . . we see as being deceitful. And one common method of doing this is they're sending in grant proposals to foundations [and] including our organization and other small organizations' names on them, saying, yes we were working with these guys—and getting money to do that, without actually including us in on the take. And we find out, through whatever channels and mechanisms we can, we see actual grant proposals with our names included on them, as working with these organizations. And then they do grants for $350,000, and we get zero of that money. So there's a lot of distrust between organizations.

Some nonprofit organizations concentrate exclusively on working with people because the organization has service work as a primary mission. In these situations, nonprofit organizations may favor some clients over others. One intern observed favoritism at her nonprofit site based on client behavior. If a client acts in ways that make him or her easier to manage, then that client is favored over others:

> INTERN: Here was a huge example which I continued to think about for quite a long time, when two individual kids were being decided upon at the same time.
>
> D. S.: "Decided upon" means allowed to stay or forced to leave?
>
> INTERN: Yes. And one of them, even though he had had sex with five other females on the unit—which only one of those would be grounds for im-

mediate dismissal—was allowed to stay on because he was a personal favorite for the site head. And I would presume I could say that was because he was . . . funny to the extent that he was a release for them and allowed them to kind of forget the pressure.

D. S.: So he eased your day on the job?

INTERN: Yes. . . . Whereas, the person they were deciding upon simultaneously had not committed any crime that was as great as this other guy, but there was a general dislike for him because he didn't happen to acknowledge the staff members. He would mumble. He was kind of dirty. He just didn't communicate with them at all and openly showed dislike for them, but he never made any comments or insults or anything like that. He had kept a solid job for a while, but the fact that they did not like him, as a sort of consensus, they were ready to dismiss him and keep the former person.

D. S.: What grounds did they use to justify it?

INTERN: Very, very few grounds to justify it.

D. S.: But they would never say that it was done based on subjectivity?

INTERN: I don't think they would say that. That would be admitting that there were no grounds for their decisions, that there were no set policies. However, in the middle of a meeting, they would just say, "How do we all feel about X" and would sit there talking about him in almost a sort of a gossipy way—"Oh, I like this, I don't like this." And I felt that none of these decisions were based on any sort of technical grounds whatever.

Nonprofit Deceptions

Nonprofit informants described many serious deceptions, such as outright misrepresentation to funders, claims of doing one thing when doing another, lying about budgets, poor treatment of lower-level staff, and deceptions involving sexism. While for-profit organizations certainly also have these deceptions, it is worth examining what variables might explain the high level of deception at nonprofits. Deception seems especially critical to the economic viability of nonprofits, and thus more serious deceptions may be embedded in the organizational vulnerabilities of nonprofits than in for-profits. The irony of the moral and idealistic nature of nonprofits being partnered with deceptive behaviors is also interesting, since a reputation for doing good may hide and obscure a potential dependence on unsavory means to achieve noble ends.

Small size, a poorly resourced environment, and greater discretion for managers in smaller organizations, such as nonprofits, may encourage greater deception. A further exacerbating factor is that nonprofits are moral entrepreneurs, so deceptions concerning diverting resources may come more easily through rationalizing reallocating funds for good purposes.

Many deceptions center on dilemmas of acquiring information, dealing with low status, and concern with upward mobility. Lower-level informants in nonprofit organizations observed more serious deceptions than did lower-level informants in for-profit organizations. A comparison of for-profit and nonprofit organizations in types and amounts of deceptions associated with ongoing operations would present an opportunity to examine the effects of size and hierarchical composition on types and goals of deceptions.

Intentional Mistakes

Mistakes are also a consistent area for deception around social credits. How do people explain, ignore, fail to report, and avoid making mistakes? One deceptive quality to errors is that people repeat them if prior mistakes have gone undetected by others and they are convenient to make, so long as they can be labeled "innocent" if they are detected. I call these "intentional mistakes." People know in the abstract that the action is a mistake, but they pursue the action because doing so serves their interests and because they can get off the hook if caught. There is a distinction between convenient available mistakes, exposing a rival's mistakes, and accidental honest mistakes.

Supervisors can order subordinates to commit mistakes such as falsifying information or neglecting to do something that a job requires. The subordinate gets stuck with the potential aftermath of the mistake and the boss gets to reap the benefits:

EMPLOYEE: The study really didn't interview enough people; our results weren't that telling . . . and my mentor or supervisor there at the time said, "We're going to add in some respondents here. So, those interviews, we're going to make that forty or forty-five." And I didn't do it, and he never brought it up again.

D. S.: Is doing this stuff with the vendors and the clients rare?

EMPLOYEE: No. It's happened every quarter; something's happened.

Higher-ups often used intentional mistakes to offer a rosier picture to clients, as this worker at an advertising agency recounted:

> EMPLOYEE: They wanted to make themselves look as though they'd been doing a good job with this product. So they present these numbers, and numbers are supposed to instill confidence and instill accuracy, saying that out of all these people surveyed, this many really like our product as opposed to these other ones. But they only ask people who use that product. And they also did an imaging study to see what personality a product has. And again, they asked only the people that use the product that they want.
>
> D. S.: But they would compare it to different brands?
>
> EMPLOYEE: Right. So they were shown the same kind of product, but it was different brands. And they were shown, here's this one brand that looked like this product—they could be old men, and that kind of thing. And then there was the product that was the client's. Again, they're shown all pictures and then—these are users of this product—and they'd be cheerful looking women, mostly, because it's a cleaning product. That kind of thing.
>
> D. S.: That sounds a little biased.
>
> EMPLOYEE: That is very biased. . . . They [the client] don't know what goes on behind the scenes. And so they're led to believe that this is an unbiased thing.

Subordinates also noticed other patterns of mistakes. One pattern is that some higher-ups don't order mistakes to be made but if they make an intentional or honest mistake themselves, they blame it on subordinates. As one informant said about her boss, "She makes a mistake, she never admits it; she blames it on the staff and turns everything around. She did that to me." Mistakes are sometimes available, convenient, and intentional actions, especially if others are around to take the fall. That mistakes can be desirable can tap into a subtle social currency.

Derogatory Information about Co-workers

Workers share comments with one another about how hard their peers work. Receiving credit for hard work and getting noticed is a critical form of social credit. Most comments, however, did not seem to be admiration for hard workers but rather complaints about workers who goof off. For example, interns to their surprise (the naïveté of youth) learned that veteran workers did not match the enthusiasm and excitement that interns had for their new work. Interns noticed that co-workers did not work as hard as they claimed they did. They observed that workers who talked about staying until ten every night and groaned about how much time they put in, actually "forgot" to factor in two-hour dinner breaks, hours on the phone talking to friends, doing personal errands during work hours, surfing the Internet, and playing endless games of computer solitaire. Clearly the amount of "face-time" spent at work does not always match up with the amount of real work that gets done. An intern at a banking firm, for example, noted that "a lot of the bankers make out like they work these huge ridiculous long hours, and a lot of that time is spent on the phone, talking to friends, or things like that." This goofing off constitutes seeking undeserved credit.

This false credit deception is endemic. Workers are always quick to count others' work, since they need to discover how much work is actually expected, to learn "what's what" and how to offer their own convincing portrayals of how hard they work. Noticing if someone slacks off also provides ammunition for potentially criticizing that person to others. These covert evaluations establish a baseline constructed from observing others that enables them to monitor how much work they ought to be doing. They make these covert evaluations by looking over others' shoulders to see what standards for work actually exist, by gossiping, and by comparing themselves to others.

Sometimes people are bitterly surprised and angry about how little some of their co-workers work. Their resentment comes from feeling that they work hard when they could have been slacking, yet others get away with not working to capacity:

> People have different ideas of working really hard, and what that means. Like, I've done so much today. What I think that means and what my colleague means could be two totally different things. If you gave us the exact same tasks to accomplish in a day, how we went about doing that and if we did it, it would be interesting to see. Because I mean, I've noticed, like when someone's out and I'm kind of covering for them in their daily duties, and I get it done in like an hour or two and I'm like, "Why do I still see her doing this at two in the afternoon?"

In trying to find out how hard others work, people sometimes never see others working at all. For example:

The woman in the office next to me, I don't know when she did work. I never figured out what she did. I mean she sat in the office next to me, and she was on the phone twenty-four hours a day, talking about every aspect of her life. I found out everything about her life, just sitting there. But she never did any work.

When peers detect slackers among co-workers, they may align themselves against "lazy" co-workers:

Somehow we got on the subject of Amy, and Jane said: "Yesterday . . . I asked her if she would help and she just ignored me. She acts like I am nothing here, but I am on staff. She thought I was an intern and started when you did, referring to me. I said, "Yeah, Amy doesn't chip in much. She only wants to read the stuff that we are working on for the long-term care project or talk on the phone to [her boyfriend]. I don't think she understands that when you work at a not-for-profit, it's inevitably understaffed and everybody has to help." Amy refuses to answer the phone too—I have seen her right by the phone when I am at the computer or on the other line, and she will watch the light until she sees that someone else has picked it up.

Amy's reluctance to fully participate incurred retaliations; she became a target for gossip and for malicious neglect: "Jane ignores Amy now. When Amy asks a question Jane will delay and answer her question reluctantly, even if it is something simple, like, where something is." People notice when others don't want to help carry the load. They also are careful about how visibly they evade their own work, so that they can avoid having co-workers denigrate them:

People say that they don't have time. And then they end up demonstrating that they obviously did have time. Maybe they don't want to work with that person, or maybe they're, at that moment, feeling swamped and don't want to do something that will distract them. But they don't want to say, "No, I can't help you." They have to look busy or lie about their inability to take time out to help—because they don't want to offend, or they don't want to be seen as being unhelpful.

Informants also denigrate co-workers endlessly for personal characteristics and appearance. Hidden insults about dress, personal habits, and the "dumb" actions of peers are common, which should surprise no one who has ever worked, although how such small-group culture may be changing because of potential harassment or discrimination lawsuits is an intriguing question. For example, insulting nicknames for coworkers that I heard during interviews included "checkout girl," "dumbfuck," "ditz and ditz lite" (a boss and an assistant insulted as a team), "invalid," "model boy," "Papa Bear," "princess," "prom queen," "little Napoleon," "snapper," "pronoun man," "Mr. Excuse," "Ms. Trailer Park," and "Windshield" (because the individual wore Coke-bottle glasses).

Men also made sexist remarks about female co-workers. Women returned the favor, including within an office where women actually scheduled sessions to ogle the only male worker at their firm (a man the informant described as being "their pet"). Men and women denigrated any peers who failed to dress to their satisfaction, although those comments are not always deceptive, since such "fashion reviews" are sometimes anticipated and open aspects of interaction in office culture. The deceptive quality there is what is and is not told directly to someone.

In settings with more white men than women or minorities, respondents reported racist and sexist comments. A banker observed:

> BANKER: There was one black person I worked with, and everyone talked about him, as soon as he would leave. There would just be comments right and left about him, just negative comments, little jokes all the time—he was very destructive, he had a drug problem. People were very intolerant about anything about women. There was one woman there, and there were sexual comments made all the time.
>
> D. S.: To her face?
>
> BANKER: Not to her face. All behind the scenes, obviously. . . . You know, she was a "piece of ass," and all this. Just negative male comments.

Certainly there is much more to say about how race and gender discrimination take place at the level of derogatory comments. The deceptive distinction here is in how much hidden backstage negative commentary takes place and the cumulative effect of that discourse on the prospects and working environment of affected men and women. There are certainly major research inroads taken and yet to be taken examining how gender and racial discrimination are overt and conscious, reflected in wage and work condition inequalities. Important work remains to be done in parsing out the interaction of deception, gender, and race in workplace culture. This book touches only lightly on those areas, noting that they exist in the organizational underlife and are connected to some patterns of deception in the workplace. Much more detailed work ought to be done in this area.

Hierarchical Resentments: Appreciation and Disrespect as Social Currency

In a hunt for sure things, you could replace death and taxes with complaining about the boss. For example, consider this description by Scott Adams, the cartoonist of the *Dilbert* comic strip:

> The Boss: He's every employee's worst nightmare. He wasn't born mean and unscrupulous, he worked hard at it. And succeeded. As for stupidity, well, some things are inborn. His top priorities are the bottom line and looking good in front of his subordinates and superiors (not necessarily in that order). Of absolutely no concern to him is the professional or personal well being of his employees.[3]

Rather than focus on the alleged flaws of bosses that are exposed, I instead emphasize how their hierarchical advantages and the hierarchical disadvantages of subordinates influence how grievances about bosses manifest themselves.[4] To stress that point, I refer to such complaints as "hierarchical resentments"—to emphasize not peccadilloes of individual managers but the hierarchical authority that they have to impose them on others. Hierarchical resentments speak first and foremost to the bitterness that workers feel about the advantages that superiors can take in their authority, particularly when they treat subordinates disrespectfully. Resentments and retaliations flow between subordinates and superordinates usually without ever being recognized officially. I first discuss some examples of hierarchical resentments and then move to some structural aspects of hierarchy that escalate the potential for deception. Of note here is how significant being accorded respect is in the decision to authentically defer to authority.

The attitude of the boss can determine the quality of the work from the subordinate, as this program assistant noted:

> Some send you a little note on their work, so you're happy to do their stuff. And then when they make a mistake, you'd say, "Oh, so-and-so, you didn't fill this out right, but I'm going to take care of it and it will be fine."

> Well, then you get the screamers, and you're like, "Screw you, I'm sending it back." And you just send it back.

Those in lower-level positions understand the expectation to defer to people with higher workplace authority. Much deference is genuine; many higher-ups can inspire authentic respect and loyalty. The issue is distinguishing between authentic and inauthentic deference, as the expectation of appearing to defer is a constant. Being treated disrespectfully will produce patently false deference. The trick for workers who feel put upon is to retaliate without inviting further trouble in return. One means of retaliation is sniping, appearing to comply while taking anonymous shots at the boss to harm their reputation among others.

Respondents described many familiar ways in which bosses disrespected them. One source of resentment was being told to do personal and trivial work that supervisors could do themselves:

> She points at Eileen's office and says, "She's doing nothing and she asks me to make her a reservation. Why can't she do it herself? That's why I hate being a secretary—you have to do all the stupid stuff that no one else will do. I hate it." She walks into the copy room. She comes back out and whispers to me, "I should mess up her reservation!" and we both laugh.

Another category of resentment emerges when workers feel overburdened by constant scrutiny:

> There was another manager, who is still a manager in the department, but he's somewhere else. And his favorite thing was to come around at 4:30, walk around the floor, and just make sure that everybody was at their desk. And people used to call him the "Papa Bear" and things like that, because he was always checking up on his little kids. And that affected people's attitude toward him. And I imagine that he didn't get what he wanted all the time from those people, because of their attitude.

Two additional categories of hierarchical resentment include supervisors taking complete credit for work that a subordinate performs and lying about the future nature of the working relationship between the subordinate and superior. The example below combines the two:

> The partner told me, "Good news, we have a new ace guy coming in. He's going to be great. You're going to like working with him. You'll get along really well." I asked, "What's the relationship going to be?" "He'll be

roughly coequal; he's not going to be your supervisor." Then I was actually introduced to him once he was hired, had lunch with him and a partner, and started talking about the relationship. And it seemed to me like it was a little different than what I had understood. So I asked, "Will he be my supervisor?" and I was told yes. And I said, "That's not my understanding of the way it was going to work." And I was told, "Oh yes, that's exactly what I told you originally." Well, that isn't what I was told originally. As you might assume, it's the kind of thing you actually pay pretty close attention to.

So this guy was plunked down in the office. And I thought fine, it's not his fault that the partner lied to me about this. So I'm not going to take it out on him; I'm looking forward to working with him. But as soon as he got in, he really wanted to enforce this relationship. He treated me like I was a very junior person who didn't know what the hell was going on, like he was Mr. Big Shot. And then there was an incident pretty soon after I came on, where I had generated a lead. And then he called a contact of his who said, "Oh, I can help you out. You need to call someone else involved in his office." He called this person and they said, "Oh yeah, let's have a meeting this week." And it was clearly something that I had identified the opportunity, I had started the thing off, and he did help the process. So I was thinking collaborative, this is a collaborative situation, this is working pretty well. His response was, "You can take that off your list—I'll handle it from here."

Of course, the classic sources of worker anger are overwork and extreme pressure, particularly when partnered with little gratitude or thanks. As an example, consider the response this intern received when he asked to take a lunch break after having worked through lunch for two weeks. His supervisor told him, "Lunch is a privilege, not a right." The intern's reaction was to despise the supervisor, bad-mouth him whenever possible, and perform poorly.

Resentment of Client Authority

Another manifestation of hierarchical resentment is deferring to clients, who are also the "boss." Consider workers in finance and management consulting organizations. Clients hire them to bring about productivity improvements, whether in enhancing a portfolio's value or an assembly line's output. Hiring the consultant naturally gives clients the right to offer suggestions and check the consultant's work. The consultant is in the structural position of having to defer to the client. Therefore, consultants greet every suggestion respectfully, even when they think the suggestion is asinine:

> CONSULTANT: You know, if we were just in our group after the client meeting, sometimes we'd have some really hilarious conversations about comments that were made, things that people said, ideas that they had said that were just completely ludicrous or small-minded or that they couldn't see beyond themselves to the scope of the project. But, of course, when you're in talking to the client, I think you definitely have to treat them like every idea that they have is crucial and important and all that.
>
> D. S.: So, what do you do to manage it, given that the consultants truly will think that some idea of the client's is idiotic?
>
> CONSULTANT: Like I said, they'll deal with it respectfully in front of them and maybe discuss it afterwards like it's kind of a joke.

Having to appear deferential, led to, as one informant phrased it, "compensating" by bad-mouthing clients backstage. For example:

> Before Ted called the guy, he explained how this guy was an asshole: "This guy I'm about to call is one of the most miserable. . . . He's one of the biggest assholes in the history of man. I could tell you stories about this guy that would make you ask why the hell I even talk to this guy. The answer is he's got money."

Workers who heard wizened veterans criticize clients soon came to draw their own "streetwise" conclusions about how to define clients:

> Fred and Jack referred to this client as being a "pain in the ass" and an "idiot." This negative sentiment was brought on because the client requested something that required more work. The client didn't just hand over his money. The only thing valued in clients is the amount of money the firm can obtain and manage from them. Also, a client is an asshole if they ask any questions about what their money is being invested in or if they make requests for information. A client is "a great guy" if they take a hands-off approach, don't ask many questions, and provide leads to other potential clients.

Another informant described deceptions involved in appearing courteous in routine service work:

> There's also putting on the show that you're such a friendly person, you're bright and happy and shiny every day, when you could be just deep

down, "This sucks, I want to get the hell out of here." But you put on this bright and smiley face. Or there might be someone that you're like, "Oh, there's so-and-so again. I wish that person would just leave and get out of here." But then you might be, "Oh, how are you doing," all happy and bright. . . . Then there's instances, where, if you know that other people have the same opinion as you, as soon as that person leaves, you might hear someone say, "What an asshole, I wish that guy would never come by here" or something.

Given the common understanding that disrespect is a depreciated form of social currency, deceptive retaliations occur. These retaliations can also become the stuff of legend, "revenge tales" as a type of organizational folklore. These tales are apocryphal stories of the "asshole who got theirs" through the collective covert machinations of vengeful underlings:

> No one really liked this one senior vice president, and he was in charge of meetings. And I found out later that this person had been discharged, or was moved down a level because he was so hostile, and he always bristled under pressure, so a lot of people didn't like this person. So, people sort of worked together to put him down in his place. He had no real allies, and as a result of that, he was moved down, he was moved out of the department. . . . That's why making allies and having friends and having people to back you up is so important in these meetings. And this one person didn't have that. And as a result, he went down.

While sharing deference is an acknowledged aspect of being lower on the ladder, there is an implicit "respect" threshold to which subordinates feel entitled. Receiving disrespect means returning disrespect. Hiding that retaliatory disrespect is more incumbent the lower one goes on the ladder. As one midlevel manager summarized: "The partners are pretty tough. . . . And so I think people are always looking for a way to bring them down a notch."

Discretionary and Dyadic Authority Relations

Some features of hierarchical relations heighten the potential for deception. The term "discretionary and dyadic authority" refers to features of hierarchical relationships that manifest themselves in one-to-one supervisory relationships. In this situation, relations between lower-level workers and managers can turn into a "personal set of procedures and understandings" that are heavily influenced by a boss's ability to use "particularistic criteria for evaluation" (Kanter 1977, 80–81). If a boss uses idiosyncratic criteria to evaluate staff, in which not being "a team player" carries weight, workers feel heightened pressure to appear extremely loyal and deferential in order to survive (Jackall 1988; Kanter 1977; Morrill 1995).

Further, when lower-level employees are new, they cannot draw on prior experience in the environment. They must depend officially on one person who is in charge that they must impress. Having only one official source, the manager, also biases what the new employee learns. When written records exist, as well as close observation of the working relationship by third parties, superiors are less likely to act inappropriately, as these documentary sources can then help support future actions against them.

Having no paper records about training can also enhance discretionary authority and aid people in evading blame. As Jackall (1988) notes, bosses attempt to push blame and responsibility down and pull credit up. As a consequence, workers use systems of subterranean education and on occasion resort to covert retaliation through acts of sabotage. In summary, when a job description, outside surveillance, criteria for performance evaluation, and record keeping are made abstract or are absent, the resulting authority relation increases the potential for deceptions.

Early Exit Labor Markets

Early exit labor markets exist when lower-level workers (entry-level and interns) remain with employers just for short time periods before moving on to other jobs. This condition is endemic in nonprofit organizations. In early exit labor markets, lower-level employees do not stay at a company long enough to compile an informal dossier of deceptive acts by superiors and co-workers. They may also not stay long enough to develop motivation to act against exploitative work conditions. They may know that they will leave soon and are content to ride out the storm in exchange for a credentialing work experience. If they are entry-level workers, they must hold on until they can move upward into more promising options in the same organization or elsewhere.

Low-level employees such as interns, entry-level workers, and secretaries may feel pressure to carry out deceptions for higher-ups. For example, bosses may ask them to spy or to lie to others. Workers may share the knowledge that a boss acts deceptively with co-workers, particularly when there is no other evidence available of a supervisor's actions. However, when entry-level workers turn over rapidly, their knowledge of deceptions departs with them. When low-level workers turn over quickly, there are no experienced workers to covertly train new workers about exploitative bosses and co-workers.

Here the machinery involved in the rotating exploitation of interns is partially revealed. New interns turn over quickly and, when around, may be asked to do dirty work. Interns leave without moving up, knowingly exchanging their labor for a work experience credential that they plan to trade up for better work elsewhere. This market perpetuates deception by insulating the boss and by ensuring that lower-level workers have scant interest in rocking the boat, since either they leave and trade in their credential payoff or they have a vested interest in remaining silent and advancing.

In several nonprofit organizations where I interviewed people, turnover was so high that some interns whose tenure usually lasted no more than two to three months became the most experienced low-level employees in the office. In such cases, a deceptive boss was protected and encouraged by a system that rotates new workers out, along with any incriminating information they possess. Naïve and less powerful workers arrive and in turn depart before sticking around long enough to potentially challenge a boss. The boss is the constant, able to manipulate subordinates who will never advance and stay on a long-term basis.

Even if a supervisor's peers are aware of his or her deceptions (for example lying to clients and other workers or misusing funds), the other supervisors often do not act against the deceptive supervisor, choosing to look the other way. In the various organizations I studied, a manager, an administrative vice president, and a director of a community outreach program all knew of deceptions perpetrated by their in-house fund-raising directors. They all chose to ignore this inconvenient information. The distaste associated with turning in a co-worker, particularly one who is "bringing in the bucks," grants superiors greater insulation from being put on notice.

Of course, the more insecure an employee feels, in terms of encountering great difficulty in getting a job outside the organization and having great pressure in the job, the more likely he or she is to act deceptively to stay employed. These deceptions may progress in two directions. First, a worker may feel that acceding to any deceptions that higher-ups request is unavoidable. Second, a worker may act deceptively in revenge for being stuck in their current work situation.

Unidirectional Social Control

Organizational higher-ups dictate the goals of internal policing in the workplace. The upward hierarchical "ownership" of social control can lead to overlooking many types of deception. Unidirectional social control, for example, may focus only on specific deceptive acts, such as crimes that subordinates commit. Organizations officially monitor deceptions as if they are constituted only by the acts of low-level workers, such as those scheming to steal time or resources, or they focus scrutiny on customers who may shoplift. Although these deceptions are legitimate targets for higher-ups to police, they represent a limited sample of the actual range of deceptive acts within organizations.

Unidirectional social control thus produces a marginalized set of sinners. Even if a subordinate knows of a superior's transgressions (which may be grievous ones), he or she may not be able to do anything about them except at great risk. After all, whistle-blowing is never called whistle-blowing unless the person whose actions are questioned is a higher-up—top to bottom whistle-blowing does not even exist as an official category.

The hierarchical nature of whistle-blowing reflects the advantages that a high hierarchical position has within systems of one-way social control. If higher-ups act deceptively, they are unlikely to arrest themselves. Getting to position the surveillance camera is a great advantage when you do not want to capture yourself on tape. Lower-ranked employees and colleagues are also unlikely to overtly challenge or report superiors. Unidirectional social control resonates with the criticism left-leaning criminologists offer that crime control efforts center on "crime in the streets" rather than "crime in the suites." Internal policing and social control efforts in organizations center on hunting the "street crimes" of lower-level workers, not on deviance by higher-ups or administrative patterns within organizations that are clandestine noncriminal deceptions.

Productivity Contradictions

When workers cannot comply with either informal or formal rules in order to attain desired individual or organizational goals they are caught in a productivity contradiction. This example is from James Henslin's *Essentials of Sociology* (1996):

Recently one of the female members of the board suggested that the company become involved in Horizons for Tomorrow, a program designed to provide internships for disadvantaged youth. Two other women and I spent many days developing a proposal for our participation. The problem was how to sell the proposal to the company president. From past experiences, we knew that if he saw it as a "woman's project" it would be shelved into the second tier of "maybes." He hates what he calls "aggressive bitches." We three decided, reluctantly, that the proposal had a chance only if it were presented by a man. We decided that Bill was the logical choice. We also knew that we had to "stroke" Bill if we were going to get his cooperation. We first asked Bill if he would "show us how to present our proposal." It is ridiculous to have to play the role of the "less capable female" in the 1990s, but unfortunately, the corporate culture sometimes dictates this strategy. To clinch matters, we puffed up Bill even more by saying, "You're the logical choice for the next chairmanship of the board." Bill, of course, came to our next planning session, where we prepped *him* on what to say. At our meeting with the president, we had Bill give the basic presentation. We then backed him up, providing the rationale for why the president should endorse the project. As we answered the president's questions we carefully deferred to Bill. The president's response: "An excellent proposal, an appropriate project for our company." To be successful, we had to maneuver through the treacherous waters of the "hidden culture," actually not so hidden to women who have been in the company for awhile. The proposal was not sufficient on its merits, for the "who" behind a proposal is at least as significant as the proposal itself. "We shouldn't have to play these games," Laura said, summarizing our feelings. But we all know that we have no choice. To become labeled "pushy" is to commit corporate suicide—and we're no fools. (110)

Productivity contradictions illustrate Merton's (1968) strain theory, which views deviant behavior as the outcome of individuals being unable to use accepted means to achieve culturally valued goals. Here, for example, the respondent argues that she cannot obtain approval of a valid proposal because she does not comply with the president's informal "rule" that worthwhile ideas only originate with men. Credit seekers must navigate their way around the productivity contradictions that often lie at the heart of needing to lie in the workplace.

Deceptive acts in fact may constitute normal organizational routines that people use as camouflage to keep from being detected by external or internal monitors. Witness the quoted respondent's comments on presenting a case to a troglodyte president—demands to act surreptitiously are familiar to experienced, savvy women in the corporation. The respondent's collusive deception with her partners is a routine strategy for circumventing perceived sexist impediments to attaining goals.

One implication, then, is that publicizing accurate knowledge of how things are really done is personally and organizationally threatening both to men and women. A second implication is that how information on useful tactics is distributed throughout the organization stratifies the organization in ways that advantage and disadvantage some people's individual mobility. For example, this respondent knew how to navigate around the chairman. That knowledge enabled her to get things done, while others who are not so savvy may be shunted aside. Of course that achievement also depends on letting Bill have all the credit.

Overlooking the "Contradictions"

Managers will also sometimes set performance goals knowing that attaining them is impossible without some recourse to deceptive cutting of corners. Setting "impossible" goals encourages deception structurally without stating that workers should lie. Such "read between the lines" instructions insert a strategic form of ambiguity into accomplishing things. Demanding that workers meet difficult goals is a camouflaged means of explicitly requesting subordinates to reduce quality, albeit without superiors having to risk guilty knowledge or responsibility by stating on the record that they have requested those actions.

If workers engage in a deception that is needed to meet production goals, and they are not caught, they are often "just doing what everyone really does." If an individual is caught, then organizational representatives can blame the individual for fulfilling their work obligations inappropriately. Blame can pass to individuals without declaring the organizational incentives that encouraged the individual's acts. Organizations can thus encourage deceptions while avoiding culpability for doing so, by blaming suddenly liable individuals.

Additionally, organizations may make unrealistic yet detailed promises about when work will be completed, the quality of the finished product, what money is necessary for delivering the product, and the organization's ability to arrive at the exact product that the client seeks. After obtaining a client's commitment, an organization may then retreat from their previously certain claims and make those claims newly ambiguous. Concreteness is strategic, used to solicit business, to make sales, or to secure grants. If specific promises cannot be kept, because more was knowingly promised than could be delivered, the larger organization can then blame individual workers for making false promises, rather than placing blame appropriately on imperatives in organizational culture.

Organizational Sources of the Information Black Market

Much workplace deception originates because information is a coin of the realm in the workplace. Knowledge is power, a basis of camaraderie, the difference between jaded experience and naïveté, an instruction manual to colleagues on how to work, and a tool of upward mobility. Acquiring accurate information is difficult because hierarchical privileges control what one can be allowed to "know." As a result, people in the workplace experience uncertainty and must become information entrepreneurs. They have to act as investigative journalists who choose not to publish most of the stories they uncover.

What is most salient is that factors such as hierarchy, incomplete resources, self-seeking behaviors, productivity contradictions, and unidirectional social control are structural roots of informal deception in the workplace. The analogy of an alliance-shifting double agent describes the dilemma workers face in having to appear to conform to different masters, while underneath calculating and collecting information for their own use and that of others.

7

GOOFING OFF AND GETTING ALONG

Goofing off—is there a more attractive oasis when confronted by having to do work? The pleasures of computer solitaire, catching up with co-workers, checking out fun Web pages, finding a secluded place to cat-nap, or taking an extended lunch are just some of the hidden joys that people can sneak into their day. To goof off and not get caught inspires in-novative schemes to hide one's sloth. In this chapter I identify some variet-ies and means of goofing off and analyze how workplace culture enhances opportunities to avoid work.

I propose three categories of goofing off. The first is doing no work at all. The second is doing halfhearted work by just going through the motions. The third is deceptively passing one's own work on to others, a practice that I call "unofficial drafting." After presenting some examples of each, I consider how people try to maintain an appearance of working hard and depend on co-workers' silence to successfully goof off.

Goofing Off by Not Working

Informants described multiple examples of their colleagues or them-selves doing no work. These included their spending time playing com-puter games, surfing the Internet, talking to friends outside work, taking long lunches, napping, and gabbing with co-workers:

> "There were times I'd play solitaire and have my hand on the Alt-Tab key so that I could click over to the spreadsheets if someone walked by."

"There were definitely times where we wouldn't get anything done in a day, that we'd kind of just be sitting around talking or whatever."

"The percentage of time they spent working and the percentage they didn't? Maybe 60 working, 40 socializing. In some cases I think it could be 50–50."

"She was the computer person, essentially. She did everything with the computers. I think that she did fairly nothing. She played on the Internet every day."

"I can't just sit there and go to sleep in my chair. I used to, when I first started working. I would go out until two in the morning, when I first graduated from college, my first job. I would prop myself up in the corner with a book. And you hear all the time, wake yourself up. But now I've gotten past that anyway. If I go out drinking, I'd call in sick."

"The goofing off is like taking lunch breaks or leaving early or making personal phone calls, pretending to be sick and going home early."

"It was very interesting to watch the managing directors hand off projects to these guys and then watch them leave, and see their projects put aside to them doing calculations about how many beers per strike or how many points per dollar" [note: referring to planning their evening bowling competitions].

Goofing Off by Working Halfheartedly

People also goofed off by making only a halfhearted effort at work. For example, one intern observed:

> Say you had to record some sort of transaction or something. And it might be that you have to record something, and if you don't do it in depth and really correctly, nothing will ever happen unless someone came and checked on it or there was a dispute on it. I think a lot of times, people will say, "Screw it. I won't do it. That's never going to happen." So there's that deception, that I plugged through all that stuff, blah blah blah. Where you actually may have just recorded the things that you're going to see; but there may be something further that you're required to do or some calculations that you never went through, just thinking that, we're never going to do that anyway.

One may argue that halfhearted goofing off constitutes doing no work, but that is inaccurate. Halfhearted goofing off involves giving a limited effort, a slacking off on how efficiently a job could potentially be done. Taking illicit shortcuts in completing a job, for example, often constitutes halfhearted goofing off. If one is supposed to check every five figures, then someone goofing off in a halfhearted way checks every ten or fifteen figures.

Halfhearted work is also a strategic choice that people make for the sake of appearances rather than just because of laziness. Workers regularly over- and underestimated how long it would take them to do a particular job. Sometimes these estimation errors were intentional, intended to produce whatever appearance the estimator thought would do them the most good.

Halfhearted work is often accomplished by extending how long a task is supposed to take. For example, if a task takes one day, a worker asks for two, as this worker described:

> Let's say that you can do it in one day. Two days is acceptable. Three days is how much people can accept, right? So you go in and say, "I could do it in two days."

When this worker requests more time than he needs, his motivation is to hoard time and cushion pressures to perform. That extra time enables him to get other work done in the interim or to learn how to do a job he does not know how to do. Also, asking for more time provides an opportunity to have extra time to goof off.

There can be many reasons for halfhearted goofing off. A worker may extend a task because she knows that if she announces that she has completed her work, she will not be able to avoid getting assigned unpleasant new tasks:

> If I say, "OK, I'm done, what should I do now?" and I know that they'll say "filing," and I know that I don't want to do that filing, then I'll either try to come up with some way of extending the project that I am working on, to do something else that doesn't really need to be done or not tell anyone that I'm finished, or come up with my own project.

Goofing Off by Unofficial Drafting

Unofficial drafting is goofing off by passing one's work on to co-workers:

EMPLOYEE: I think a couple of the people didn't know what they were doing, even if they kind of finagled their way through by asking other people.

D. S.: How would that work?

EMPLOYEE: Getting other people's help to do it.

Unofficial drafting is not about asking questions for educational purposes. Unofficial drafting involves asking questions with the explicit intention of getting someone else to eventually perform your work through their answer to your question. Some informants described unofficial drafting as their purpose when asking other people technically oriented questions. They would ask questions about how to run a particular statistical or spreadsheet function and hope that the other person would volunteer to do the involved work. An ideal response to a question, in the requestor's mind, is, "Well, the best way for me to teach you is to do it myself to show you." Once the person does the work, the requestor has passed their work on successfully, without admitting that doing so was the primary motivation behind asking the question. "To learn" sounds better than "I'm lazy," particularly when you have taken advantage of someone.

Unofficial drafters try to cultivate useful people to co-opt. People will try to ingratiate themselves with skilled co-workers in part to set the stage for getting them to help with difficult work. One informant described participating in a difficult technical course on computer operations for his job. The strategy he adopted to handle the class was not to study harder but to set himself up to exploit his more adept classmates:

> The class that I'm in, I'm not really qualified for at all. But I knew that there were several individuals who were very proficient and I made it a point to really talk to people at the class, to get there early and try to make friends with everyone. Because I knew eventually I would need help.

This informant then went on to describe how, by ingratiating himself, he set the stage for participating in their study group and siphoning off their brainpower.

Unofficial drafting is an understudied type of exchange relationship in the workplace. In the previous case, the classmate took advantage of classmates. But this individual does work hard, so to speak, in ingratiating himself with chummy remarks and feigned interest, to be in a position to expropriate the labor. In that sense, goofing off by unofficial drafting is not the same thing as an absence of work effort, even though this is not actual work that he is paid to do. The drafter still must exert himself strategically at ingratiating. It is substituting ingratiating for actually learning that becomes an interesting fiction of his relation to work. Just how much a part of work is ingratiation? There is also the tacit exchange that Blau and others identify of people trading functional technical skills in the workplace for social rewards of affiliation that may be difficult for them to acquire otherwise.

An unofficial drafting by superiors occurs when there is no acknowledgment that work is being passed down:

> Jim sat down with this deceptive person and said, "OK, you know, we need an AA (administrative assistant). She is not around. Why don't you take this search on? Do you want to take responsibility for actually coordinating the process of the AA?" And she said, "Sure." And then she went to my assistant [Mike] and said, "Well Jim and I have decided that we thought . . . " And Mike probably said to her, "Well, work with this other person on it." But she went to the other person and said, "Well, Jim and I have decided that it would be a really good thing for you to take responsibility to do this search." In other words, she pushed it all over into her group. She didn't want to deal with it. And that type of stuff happens pretty regularly.

Accusations of unofficial drafting also are a form of derogatory information that subordinates spread about superiors. One route of explaining away a person's success is to accuse him or her of not really being responsible for the work. The people who accomplish work should be praised, not people who get the perks of others invisibly accomplishing their work:

> I think that oftentimes a manager, or someone in a higher-level position, might be less competent in doing the day-to-day or essential task[s] of that business. Maybe they were good at schmoozing the executives, and they have been put ahead of everyone else so that they were put into this position. So they might not really be the cornerstone that you could rely on, but they might be good at . . . really fooling other people into thinking that they know more than they do. . . . Maybe a couple of years back before this person was at that level, there would be someone above that person saying, "Here, go do this assignment." And they were able to go up to so-and-so and say, "Could you help me out with this?" And they'd get something else, and they'd go to someone else.

Goofing-Off Strategies and Authentication Practices

To goof off without getting caught requires crafting strategies to create a busy appearance. To do so, successful goof-offs use authentication practices that create a convincing image of busywork. For example:

Nobody really gets up to walk over to the next cubicle. But, you know, they'll just call each other on the phone, and they could be talking about anything. I imagine part of it is laziness, and part of it is to try to look busy. Because if a manager walks by and you're on the phone, you're busy, at least that's what goes through their mind.

Informants use papers and phones as props to look busy. Informants also avoid giving off telltale signs of goofing off, such as having screen savers visible on their computer screens:

We'd always keep tabs on the screen saver, you know. If it jumped on, you'd just bump your mouse real quick to make sure it went off right away, just in case they'd come by. And you'd always have your stuff laid out, so that it wasn't that obvious that you weren't doing something.

More collusive forms of covering up include peers who offer warnings of "incoming" supervisors:

We'll cover for each other all the time. A bunch of us may be sitting around goofing off, checking out websites or talking, and there'll be a guy at a far desk near the supervisor. If the supervisor comes around, he'll signal us.

Other forms of collusion in goofing off involve concealing that people do not have enough work to do. Below, in a dramatic example, a respondent describes a conspiracy he observed during his summer job working for the state, clearing a river of debris, that involved feigning the appearance of having work:

EMPLOYEE: If you don't find enough wood, if there's not enough wood floating around, maybe one of these boats would be grounded, and not go out any more. And people would lose their jobs. So, a lot of times, we would have an agreement, it's a secret agreement with the fire department. Some local fire department would go there, pull into their secret little dock [and] put wood in our boats, wood that they'd found in houses, different wood that they found. And the captain would tell us to hose the wood down, make it look like it was wet, and [say] we got it from the harbor. The captain would tell us this. And we'd hose down this dry wood, and we'd take it back and the people [would] weigh it, make a metric ton estimate, and go down and boast, that this was wood that we found in the river. So there'd be a lot of that. And that'd get done in the morning [and] we'd go to lunch.

D. S.: So that it would look like you had done something? So technically, there wasn't really enough work for the three boats, but the idea would be to . . . pretend there was?

EMPLOYEE: Exactly. There was a lot of pretending about the amount of work. This job just depended on the work, period.

D. S.: So it was a form of busywork?

EMPLOYEE: Yeah, for sure. This was just outright deception, but everyone knew about it, except obviously the ultimate higher-ups. But I think people three or four levels above me knew what was going on, and I think people even higher had hints about it. . . . But as long as wood was being found, jobs were being saved; that's all that mattered.

This example involved an unusually complex conspiracy that involved many people. More often, the types of stories I heard concerned individual strategies to avoid getting caught. In one case, I interviewed a computer software consultant who said that "my real goal at work is to do as little work as possible while getting paid as much as possible. That's it, and I don't feel bad about it at all." I asked this man how he hid not working at his job. He then outlined a lengthy series of rules that enabled him to mimic working while not working:

D. S.: What are the strategies, while you're at the office, to do the least work possible? I know that you do the work in blocks, so what are you doing?

CONSULTANT: I guess you gotta figure out what you have to do for the day, or what people expect. There are always emergencies, especially in the computer business. And they come and say, "Mr. [Jones] has to have this included into it, and we need it right away." I'll sit down—it can take me the rest of the day.

D. S.: So rule number one is, handle emergencies always.

CONSULTANT: Right.

D. S.: Rule number—imagine you're writing a book on how to do this.

CONSULTANT: Rule number two: figure out the things that need to be done for the end of the day that people are expecting for tomorrow.

D. S.: Know what people want. . . .

CONSULTANT: You have to always know what people are expecting. . . . Sometimes there are weeks when all the people are busy, and they forget about you entirely. Those weeks, I pretty much don't do any work at all.

D. S.: But you're still sitting there.

CONSULTANT: Yeah, well, you do gotta go in to work and collect the money, or you can't pay your rent.

D. S.: This is the specific strategy part I'm interested in looking at. What do you do that day? I know you've talked about the Internet, but what is it you take advantage of that enables you to do that?

CONSULTANT: I really don't do much all day. Like on a day when people are out of the office or at a meeting . . . I'm a consultant, so I don't go to the meetings.

D. S.: So do you think you have a special ability to do this because you're a consultant? That you'd ever be able to carry it off in a regular . . . ?

CONSULTANT: No, it happened when I was working for them full-time. If I'm not involved with something and everyone's off doing their own thing they don't expect anything—it seems that way, anyway. Those people, they're so concerned with their own little world, that if you didn't produce anything, they'd still think you've done something, because they've been busy all day.

D. S.: So one reason is their lack of technical expertise?

CONSULTANT: No, they're almost always just as technical as I am. Except that, they seem so busy, that I guess they assume that I'm busy as well.

D. S.: So one thing is that you can claim. . .

CONSULTANT: I can always fall back on, "I ran into a problem." That's for my own mind. Because I can't imagine them saying, "It's not ready yet?" Unless you have a specific deadline, like a whole project's coming and it's due the middle of the month.

D. S.: But you could say, "I'm working on a bug."

CONSULTANT: Exactly right. But I can't remember a time when they really said . . .

D. S.: OK, so that's a default.

CONSULTANT: I have it available. . . . . I guess, for my own sanity, I know what I could tell them, if they ask me what I'm doing during the day.

D. S.: So some of the stuff that you're doing during the day is actually like busywork? Like appearance stuff?

CONSULTANT: On the days when people are out and not expecting the product at the end of the day, I'll just sit there [and] type a mail message. Every once in a while I'll do stuff for myself, but it's rare. Like I'll write a small software program. I did this a couple weeks ago. When I download stuff from the Internet and it's in a format I don't like, I wrote a little program to get rid of all the junk. . . . And it looks pretty nice, kind of formats it nice. And I did that. Took me four hours to write that. Not work related at all. But it sits there on my thing. If I ever want to use it I can use it. And I won't take it with me because I'll just write it again, next job, as a time filler. There's only so much walking around the hallways you can do and going to get a Coke. Say I work a nine-hour day, and I take an hour and a half for lunch, so it gives me seven and a half hours to work. I could probably only walk around the building maybe half an hour out of all that. Or I could go up and get a printout for about an hour and a half. Walking into people's office, shooting the breeze. I mean, I can fill up my day pretty quickly. Or, I'm playing on the Internet and someone walked down the hall, I just click on my one other window.

This informant's goofing off routine reveals several ways to goof off without detection. One rule is to be aware of the expectations others have of your work. If you know those expectations, you know what margins for goofing off you have. Second, have decoys and defaults available; for example, be ready to invoke "problems" in a software program. Third, take longer to do everyday activities, such as using an hour and a half to get a printout. This informant also identified several perceptions in the workplace that benefited him. The first was a perception among other workers that everyone is busy. People may be too busy with their own work to notice what other people are doing. Of course, other people also could be goofing off and choose not to monitor others too closely in a "you scratch my back, I'll scratch your back" informal détente.

The Dramaturgical Infrastructure and Social Currency

How do people get away with idling? These types of goofing off, and the clandestine actions in the previous chapters, all depend partly on co-worker "dimmed vision" and the shared risk of mutual incrimination. Actual conditions of work also create little pockets of opportunity.

The Expectation of Autonomy
Bestowing autonomy on successful workers is seen as a reward for productivity. Autonomy extends the backstage and grants the actor independence from continued scrutiny, while also distancing others from any sense of immediate responsibility for the autonomous worker's actions. That partnered estrangement helps propel deviance through insulating a person from observation, while allowing outsiders to avoid monitoring, which circumvents scrutiny and pressure to expose behaviors such as goofing off.

Taken from a social control standpoint, autonomy also means that there is little monitoring of whether trust is misplaced. Further complicating the picture is that as long as people are successful, managers may not want to discover that rules are being broken. Delivering profits can then, in a vicious circle, accelerate granting more autonomy and opportunity, which then leads to more potential deceptions.

Technical Complexity

That some people rise "above" routine observational social controls lays open the general issue of how social control exists in everyday business practices and acts. When records, supervision, and performance criteria are complex, abstract, or under the aegis of the policed professional, there is tremendous wiggle room for deceptive activities. Shapiro (1987a, 1987b, 1990) documents these vulnerabilities very well in her work on white-collar crime. A steady progression toward using sophisticated computer technologies enables people to conceal crimes in technical complexity. Increased electronic commerce also creates social control difficulties in which offenses are enacted completely through electronic machinations rather than by multiple human participants.

In her book *Challenger Decision*, Diane Vaughan (1996) concludes that demanding more information can result in people knowing less, rather than more, about what's happening. If people are overloaded with information, they start to pay less attention to the particulars of the information swamping them. A second dilemma Vaughan identifies is that technical reordering and presentation of information can result in "obfuscation parading as clarity" (250). When records are overly complex, warning signs can disappear in overflowing details. In terms of credit and social currency, technical complexity can leave audiences unable to render proper evaluations, with deceptive actors concealing lies beyond the range of an observer's sight. There is room to lie because people do not have access to the evidence of a lie. Technical complexity is an indecipherable front stage and backstage for the uninitiated. A computer shirker can write his own program for his own purposes and have others be clueless that this work is unrelated to his job duties.

Ease of Conversion

A further aspect of workplace structure that escalates the capacity to goof off is whether it is easy to convert organizational resources to personal use. Some employers pay an incredible amount of attention to this problem. Casino dealers, for example, are some of the most heavily monitored nongovernmental employees—their pants even lack pockets to make it more difficult for them to walk off with money. How easy is access to converting company assets to one's personal use? For example, are means available to "wipe" Internet cookies and history files that could tip supervisors off about personal surfing on the Internet?

The anonymity available in a large-scale organization also helps conceal goofing off. This problem is also aggravated by the "who guards the guardians problem" that Shapiro (1987a, 1987b) identifies, in which actors who are supposed to monitor for breaches of trust may goof off themselves, because of their superior access to subverting social controls. If the thief is in charge of inventory, it is a safe bet that things will continue to get lost.

Individual Tactics of Concealing and Engaging in Misconduct

All individuals engage in a measure of concealment and deception in everyday life. An individual worker's ability to maintain a trustworthy and creditable appearance is assisted by structural factors. First, the status associated with a position may offer insulation from observation, either through autonomy or technical complexity. Second, people who are responsible for watching may be uninterested in raising any alarms. If they detect co-workers goofing off, they may avoid exposing them because doing so would carry greater penalties for them than keeping quiet. Third, technical complexities and a potential overload of information may make distinguishing between legitimate front stages and backstages very problematic. As with the classic dilemma in principal-agent relations, an individual may be able to hide acting in bad faith by having an asymmetrical advantage of knowledge over laypersons.

Understanding these contextual forces complements analyzing how individuals manage their impressions to fake trustworthy performances for particular individuals and audiences. What are individual techniques and abilities for doing so? What social variables, such as prestige, wealth, race, and gender, can people manipulate to appear more or less credible for a particular audience? As workplaces structure the identities that employees need to portray to consumers, they also structure the performance that someone needs to put forth to create a convincing appearance to co-workers. Emotional labor is not just for customers—it is also for the boss. Some forms of emotional labor are more necessary than others for acting deceptively. For example, adopting an aggressive and obnoxious persona discourages confrontation, a fact of office life that some people count on to avoid scrutiny. Research on con artists has uncovered a range of techniques for avoiding discovery, including cultivating and exploiting greed in victims that diminishes their desire to report being conned. Efforts to avoid appearing suspicious may also be unnecessary, since audiences may be oblivious, apathetic, or lack the expertise to detect deception.

A final note here is that those in charge of discovering goofing off may not be human beings. The "duped" party may be nonsentient and easy to fool, such as a written record, computer software, or a video camera. In such cases, a performer must know loopholes in those safeguards to circumvent them. The distribution of such information may well come from more experienced conspiratorial co-workers.

8

THE EVERYDAY ETHICS OF
WORKPLACE LIES

In the aftermath of savage human actions, we often ask, "Who could do such a thing?" We agonize over people's capacity to do evil to others and we hope we can uncover and control whatever forces can turn people into monsters. Our culture usually explains wrongdoing by segregating responsibility—we hold "bad" individual actors culpable and fault to a lesser extent the larger society from whence wrongdoers come. This separation of individual and group flatters society by allowing us to displace blame to individuals while disregarding ways in which social groups bear some responsibility.

The capacity to do wrong is a collective act. It takes more than one person to produce harmful acts ranging from the ultimate crime of genocide to white-collar, occupational safety, and environmental crimes, even if one or two individuals at the top are the initiators. When we spotlight only the most egregious individual offenders, we risk neglecting social contexts that make committing offenses possible. Understanding these obscured contextual forces is critical for answering a general question that the sociologist Everett Hughes (1984) posed, which, to paraphrase, is: How can people do wrong and still view themselves as "good" people?

There is an important difference between the organizational underlife explored in this book and an organization's potential criminal underworld. But the aspects of the workplace that encourage and tolerate deception as an everyday mechanism of social interaction at work may represent important microsociological features of workplaces that help in carrying out and rationalizing more serious deviant activities. Are the mechanics of rationalizing everyday deception useful in understanding criminal wrongdoing in the workplace?

In chapter 3 I explored how workplaces enable people to justify lying for work-related purposes without viewing themselves as being immoral. Examining a similar process in informal deceptions is useful for learning about lying and criminal behavior. Organizational culture does influence misconduct. Exactly how does it do so? In this chapter I examine a range of rationalizations in the workplace for informal deception—the sources of an everyday ethics that favors workplace lying—and suggest some connections between the source of those rationalizations and their potential role in perpetrating misconduct.

That people use a range of preemptive and post-hoc excuses and justifications to avoid or to repair a spoiled identity is well established.[1] However, what must be elaborated further is the organization's contribution to those accounts. The distinction here is between an individual's motive and the opportunities and encouragement that an organization provides to pursue that motive.

Consider three managers who are caught embezzling. One might embezzle to fund a gambling addiction, another to seek revenge against the employer, a third because of greed. The individual motives vary. What is analytically relevant, however, is that all three had the problem of having to subvert some set of social controls to commit the act. They had to feign trustworthiness so that co-workers did not notice anything out of the ordinary, and written records had to be vulnerable to fraud.

I suggest that organizations inevitably have structural and cultural blind spots in their social control, in part because casual deceptions are so important in an organization's dramaturgical infrastructure. This infrastructure allows productive deceptions and possibly permits people to act on and rationalize much more serious offenses and opportunities to subvert social controls.

In the introduction I introduced the term "ethical disengagement" to describe a process through which people neutralize ethical mores so that they can engage in deceptive actions. This category references the moral reasoning that surrounds workplace deception. Routine organizational operations permit an everyday ethics that both encourages and mitigates deception. What is crucial about this ethical disengagement is that it reflects an underlying social organization of irresponsibility. By blaming only individual bad actors, ethical disengagement is often perceived as being the product of faulty moral decision making by individuals, while the underlying social organization of irresponsibility is overlooked.

There are many sound reasons for this attribution. First, individuals do decide to carry out wrongdoing and are culpable for doing so. Second, responsibility is often viewed in individual terms. We prefer to reduce social complexity in criminal offenses to single actors, which is what our system is set up to adjudicate. Neo-Marxist theorists, on the other hand, view the amoral individual model as promoting a false idea of who the real economic criminals are—exploitative capitalists and the capitalist system. By focusing on frequently apprehended individual offenders, systematic economic pillaging by rich elites receives less attention. We should try to reveal an underlying system whereby workplace cultures can subtly encourage the rationalization of misconduct.

To that end, I suggest analyzing ethical disengagement as a process that is sponsored by informal organizational culture and norms. Individual excuses and justifications are a symptom of an underlying set of organizational mechanisms that allow both individuals and organizations to detach themselves from adverse moral assessments of deception. These mechanisms of ethical disengagement exist to preserve individual workers and the organization's "identities" as ethical. I believe that these systems of ethical disengagement are often mundane and apply mostly to slightly questionable behaviors. However, these stable systems of ethical disengagement may escalate into propping up an organizational culture of misconduct that is an important and understated accomplice in explaining workplace crime.

How Do Good People and Bad Behaviors Coexist?

Jackall (1980, 59) argues that bureaucratic administration influences moral consciousness by "making the moral classification of right and wrong irrelevant and replacing it with the technical classifications of correct and incorrect, logical and illogical, efficacious and non-efficacious." Bureaucratic organizations stress pursuing rational goals and administration, which may produce a tunnel vision that substitutes an imperative of productivity for a responsibility to the general "good." The danger here is that workers, on their own initiative, will fastidiously follow unethical or illegal means of accumulating profits while remaining concertedly blind and callous to the possible negative consequences of those means.

The tendency to emphasize rational efficiency can diffuse responsibility further by allowing people to make "efficiency" culpable for any questionable activities that are required on the job. The use of "legality" as a default account by private detectives is an illustration. Jackall (1980, 58) concludes that bureaucracies invite deceit because "managers and officials come to internalize the bureaucratic morality, based on the rational/technical ethos and on the compartmentalization of actions from their consequences."

As the bureaucratic ethos makes clear, ethical implications are also not immediately apparent when they are subordinated to technical ends. Gioia (1992, 137) notes about the Pinto, "The person who decides to let the assembly line use substandard cord in the fabrication of radial tires is not thinking of the accidents that the decision could cause, but simply keeping the assembly line moving." Further, keeping one's job is a strong incentive. As Vandiver (1982, 138) recalled, in his experience of faked AD7 airbrake tests, workers' livelihoods depended on following orders. As he succinctly notes, "Your conscience doesn't pay your salary." To quote a helpful reviewer, as written in *Threepenny Opera*: "Erst kommt das Fressen dann kommt die Moral" ("First food, then morals")—"expresses Brecht's insight that there are situations where one simply cannot afford to act morally."

At the extreme end of a nightmarish spectrum for the bureaucratic ethos lies Kelman and Hamilton's analysis (1989) of the three dimensions of organizational culture that contributed to the My Lai massacre, which can be applied to the workplace: *authorization*, which imposes a structure of authority on workers and a dictum in which obedience requires not asking questions of authority; *routinization*, in which tasks are compartmentalized and actors focus on a job's details rather than its meaning; and *dehumanization*, in which organizational influences lead workers to see an organization's targets as less than human and deserving of little consideration.

Financial and Moral Sunk Costs

Business ethicists cite both moral and financial "sunk costs" as motivating misconduct in workplaces. In competitive industries, implementing deceptions may offer a winning edge. There is also a related but little acknowledged moral sunk cost in rationalizing serious deceptive wrongdoing because of loyalty to co-workers to a workplace mission. For example, if nonprofits are highly invested in a particular cause, they might be willing to mislead a donor to maintain a financial commitment to that cause. That deception sustains a particular organizational mission that some perceive as a vital and collective moral obligation.

An interesting example of a moral sunk cost is when a worker gets involved in misconduct involving others, creating a new obligation to help cover up the action. This moral sunk cost begins with what we might call the "aftercrime"—engaging in even more deceptive activity to cover up the initial act. A police officer, who out of loyalty lies about another officer's unwarranted actions, is not guilty of the primary offense, but he or she is guilty of the aftercrime of covering up the offense.

External Market Pressures

External market pressures also trigger an escalation into more serious workplace deceptions. Companies operate in competitive markets that entice workers to deceive. Such deviance seems to be a rational choice for companies. What if competitors use illicit practices to a company's unfair advantage? Isn't deceptive reciprocation inevitable? Further, if an organization can reap massive profits while risking only slight fines for misconduct, that incentive may be too strong to decline.

External pressures may lead to suddenly employing deception as a means of crisis management. When a product or policy experiences a disastrous and unexpected outcome, deception often emerges as a managerial remedy, one that ends up worsening the situation rather than improving it. Those companies are the ones that deny having any prior knowledge that their products could have adverse effects.

The Workplace Virtues of Deception

The functionality of deception makes rationalizing lies easy. The workplace virtues of engaging in informal deceptions are at least fourfold. First, deception enables flexibility in bureaucracies. Second, workplace culture can punish honesty. Third, efficient work may demand deception. Fourth, self-interest, including fitting in with co-workers, encourages people to lie. The interaction order also requires people to engage in polite fictions relating to getting along with one another. Hence people are deceptive about how much they like or dislike someone, about the amount of gossip they engage in and its nature, and about how hard they work. Employees also try to conceal potentially discrediting attitudes that others could criticize, such as being ageist, racist, sexist (or none of the above) or being too liberal or too conservative. The very normative expectation of deception makes lying a coin of the realm that becomes its own rationalization: not only should you lie because it is expected that you will, but you are foolish if you don't, because "nice guys finish last." The question is, What does learning to lie as a routine mean ethically?

An escalation into criminal misconduct can certainly emanate from routine lying. People want to appear at their best in their workplace roles, which means that concealing discrepant information is already part and parcel of their job. As a consequence, the organizational underlife can be an organizational underworld in the making. The work team that helps its members slack off may be a natural breeding ground for formulating group norms that could lead the group to work together to steal from or otherwise victimize an employer or consumer or steal from the employees in the case of management conspiracy, as in Enron, for example. The perceptual blind spot that collective goofing off creates may be used for mild malfeasance, such as long lunches covered up by co-workers, but that same blind spot can also be spun off for darker purposes. Deception produces a diffusion and fragmentation of information, and consequently of responsibility for prohibited behaviors. The more familiar learning not to see moral problems becomes, the more callous one may become to both moral inhibitions against them, as well as to their consequences.

Preserving Individual and Organizational Images

Identifying how workplace culture sponsors both overt and subtle pressures to informal deception is the first part of the puzzle of explaining how good people and bad behavior can coexist. A second part of the puzzle is examining how individuals and organizations strive to avoid responsibility for deceptions, even though the workplace might demand them. The mitigation of formal and informal deception is a two-tiered phenomenon. Individuals and organizations both attempt to preserve a positive identity in the wake of revealed deception. Jackall (1988) notes that managers disassociate their private individual morality from any unethical or distasteful actions that they are expected to perform in their jobs. Conversely, organizations tend to treat deceptive workers as aberrant, as rogue bad apples. Both the worker and the workplace may claim a moral purity sullied by the other. The processes through which both disentangle blame from themselves and lodge culpability with the other is a crucial component of workplace culture, because the capacity to whitewash deception allows people to keep on acting deceptively.

There are of course situations in which deception is acknowledged as a shared, joint enterprise. Those scenarios, as private detectives illustrate, occur when deception is the authorized work of an organization or profession. In more informal situations, managers may also request that employees engage in deceptive behaviors as an unofficial but important work task. For example, in advertising and sales-oriented organizations, managers asked interns to pose as potential buyers in order to acquire pricing information and other data from competitors. As one informant described:

> They would have me pretend to be a student and ask questions of different companies to find out what things were being bought more and that kind of thing. That was definitely a deception, where the [supervisor would say] don't tell them you work at an advertising agency.

Another organization asked interns to pose as children and as teenagers in children's or teen-only chat groups and websites in order to gather information—the premise was to do essentially unannounced market research with unaware and spontaneous "focus groups" to learn what products and cultural figures were in demand.

Superiors can insist that subordinates engage in deceptions on their behalf. The higher up one is in the hierarchy, the greater the opportunity he or she has to acquire good credit while pushing undesirable credit downward. Willing and unwilling shills offer higher-ups the chance to not have any impropriety associated with them for illicit behaviors they put into motion. Fall guys is the common term for describing those workers as disposable pawns. Such scapegoats help higher-ups to appear honest while they maneuver dishonestly behind the scenes.

How Organizations Play Dumb

Organizational ethnographies have documented how criminal enterprises become informally organized within the shadows of bureaucratic administration (Dalton 1959; Mars 1994; Punch 1996). Theorists recognize

that organizations typically have a submerged set of informal administrative practices, loyalties, and arrangements that take on double lives as
criminal enterprises (Dalton 1959; Mars 1994; Perrow 1986). A shadow organization carries out illegal or deviant enterprises that are compartmentalized from the legitimate administrative actions of a company. The need
to disguise shadow organizations means that they operate using covert
administrative means, such as secret memos, double-talk, and meetings
outside the office. Punch (1996, 97–98) discusses the General Electric price-
fixing case in this regard by describing how conspirators essentially cre-
ated an informal headquarters in hotel rooms in order to strategize and
carry out their plans.

Just as "Chinese walls" keep inside knowledge of impending mergers
from investment bankers and traders, managers who engage in misconduct also construct Chinese walls to separate shadow enterprises from
legitimate ones. In other cases, employees and managers are motivated
to build Chinese walls to conceal incriminating efforts from regulators,
auditors, and internal watchdogs.

People in various positions on the corporate ladder compartmentalize
responsibility for actions differently. As Jackall (1988, 246) notes, "To live in
this world, you have to live by the operational code while mouthing convincingly the tenets of the myth system." This operational code prioritizes
the practical importance of appearing loyal to superiors, who also have
the important hierarchical advantage of being able to assign work, declare
mistakes or the nonexistence of them, and who can insulate themselves
from any improper actions committed by their subordinates. Hierarchy
protects against appearing to have guilty knowledge. As one of Jackall's
informants put it, bosses do not have to, or necessarily want to, know in
detail "all the eggs that have to be broken." Hence shadow organizations
and hierarchical inequalities are the prime movers in compartmentaliz-
ing accountability. Rationalizations emerge that deception was aberrant
rather than a typical and ongoing process in the workplace.

Workers and Socially Organized Irresponsibility

Workplace culture does supply workers with subtle means to help them
avoid taking responsibility for their deceptions. These means include
various accounts and an overall ability to use organizational features to
diffuse individual responsibility. How do working conditions encourage

people to see deception on the job either as morally neutral or beyond their control?

An important diffusion of responsibility lies in an organizational variation on the belief that "boys will be boys." In this variation, workers expropriate the knowledge that a competitive environment and internal organizational culture can provide a rationale for engaging in an occasional "low blow." People will excuse themselves as they are only "acclimating" to the requirements of the working environment. One informant described how his superiors demanded a competitive environment:

> EMPLOYEE: It's just that . . . they like a very intensely competitive environment. And if sometimes that means shading things, people not telling each other the straight answer, they really don't care. Now, outright crookedness, that's a different issue. But competitiveness—like in boxing, occasionally there's a low blow. And if it happens once in a while, it was an accident; it's not a problem.
>
> D. S.: Even if it wasn't an accident?
>
> EMPLOYEE: Right, right. We'll just let it go.

On an individual level, people may also act deceptively by invoking an abstract organizational "reason" to explain an unpopular action. For example, one manager had a regular policy of denying people's requests. He would not identify himself as the reason why individuals couldn't do something that they wanted. Instead an abstract "they" wouldn't allow it, or "they" put him in a situation that forced him to deny their request. As he put it, "I can't even think of a situation where I've said to someone, 'I'm sorry, you can't do that.' What I'll say is, 'I'm sorry, they won't let us do that.'"

This manager's technique is to shift blame to abstract parties within the organization. In his own actions, just as in the case of some private detectives, he is a neutral agent of "their" machinations. The manager disguises his own discretion and desires as someone else's dictates. This belief then makes the organization itself culpable, not the specific individual enacting "their" requirements.

Consider how common it is to arrange a surrogate for one's own deception in the workplace. Employees often complained that other workers asked them to deliver bad news for them. In the case below, a manager analyzes what happens when workers ask him not to assign a disliked individual to their group. They want the manager to break the news to that person, rather than informally doing so themselves. A manager comments on their motivation:

> What they really want to say is, "Don't attribute it to me. If possible, I don't want to have to pay the dues of having it be known that I didn't want to work with that person." Now it becomes my problem . . . without making that other person the bad guy.

The above technique is a form of deception that people use to obscure responsibility. Not only is this surrogacy for deception available, it is a crucial form of good people and bad behavior coexisting.

Workers also take advantage of traditional organizational doublespeak for their own benefit. For example, they may use abstract descriptions to communicate ill will without having to state their real feelings explicitly:

> EMPLOYEE: People would say things like, "Well, he's not as flexible." Or they would just make a facial expression like, "Oh my gosh, yeah, that was quite an experience, working for them." And you can infer from that that it wasn't really a positive experience.
>
> D. S.: And that's really the clear message that they're conveying?
>
> EMPLOYEE: Oh, it's definitely a clear message, without coming out and actually saying . . . anything.

Workplace Culture and Disowning Deception

Both individuals and organizations seek the ability to disown deceptions. That capacity to disown deception is at the heart of ethical disengagement and is built into everyday workplace culture. If a supervisor engages in unacknowledged discouraging and a blunder results from the new worker not knowing what to do, then the supervisor can say, "Well, if you had a question, why didn't you ask?" Built-in disincentives for asking the superior questions blunt them. The supervisor can then disown responsibility by stating that the learner should have asked questions.

Another means that workers use to deny responsibility for acting deceptively is consciously choosing not to label a behavior as deceptive in the first place. If an act is not really deceptive, then what's the problem? Many informants defined a behavior as deceptive only if it was malevolent. As one worker noted:

> My feeling is if you do what needs to be done in the workday, and you do your work on a consistent basis and get it done in a timely manner, and

it's accurate—what's the issue? [There are] the small, small deceptions of I'm on the phone looking very serious but I happen to be talking to my best friend from home [yet] I'm getting my personal time and work stuff done at the same time. So, to me, you get called on being deceptive if you're not accomplishing what you're supposed to be doing.

In another illustration, employees described keeping contemptuous feelings for a co-worker hidden (even though they gossip about that person behind their back) as not being deceptive. Instead they are being "civil," which includes acting friendly toward the individual they dislike.

The obvious benefit is to avoid an adverse moral judgment. A metaphorical equivalent is the idea that telling white lies is unselfish because the liar spares a person's feelings when lying to them (such as telling someone that they look great wearing some article of clothing when they do not). Left absent is that telling a white lie is self serving. By telling a white lie, the liar does not have to deal with the aftermath of angering the other person by telling the truth.

In many cases, telling white lies is appropriate etiquette and an expected means of achieving civil interaction. In other cases, telling white lies is a means of avoiding confronting people who should be confronted, such as workers who are performing poorly. Not telling them that they are doing a bad job may spare their feelings, but in telling that white lie liars avoid an unpleasant requirement of their own jobs. A false compliment is "deceptive" and based in a self-interest that is obscured by claiming kindness.

One worker said that his employer "does not tell lies about the products, even though they might not tell the whole story." The product involved is a bank card. The relevant question is whether a cardholder from that bank is charged for bank machine transactions:

> EMPLOYEE: They don't tell lies about the products. They might not tell the whole story, though.
>
> D. S.: What would be an example of not telling the whole story?
>
> EMPLOYEE: When you say, "We're not going to charge for transactions if you use our network." But you don't mention the fact that they still charge you when you use other networks, and they charge you more, actually, than they did before. They have control over the information.

In this case, the company misleads the customer without lying. Strategically, the company answers the customer's question by using the ambiguous term "network." The company does not consider it deceptive, even though the aim is to prevent the customer from hearing that charges exist.

In diffusing responsibility, workers sometimes blame having to deceive on the organization. If a boss orders you to "spy" on competitors or to lie to get around regulations, the organization is responsible for your acts. Companies, in turn, can blame individual workers for their deceptions. Organizations can insulate themselves from being labeled deceptive because organizations can suddenly disown an individual worker and state that the individual acted deceptively on his own accord. Say there is intense pressure to land a contract. If a sales agent offers a bribe to get a contract, and no one finds out, his employer benefits from that deception. However, if the agent gets caught, the employer can claim the worker acted on his own initiative.

An organization may apply pressure through managers to have favored opinions echoed in meetings. If people agree in a meeting that a strategic plan should be followed, even when they disagree privately, there is a deceptive appearance of consensus. The appearance of consensus allows the company to move forward with the plan. Should the plan end up failing, then organizational representatives can say that they would not have approved the plan had individuals at the company meeting stated their problem with the plan. That honesty is penalized within that organizational culture is significant in this story but not made explicit. Deception is unrecognized in the process and easily disowned.

An important point in considering how organizations avoid responsibility for deceptions is that an organization may consider itself a single entity or an entity made up of individually culpable actors. An organization as a sole entity supplies particular ideologies that encourage people to act deceptively. However, should there be fallout from deceptions carried out on the organization's behalf, there is suddenly no "organization" motivating that individual. There is only the one amoral individual, judged as if his or her actions were carried out in a social vacuum.

Individuals and organizations exist in a social context that sponsors deceptive behaviors, yet both individuals and organizational representatives attempt to disown any moral responsibility for engaging in those discrediting deceptions. Routine workplace interaction sponsors deceptive appearances, and from that infrastructure darker ethical dilemmas can emerge. The sociology of workplace deception is not about analyzing aberrational conduct but about delineating the basic terrain of workplace culture that can rationalize it.

9

APPRECIATING DECEPTION
IN THINKING ABOUT
ORGANIZATIONS

Deception offers people hope that perceptions can replace reality. Deceivers want how they seem to be taken for how they are. The social machinery of status makes many people fearful of losing their place or of never gaining position. Deception offers the hope of escaping that fate.

Workplaces constitute a social system that demands outward shows of appearance from individual workers. In this book I have described many ways that working is organized around an infrastructure of appearances, whether in undercover operations or lying to a client. The sheer volume of deceptive impression management that is present in the workplace should prompt us to revisit and reinvigorate existing theories about how people act at work.

In this chapter I offer creative thoughts about new ways to extend existing organizational theories. Sweeping and inclusive definitions of deception are standard in the scholarly literature. In this book, a qualitative exploration of how people mislead others in the workplace—a broad definition of deception—has been most appropriate. People act deceptively when they engage in an activity that is intended to make others believe something that is not true, whether they are working hard when they are not, claiming more qualifications on a résumé than they have, or flattering a boss they think is a moron. These are different situational acts, but they share a broad commonality—they represent a workplace reality where people intentionally mislead others in a wide variety of ways. The key issue here is that deception is common throughout workplace culture and administration. Reining in a definition of deception would move the importance of deception to the sidelines. My aim is to prompt a debate on the scope and impact of what should be considered deceptive behavior in the workplace, an issue that is overly neglected and viewed too narrowly, in direct contrast to its importance. If I have ended up taking that concept too broadly in order to oppose the neglect of deception in the current literature, then I welcome other scholars correcting the balance.

Summary of Major Points about Workplace Deception

1. Individuals deceive in order to gain more autonomy than their working conditions authorize. Hodson (1991, 2001) argues that workers are neither anesthetized into submission nor constantly rebellious. I support Hodson's view by focusing more specifically on how acting deceptively enables people to "freelance" outside the rules to try to get more flexibility at work.

2. Deception is a survival tactic in many ways. Superiors punish subordinates who reveal problematic information. Not all people welcome the astute critic. Being aware of the dangers of "messenger-blaming" is a marked difference between innocent "Boy Scouts" and workplace veterans.

3. Workers identify colleagues as trustworthy if they help cover up violations. Keeping secrets and covering up evidence helps maintain harmony within a work group. Workers decide what side to be on in a given situation, and they will sometimes switch sides as needed.

4. Employees cannot accomplish all that is required of them if they follow all of the company's rules. Yet employees acquire legitimacy and security from appearing to work at least somewhat within the rules. Deception helps solve this dilemma. Deception about how things are really accomplished covers up the flaws in formal rules while preserving the illusion that everyone is abiding by the rules.

5. Workers must use impression management to appear legitimate and competent in their occupational and professional roles (Hughes 1984, Abbott 1988). Impression management requires demonstrating desired attributes and concealing undesirable ones. People fake competence strategically to try to appear legitimate. Workers may act deceptively to

exclude information that threatens a legitimate appearance while substituting rosier information in its place. Socialization into organizations is often training in learning what impressions are most useful. Later this information informs how individuals pursue upward mobility, as success is based in part on appearances and putting on a facade that reflects organizationally desirable personality traits (Bosk 1979; Jackall 1988).

6. Employees who commit illicit acts use deception to foil social control efforts both within and outside the organization. Efforts to safeguard trust, such as contracts, surveillance, screening, patrols, self-policing schemes, and external guardians of trust, all attempt to coerce honesty. Deceptions occur to thwart these tactics—why they succeed in a microsociological sense warrants additional research.

7. For some occupations, deceptions are the professional product. Many types of work require official deception, from the physician's placebo to the public relations firm hiding a client's warts to a quarterback's faked handoff. Acting deceptively is a legitimate aspect of some professional work, particularly in adversarial professions.

8. Position within a hierarchy affects one's ability to deceive. Higher-ups can "officially" have more organizational resources to use in their lies. Organizations have one-way social control systems in which the actions of lower-placed employees face more scrutiny than those of higher-placed workers. Hierarchical position bestows particular advantages and orients particular performances, phenomena that I reference, from an informant's term, as a position's "social rights" in the workplace. Deception is a crucial element in avoiding and managing hierarchical impediments, from incompetent bosses to exemplary ones.

9. People use subterranean educational networks to exchange honest views and socialization tips for work. People also use subterranean education to exchange tips on handling difficult situations and on how to perform work. Information in organizations is a resource that some workers are allowed to have more custody of than others. Discrediting information has a vital role to play inside organizations, so that workers can factor the "flaws of the land" into a clear understanding of how to do their work and propel their own interests.

However, when workers hide flaws, such as not knowing how to do a particular task, or a manager ignores that insufficient resources exist for a subordinate to complete a job, the unclear picture of these real operating conditions can spell disaster. Hence one must learn the art of acquiring accurate information in an environment where accurate information is hidden. People must also hide their own embarrassing information as they are always working to retain their own secrets while trying to dislodge secrets from others.

10. Deception speaks to the moral culture of workplaces. How do deceivers reconcile themselves with the pejorative connotations of acting deceptively? The dramaturgical infrastructure contains within it enabling conventions, accounts, and rationalizations that sustain the ability to act deceptively. In this book I have explored some specific ways that people and organizational contexts rationalize acting deceptively as a legitimate and illegitimate aspect of their work.

11. Deceptive acts can have significant structural consequences for classic organizational outcomes. Who gets ahead, budget allocations, systems of covert discrimination, cheating of customers, and bases of solidarity among workers are in part associated with deceptive behaviors. A subterranean educational system exists in counterpoint to administrative and hierarchical controls on the distribution of information. The implication is that drinking from that stream of secret information helps some workers get ahead while others will not. Gossip can be a deceptive and hidden mechanism that affects others—a decision channel that goes unarticulated.

12. Effective deception takes work. There is a social architecture implicit in telling believable lies. Mechanisms for constructing convincing deceptions— authentication practices—warrant further exploration in studying lies that are specific to particular jobs and for understanding vulnerabilities in trust relationships more generally. The literature on passing is of key interest here. Why fakers simulate authenticity so well is a question that we can pursue through reverse engineering. Take the lie and unpack its components. We should learn what kinds of lies work or fail, what makes them tick, and why audiences can be taken in or why they may choose to be fooled by them.

Integrating Deception into Organizational Theories

Theories of how workplaces operate need to take into account more of the nastiness, scheming, illusions, and moral sacrifices that pepper the working world. No one is surprised to learn that people can goof off, exaggerate on résumés, flatter people falsely, mislead clients, hide their loyalties, or disguise their incompetence. The presence of these broad forms of deception is acknowledged. What is omitted is thinking of these acts as a cumulative and systematic phenomenon in the workplace instead of as an individualistic one. Fake appearances are a system of social communication in the workplace. Taking deception seriously as a cumulative infrastructure in the workplace means invigorating theories where deception has not been acknowledged to the extent that it should. I now review several existing approaches for analyzing organizations to illustrate ways to take deception's cumulative importance more into account.

Theories of Emotional Labor and Interactive Service Work

Research on emotional labor and interactive service work (Hochschild 1983; Leidner 1993) shows that a worker's emotional performance, whether in an airplane, insurance office, or restaurant, is part of a service landscape in which organizations deliver their products. Many workplace products include an emotional performance, whether in a doctor's display of professionalism, a professor's capacity to entertain students, or a river-rafting guide's "aren't we having fun" demeanor (see Arnould and Price 1993).

The emotional labor of workers plays a major part in determining the productivity of services marketing, sales, and workers (Grayson and Shulman 2000). Turnover in the workplace is also linked to burnout from burdensome emotional labor (Hochschild 1983; Leidner 1993). Excessive demands for emotional labor from ethnic and racial minorities (don't speak so "ghetto") and/or women ("just smile, honey") also constitute forms of gender and racial inequality.

Deception is an intrinsic part of emotional labor. Some workers must create a working personality that is very different from their authentic selves. Whether one feels happy or not, one has to smile for the customer, and maybe more so for the bosses who act as the emotional labor police and monitor the performances that are put on for customers. Effective displays of emotional labor for bosses sustain continued employment.

Some workplace identities may match up with who a person feels he or she is privately. But workers also may feel alienated from the fabricated identities that their workplaces impose on them (Hochschild 1983). As a consequence, discovering how people mount inauthentic performances successfully is important. Examining deception at work contributes to understanding developmental and strategic aspects of emotional labor—the techniques involved in putting on a good and credible show in order to do one's job. Putting on a strong performance results in positive outcomes such as increased sales and favorable performance reviews. In emotional labor, deceptive impression management strongly affects how well an organization succeeds in delivering a product. What authentication practices are involved in emotional labor?

The Informal Relations–Negotiated Order Tradition

Developed by Anselm Strauss and colleagues (1963) and articulated further by symbolic interactionists like Gary Alan Fine (1984) and David Maines (1982), the "negotiated order" perspective stresses the socially constructed nature of formal and informal administration in the workplace. Strauss (1978, 5–6) argued that the negotiated order "could be conceived of as the sum total of the organization's rules and policies, along with whatever agreements, understandings, pacts, contracts and other working arrangements currently obtained. These include agreements at every level of the organization, of every clique and coalition and include covert as well as overt agreements." The negotiated order approach "emphasizes the construction of organizational culture, through analyzing how workers create the meanings that are embedded in routine organizational activities" (Fine 1984, 247).

This tradition analyzes how people organize themselves to accomplish work "by the book" and how they "freelance at work" by negotiating informal working arrangements within a given organizational structure (Fine 1984). This orientation was a response to criticisms of formal understandings of how people work. The negotiated order theorists believed that traditional explanations were at odds with how people actually negotiated and put into place informal understandings of how to really accomplish work. Documenting this latter aspect of working, which I have dubbed "shadow administration," is a hallmark of this tradition in organizational ethnography. In negotiated orders, deception occurs in deviations from the formal rules of how to work.

The informal administration of work always surprises the uninitiated. To paraphrase an old cooking aphorism, if people knew how restaurants really prepared their meals, they might not eat them. The customer who enjoys her or his dish might never know that cooks insert their fingers into their food for tasting and presentation purposes. The customer might also not know that it would be impossible for cooks to wash their hands as often as is desirable, that restaurant kitchens use tremendous amounts of butter to flavor dishes, canned or frozen products substitute for "made from scratch," dinner bread is recycled from other tables. These aspects of informal administration affect the product but are not disclosed as part of the working formula. However, they are routinely important in producing food quickly and arguably well. Those backstage realities are important for production, and they must be kept secret.

The deviation from rules represents covering up a hidden infrastructure that actually carries out work. Although the negotiated order tradition clearly states that deception helps constitute this shadow form of administering work, detailing how deception helps get work done and aids in productivity requires greater empirical and theoretical attention. Deception should not be treated as an afterthought of this tradition but as its main engine.

No organizational sociologist is surprised when people state one set of official procedures for working while in actuality following others. In Melville Dalton's *Men Who Manage*, for example, workers consistently bypass "onerous" regulations through shadow administration. These informal systems of administration exist to distribute unofficial rewards to valued executives, to forgo safety requirements, and to stave off disputes between union and management. Deception is clearly implied and acknowledged here, yet again it hides in plain sight as a theoretical phenomenon in its own right.

Business Ethics and Worker Morality

Recent surveys demonstrate a prevalence of deceptive and unethical behavior within organizations. In the American Society of Chartered Life Underwriters and Chartered Financial Consultants and Ethics Officer Association 1998 survey "Sources and Consequences of Workplace Pressure: Increasing the Risk of Unethical and Illegal Business Practices," 56 percent of workers reported feeling pressure to act unethically on the job and 48 percent responded with unethical behavior, most prevalently in "cutting corners on quality control." In the Swiss cooperative KPMG's 2000 survey on organizational integrity, 49 percent of respondents reported observing illegal or unethical conduct on the job. In a 1999 business ethics study by the Hudson Institute (in conjunction with Walker Information, Inc.), 30 percent of respondents reported knowing or suspecting ethical violations in their organizations in the past two years. The violations included unfair treatment of employees, lying on reports or falsifying records, lying to supervisors, theft from employers, conflict of interest, sexual harassment, and abuse of drugs or alcohol. Surveys reporting that a third to half of employees observe unethical behavior justify exploring deception more deeply. Recent scandals at Arthur Andersen, Enron, and WorldCom, among others, offer painful reminders of the widespread prevalence and impact of illicit deceptive practices in major corporations.

What we do not yet know about the organizational contexts of workplace deceptions warrants further investigation. For example, the organizations surveyed in the above studies tend to be larger ones, usually of well over fifty people, so we know little comparatively about reported unethical behaviors among smaller businesses. There is also no focus on unethical behaviors in nonprofit organizations, which are not immune to such behaviors and are also workplaces. These surveys also focus on unethical and illegal behaviors, which are only a subset of deceptive behaviors at work, and are particularly unconnected to ones that people view as less discrediting, such as exaggerated accomplishments on résumés or lying about how long a task takes to do.

We need to know more about how unethical deceptions work and to expand the territory of what is thought of as deceptive behavior. We can distinguish three orientations regarding deception in business ethics scholarship. One tradition articulates some set of best ethical practices and values for businesses to adopt, sometimes advocating them as social responsibility strategies or as codes of ethics. A second tradition emphasizes case studies, seeking to discover and inventory causes of malfeasance from secondary analysis of infamous cases of ethical misbehavior. A third tradition focuses on everyday counterethics; it is one that should emerge more prominently.

Some writers, influenced in part by Albert Carr's famous article "Is Business Bluffing Ethical?" (1968), argue that business ethics and personal ethics are not the same. Hence people feel freer to take actions (cheating customers or competitors) in their workplace than they would in their private lives.

Such approaches emphasize studying what I reference here as "counterethics"—routine deceptive behaviors that are encouraged in the workplace. Research in this tradition examines what factors within individuals (i.e., personality variables) end up combining with organizational factors to produce unethical behaviors. Rather than studying infamous cases in business ethics here (such as the Ford Pinto or AD7 air brake), scholars ought to focus on routine malfeasance in certain professions, such as in sales (Carson 2001) or by purchasing agents (Robertson and Rymon 2001). This tradition dovetails most with this book's orientation of trying to uncover the influences that immediate and daily organizational context has on unethical behavior.

An abstract ethical code literature adopts a perspective that "we" (the ethically high-minded) must identify proper ethical values. Once this moral entrepreneurship is complete, companies that are sick with unethical behaviors can be vaccinated with an injection of proper morality. The idea that educating organizational employees about the difference between right and wrong, as if people will suddenly stop in their tracks because they now "learn" that stealing is wrong, is simply naive. What workers ought to ideally think about ethics is a question for philosophers and business ethicists. *Investigating* what people actually *do* on a day-to-day basis that may be unethical and why they do it is a better issue for social science researchers.

Trust and Workplace Ethics

Trust maintains social and business relationships, hence, the problem of how to safeguard trust attracts great interest from sociologists of law, organizational sociologists, and economic sociologists. Because organizational deviance is a breach of trust that may go undetected, the problem emerges of understanding how people construct convincing but fake trustworthy situations and identities. We need to identify how deceptive people quell suspicions through their physical, verbal, and written interactions at work. That analysis will reveal blind spots and vulnerabilities in social control.

What are the microsociological aspects of committing ethical violations? As Cressey (1950) observed in studying embezzling, managerial offenders must be trusted before they can commit their crimes. What do offenders do "right" to avoid giving away their real intentions and activities? People can exploit organizational resources if they avoid tripping any social control alarms, which includes knowing whether their co-workers or social control agents will respond to any alarms. A microsociology of trust violation is needed to learn how offenders manipulate credibility and how they identify and exploit indicators of trustworthiness within organizations. Given the potentially severe consequences, faking a legitimate appearance should be theorized more completely.

Research findings in studies of white-collar crime, ranging from Sutherland (1949) to more recent studies by Benson (1985) and Jackall (1988), all conclude that white-collar workers do not feel much individual responsibility for having engaged in their actions. There is a disassociation of individual character and morality from objectionable organizationally based actions. What factors in organizational life cause ethical disengagement, such that individuals (and organizations) can engage in unseemly activities yet disassociate themselves from feeling personally responsible for those actions? Further, what processes of ethical disengagement are associated with workers at lower levels in the organizational hierarchy, and not necessarily with the criminal elite (see Mars 1994)?

C. Wright Mills (1963) argued that bureaucracies constitute vast systems of organized irresponsibility. Punch (1996, 215) notes that organizations require "deception and the necessity to engage in institutional impression management through creating legal, cultural and social facades." Hughes (1984) notes that all work carries with it some "dignifying rationalizations" that help to mitigate the shameful implications of having to perform "dirty work," such as tasks that are physically disgusting or morally degrading. Ethical disengagement encompasses this "legitimating work" both at the individual and workplace level and ought to be explored further.

Deception as a Tactic of Resistance

A neo-Marxist perspective in organizational sociology addresses how workers react to overarching managerial control. Most recently in this vein, Randy Hodson's *Dignity at Work* (2001) examines how workers act to restore dignity to their work through tactics of resisting difficult working circumstances. Their resistance, for example, can take the form of "effort bargaining" (deciding how much work will actually get done) or acts of sabotage.

Workers must keep secret some of their dignity-attaining mechanics to avoid running afoul of social control, while employers must also at times keep their own abuses concealed (Hodson 2001, 107). Yet Hodson neglects to analyze the deceptions themselves that are necessarily involved in this dance between organizational control and worker agency. That omission can be rectified by analyzing how people lie at work, how workplaces structure those lies, and how lies are a part of the worker agency at the heart of Hodson's arguments. To do so requires paying special attention to deception as the tactical playing field on which management and individual workers battle for advantage.

Is it also possible that the actions Hodson describes as resistance or as sabotage occur first—as worker self-seeking—without necessarily being retaliation for a hostile work environment? Deception is more than a tactic of resistance or revenge against workplace affronts—it also serves as a tool of self-interest and self-promotion. Deception is a basic aspect of work. Its role in maintaining dignity constitutes just one part of its impact in the workplace.

It is important to highlight that Hodson does distance himself from a pure resistance model, seeing that tradition, as well as other organizational theories of work, as "straightjacketing" workers by neglecting to consider their creative and autonomous attempts to make work a more dignified setting. For Hodson, work is not universally oppressive, nor is the worker only a desperate resister—work can be a meaningful creative place:

> In order to understand workplace behaviors, we need a theoretical model of the worker that is neither anesthetized nor limited to resisting management strategies of control. Such a model must include central roles for pride in work and for the struggle to create autonomous spheres of activity. Autonomous activity is an essential requirement both for workers and for the vitality of organizations. . . . Employees are active and creative human beings. (266)

Hodson hammers this point in a model that incorporates the vision of the "active worker" and of agency, which he believes is dramatically neglected as a theoretical perspective. However, there are also those who premeditatedly shirk, do not do their work well or legitimately, and who have no problem lying about it to avoid accountability. Some "active" workers seek creative autonomy not merely to realize meaning at work but to avoid getting caught for finding no meaning there. This point does not reinforce wholeheartedly any "lazy, rotten workers" allegation—it merely acknowledges the reality that some individuals, for a variety of reasons, could not care less about doing their jobs, whatever the management. Conceiving the active worker is one thing; there are also inactive workers who appear active only to save themselves from tripping any alarms leading to punishment.

A system of subterranean education exists, through which people learn schemes of becoming "recalcitrant workers" and how to practice "work limiting" or "effort bargaining" or being "absent at work." We must analyze how people learn to undertake collective acts of deception and wrongdoing. Ackroyd and Thompson (1999, 54) argue that the field of "organizational misbehavior," as they call it, ought to be analyzed as processes of "self-organization," referring to the tendency of groups to form interests and establish identities and to develop autonomy based on these activities. This argument is certainly reasonable and appropriate to develop, just as we should not neglect lone wolves who also busy themselves with misconduct.

Workers in production facilities are in collectivities with joint interests; the very nature of their work consists of tasks that they accomplish together. They are also a group with a shared vulnerability to managerial encroachment on their autonomy. However, there are other types of workplaces and other types of work. Solo practitioners of various sorts, such as salespersons or private detectives, are individuals who may work alone. They also lack the controlling supervisors that factory workers have. If they work for themselves for autonomy, that is one argument; if they do so to reap profits as their own managers, another explanation is needed.

The war of all against all, of individuals who keep secrets and who only partly trust their fellow workers, must be acknowledged. Even groups with goals of collective autonomy have individual differences including the secondary autonomy of individuals who seek to better their place within the "self-organization" around them. What about people who pursue divisive strategies against fellow workers rather than against managerial control?

"Self-organization" is an outcome and cause—how self-organization happens and its details are part of an as of yet untold story of impression management strategizing within an organizational context. All misbehavior is not symptomatic of gentle or harsh rebellions against managerial control. Misbehavior is also at times an organizational mandate, in which a worker collectively sides with the organization, combining both his or her own and an organization's self-interest by lying to third parties. Misbehavior is also a socially contingent behavior; a consultant who dishonestly portrays respect for a client's "dumb" idea is acting appropriately, even though she or he is falsely portraying their opinion of the client and of the client's idea.

Embeddedness

Granovetter's (1985) embeddedness argument criticizes oversocialized (people are norm-driven robots) and undersocialized (people act only in their self-interest) theoretical explanations for how people maintain trust. The term "embedded" refers to affective or economic relationships between partners who know one another and are ensconced in a network of reciprocal obligations. Granovetter summarizes three reasons to explain why interdependence and familiarity in embedded relations helps maintain trust:

> 1) information is better, 2) that individuals with whom one has a continuing relation have economic motivation to be trustworthy, so as not to discourage future transactions, and 3) departing from pure economic motives, that continuing economic relations often become overlaid with social content that carries strong expectations of trust and abstention from opportunism. (481)

It is reasonable to hypothesize that familiarity breeds better information and shared interests, and that fear of losing future transactions and social expectations inhibits betrayal. Yet there are limits to these arguments. Granovetter (491) notes that "trust engendered by personal relations, presents by its very existence, enhanced opportunity for malfeasance."[1] How effective is "embeddedness" overall in maintaining trust? This question is unexamined across many types of embedded relations. Imagine reversing the question and asking what conditions of embeddedness make deceptions more effective?

For example, one condition under which embeddedness fosters deception and helplessness is in monopolies. Workplaces also model such situations in trapping people in lines of authority. Fear of losing future transactions may fail to suppress malfeasance in personal relations if someone cannot switch partners. People trapped in inflexible superior/subordinate relationships may lack alternatives to their current relations. If bosses have a monopoly over subordinates, as they do under systems of one-on-one authority, then embeddedness does not guarantee trust but instead may provoke exploitative deception.

Granovetter's point that "information is better" (490) in personal relations depends on individuals being able to use their "better" data. People do have more information about familiar persons with whom they have existing relations. However, having substantial knowledge does not mean that people use it well or that one's substantial knowledge is accurate. When embedded participants lack appropriate evaluative skills, they may overlook deceptions that experts would catch. Learning whether information is actually good (depending on one's individual interest) and being able to appreciate the interests and ambitions that the information providers may have tempers the "guarantee" of trust that familiarity is supposed to provide.

The powerful pressures that are supposed to prevent people from malfeasance fail to note that social pressure also prevents exposing malfeasance. Cover-ups and codes of silence are common, often to protect group solidarity against outside threats. A willingness to participate in internal and external cover-ups may be required in order to sustain a full and continued group membership.

A better empirical and theoretical examination of deception would clarify these conditions of embeddedness. First, it would explore collusion in deception itself as the basis of an embedded relationship (for example, in collective "goofing off" partnerships). Second, studying existing deceptions among embedded actors reveals characteristics of "exploitative embeddedness," in which asymmetries of influence, information, power, and resources between embedded partners can actually imprison people in deception.

Network Approaches

A broader assessment of workplace deception contributes to network ideas by considering the effects of negative ties. Deceptions exist in negative ties (ties involving covert and overt negative sentiments between employees in organizations). Organizational politics is a classic arena in which negative ties hurt actors. People may camouflage vendettas and other "irrational" grounds for decision making to appear to comply with legitimate, rational, and bureaucratic criteria for actions (Morrill 1995). Hence, the power of negative ties remains hidden. One can anticipate multiple consequences of negative ties, some predictable, others less so.

For example, negative ties can produce odd positive outcomes. Managers may write good references for bad workers to hasten their departures. Or a colleague's mutual hatred of a co-worker can be a tie that binds, and in organizations, those bonds have hidden effects on job performance and turnover. Also, negative ties exclude some workers from important information, such as how to perform certain procedures or about the idiosyncrasies of important managers. Informants report that negative ties explained "irrational" promotion decisions. Negative ties are a crucial justification for using adversarial tactics on co-workers, a company's clients, and competitive rivals.

Considering how negative ties operate in more detail also reveals how deceptions help distribute power and rewards in a network. The hidden nature of negative ties disguises tacit mechanisms of organizational power. Two such mechanisms discussed here are the ability to collude with co-workers in useful deceptions and the ability to cultivate relationships with powerful mentors, even if doing so involves insincere deference. My informants frequently recounted how workers used deceptive actions to press grievances against others.

Granovetter (1973) argued that the strength of weak ties is in transmitting information about employment opportunities. Exploring how networks and ties of varying strength affect and transmit negative information is a further question. How does one access or distribute the negative information one needs? What are the unofficial and official, collusive and naive, links through which deceptive information travels? In examining subterranean education, worker's strategies and motivations for acting on, distributing, and revealing negative information can be explored further.

The New Institutionalists and Legitimation

The new institutionalist approach decouples the areas of organizational legitimacy and technical production. Meyer and Rowan (1977, 46) wrote that "institutional rules [may] function as myths depicting formal structures as rational means to attain ends." Thus organizations often have administrative dimensions whose purpose is to legitimate and maintain useful appearances. Organizations and workers both fake a legitimate appearance by hiding flaws. But what are patterns of deceptive legitimating? A new category of "fraudulent isomorphism" should be added to the coercive, mimetic, and normative categories that DiMaggio and Powell (1983) offer.

Isomorphism refers to the tendency of organizations to take on institutionalized forms that make them resemble one other. *Fraudulent* isomorphism occurs when insincere and inadequate attempts to conform to isomorphic standards exist. Informants, for example, sometimes described their employers as claiming to offer a "state of the art" technical capacity in order to obtain business. These fraudulent attempts to mimic isomorphic standards involve deceiving clients. Because resource-poor organizations and professionals have less ability to copy other organizations that are resource rich, fraudulent isomorphism is substituted.

Analyzing deception also helps identify criteria for officially legitimate deceptions. If deception constitutes official work for some, what criteria exist to determine a legitimate performance of "illegitimate" techniques? In chapter 3, I identified several occupational accounts that represent practitioners' efforts to circumscribe and legitimate standards for official deceptions.

Accounts and Passing

In this book I have made frequent reference to the ideas of accounts and passing. Both ideas should have a greater currency in organizational studies. I suggest that accounts be studied as systematic ways that workplaces and professionals attempt to preserve the right to engage in deceptive and adversarial work. I argue that accounts, at professional and organizational levels, offer a system of label laundering so that ultimately no one takes responsibility for deceptive behaviors. A greater exploration of both the cumulative and label-laundering capacity of accounts is needed.

The concept of passing, like that of accounts, has a rich history in symbolic interactionism. In this book, I argue that passing reveals "authentication practices" that everyday deceivers use to craft convincing fabrications.

Authentication practices expose the criteria that people use to socially construct what they take to be true. These practices reveal how people manipulate those grounds of assessing reality. A social architecture of lying needs to be developed to understand more about why workers are susceptible to lies and how workers tell convincing lies. Additional studies of passing also would shed light on important issues of trust and embeddedness. Scholars want to understand how people can feign trustworthiness. Authentication practices offer a microsociological tool to research that question, which ultimately could produce better knowledge of some of the shakier foundations that can exist in relations of trust.

Some Final Thoughts

While writing this book and thinking about particularly acerbic points that respondents made, I sometimes scribbled down private cynical aphorisms about workplace culture, somewhat along the lines of a Dilbert-inspired version of *Poor Richard's Almanac*. My summary reflections bore sardonic fruit, including:

"My advice for surviving workplace culture: Identify what rationalizations your superiors use and then support them to the most craven extreme while in their presence."

"There is no molehill that some troublemaker doesn't want to make into a mountain."

"Asking some managers to offer 'constructive criticism' about their co-workers and subordinates is like giving gasoline to an arsonist."

"Rules are elastic—they bend enough to let powerful people slip by and then snap back into shape to prevent less powerful people from doing the same thing."

"Telling other people that you are insecure or that you lack confidence is an invitation for them to disrespect you that they will never refuse."

"The bigger the ego, the harder the fall."

"When someone in the office urges you to confide in him or her, treat it like a shark asking you to put some ketchup on before you jump into the water."

"The most persistent research anyone does is always on the subject of colleagues' flaws. Co-workers inventory this information as if they are the most efficient bureaucrats dedicated to a task in the entire world. No defect is too minute to escape notice; no psychological profiling too off-limits. Whatever a person's line of work, they always double as an expert in the character flaws, failings, and inability to measure up of their colleagues. Everybody speaks criticism."

"Some people flee their responsibilities like vampires avoiding sunlight."

"Any system that ends up punishing responsibility isn't going to effectively generate it. On a good day, you can interpret this reality as an unintentional misfortune; on a bad day, you can see it as the absolute intention all along. Misunderstanding this is a lie served by the notion that managers have an open-door policy and that one should come forward if there are alarms to sound. Just because you invite people to put their heads on the chopping block doesn't mean that they are stupid enough to accept your offer, especially after they can see the head of the last person who did rolling down the floor."

"The problem isn't being paranoid—it's going public with your suspicions."

"Bitter, seething resentment is the proverbial elephant in the room of professional relations."

As I think about these aphorisms now, I don't disagree with many of them, although I recognize that they do not paint a complete picture of interpersonal dynamics in the workplace. Workplaces are also authentically places of friendships, support, feelings of accomplishment, and the like.

I make no claims of knowing the ratio between the honest and the Machiavellian aspects of working. I do know that the Machiavellian side exists and is overlooked far more than it should be, given its significance in everyday work. There is intrigue in workplaces, and people frequently engage in infighting and politics. Of scholarly interest here is that this hidden subterfuge is of practical and overlooked significance in people's workplace experiences. We manage their hidden dark realities in our impression management at work—and they are the proverbial elephants in the room in many of our workplace interactions.

Appendix

RESEARCH DESIGN

Social scientists know that capturing the straight story from respondents can be a vexing and persistent methodological concern. So how did I manage the process of asking private detectives and dozens of workers to discuss their deceptive behaviors? Further, what sense do I have that I gathered, irony noted, authentic accounts of deceptive actions? The short answers are that I used multiple sources of data and that I guaranteed anonymity. To quell informants' concerns, I was adamant that I had no interest in identifying any individuals by name with any incriminating or stigmatizing behaviors. I clarified that I only sought to understand what deceptions people confront and manage in order to perform their work. Finally, I also relied on participant-observation to supplement interview data. I turn now to reviewing the research design that I used for each case study.

Case Study 1: Private Detectives

I have completed a prior ethnography of private detective work. I use that data in this book to identify and analyze the deceptions that private detectives use. Private investigation is a state-regulated and licensed profession where deception is a necessary practice. Private detectives represent a category of workers that I identify as adversarial professions.

Clients hire adversarial professionals to act as their agents in conflicts with other individuals or organizations. Adversarial professionals incorporate morally contestable techniques, including deception, to accomplish their work. Some other adversarial professionals include collection agents; insurance investigators; some lawyers; public law enforcement; military personnel; and political and public relations consultants. To study deception as a type of formal professional work sheds light on the understudied practices of these professions.

However, I did not anticipate coining a term like "adversarial professions" when I first became interested in researching private detectives. My motivation did not come from film noir, Mike Hammer, or Sherlock Holmes, but instead from a source that I would not have predicted. My decision to study private detectives began when I solved the case of the lying comedian.

I had been studying a group of improvisational and stand-up comedians in order to research how people learned and taught themselves to be funny. In doing that work, I learned that one of my informants lied to me about his income, day job, and career prospects. I discovered these misrepresentations through realizing that I walked by the location of his stated "day job" as a high-end computer consultant and could easily see through a store window over a period of weeks that this individual was a cashier, which, even with an extremely lenient interpretation of technology, is a far cry from being a computer consultant. His claims of income quickly fell apart when I learned more about what performers were paid, if and when low-level comedians even got paid (hardly ever).

The methodological problem of people lying during interviews has always fascinated me. How are fieldworkers supposed to get honest responses when they ask people questions about drug use, income, sexual activities, or prejudicial attitudes? While I know that various methodological antidotes are touted to deal with this problem, I began to think about the issue differently from most researchers. I asked myself: What do professionals outside academia do to deal with liars? What do police officers do when they hear people perpetually claim innocence? What do psychologists do when previously suicidal patients now claim to have no desire to harm themselves? What range of techniques do professionals use to figure out what the truth is?

I then thought about which professions might already have broadly applied and well-articulated repertoires of investigative techniques to tackle deceptive behavior. Private detectives came to mind as they perpetually confront people who act deceptively because they have something to hide, such as adultery, employment theft, skipping bail, and so forth. Private detectives selling their creative services to the private sector presented an interesting contrast with police detectives, whose targets are mandated by law.

I decided to interview private detectives and observe them at work in order to learn about their techniques for penetrating deceptions. I learned that private detectives penetrate deceptions by being even more adept at deception themselves. In essence, private detectives have to "out lie" liars. As one respondent told me: "If you call someone up and say, 'Hi, would you mind telling me where your brother is, so that I can put his ass in jail for the next five years,' you won't last too long in the private detective business."

The Interview Data

I started by writing introductory letters to private detectives who advertised in the phone book in a large metropolitan area. The letter requested an interview, described the scholarly emphasis of the research, my academic affiliation, and stressed confidentiality. After two weeks, I followed up each letter with a phone call.

I interviewed twenty respondents, three women and seventeen men. Nineteen respondents were white. One male informant identified himself as "nonwhite" but did not identify himself with a specific "nonwhite" racial group. There were also seven interviewees who held permanent employee registration cards (PERCs). PERCs are licensed apprentices who carry out investigative operations under a primary license holder's supervision and liability. PERCs do much of the investigative legwork and are important sources of information about applying deceptive investigative techniques.

My interview approach was semistructured and involved asking informants a range of closed and open-ended questions. I used closed-ended questions to identify specific characteristics of professional practice. These questions enabled me to identify particular types of investigations, such as missing persons or undercover operations, that a private detective engaged in, their career background, investigative experience, and so forth. The open-ended questions probed more of the in-depth feelings and interpretations they had about their work. The open-ended data enabled me to conduct a domain analysis (Spradley 1980) to contrast different ethical views of investigations.

The interviews averaged an hour and a half and were almost all taped and transcribed verbatim. I could not tape three interviews, as one informant did not permit recording, another interview took place over the phone, and the third interview took place in a bar that was too noisy to make recording possible. I interviewed a range of PERCs, full license holders, and phone book and non-phone book private detectives.[1] By doing so, I ended up talking to informants across a range of specializations and practical experience. Consistent with methodological procedures of member validation (see Emerson 1983), I reinterviewed several respondents, asking them in particular about my interpretations of private detective work.

Observational Data

I did not rely solely on interview data. I also conducted participant-observations of private detective work. One of my initial interviewees told me that his agency had an in-house training program for investigators. He hoped to spin off the agency's training program to the public as a for-profit educational program for people interested in pursuing a private detective license. I pounced on his offer to let me participate in this program. Doing so gave me the chance to observe how this specific agency trained new operatives. These observations involved attending more than twenty-five hours of in-class lectures and training films, group discussions, and training exercises, such as weapons training and the rehearsal of scenarios that might occur in the field. The lectures covered legal and technical aspects of private detective work, including interviewing, investigative techniques, and protocol.

Private detectives often come from the ranks of law enforcement agencies or the military, with many having been police officers or, in more elite cases, homicide detectives. They often have more than a glancing familiarity with investigative techniques. The in-house agency training sometimes involved discussing how investigative techniques associated with public law enforcement translated to private sector work, often centering on what private detectives could do or not do, as opposed to law enforcement agents.

To balance the potential bias of participating in only one agency's training regimen, I observed private detectives working at different agencies and I also sought training materials. Thus, my observational data overall included participating in a component of in-house training at a private detective agency and observing private detectives at work at several agencies.

What kind of private detective work did I witness? I observed private detectives conduct surveillance, interview informants, interact with clients, testify in court, supervise operatives, and acquire credit reports and unlisted telephone numbers. Put in terms of cases and events rather than techniques, there was everything from the worker's compensation fraud case that involved driving several hours to watch a person's home and his outdoor activities, to watching an investigator testifying in court, to watching a private detective sweet-talk a corporate client about an investigation's progress.

Doing ethnography means getting into the nitty-gritty of people's real lives as opposed to simply listening to their recollections. Doing participant-observation meant being a fly on the wall. Accordingly, I also spent some time "off work" with several private detectives, drinking and eating meals with them and accompanying them to after-hours events such as target shooting and gun purchasing. As an example, one detective who didn't own a car called me for rides, which allowed me to make an implicit trade of conversation for transportation. As fieldworkers know, those types of interactions provide tremendous opportunities to listen to shop talk about work. I also examined completed investigation case records using reproduced copies with the real names blacked out. Some of these case files came from the training program. Access to these materials allowed me to compare interview comments with written records of cases. I also reviewed in-house training materials from some agencies.

The reception I got from contacting private detectives varied. One private detective accused me of spying on him and threw me out of his office. Another checked up on my academic affiliation and demanded to see copies of articles so that he could verify that I was not "full of shit." I learned that there is no love lost between some private detectives and some journalists, as both of these detectives suspected me of initially being an investigative journalist out to make them look bad. Others treated me with interest, as an unusual presence in the routine of their daily work lives. Though some respondents told jaded tales of investigations with swaggering bravado, most respondents treated their work as mundane but took seriously their applications of techniques to produce results. There was a restriction on my observations in that I was not allowed to go on some jobs where there was a potential for violence. I do wonder what the experience would have been like if my presence on bail enforcement roundups had been allowed rather than forbidden at the last minute by the agency head.

The observation process does offer some reassurances that one is getting the straight story. Though respondents could conceivably wish to deceive me in interviews, no one would create a completely fraudulent training program for their own agents just to fool me into thinking the right things. I just did not pose any sort of threat to warrant that effort. Further, when working on a case, the ramifications of doing inappropriate work apply directly to the bottom line, so there are no incentives to act abnormally just for my benefit. There are also too many people involved for the required choreography of putting out falsehoods solely for my benefit. Finally, there is the classic reassurance of hearing and seeing the same thing over time from a variety of informants. When people describe investigating adultery and how one can acquire credit reports in synonymous fashion, you have a growing confidence in those accounts. Hearing similar responses to the same questions about investigative techniques stood as a confirming comfort to me.

Case Study 2: Informal Workplace Deceptions

People who encounter lies and act deceptively in less exotic jobs than private investigation are the second case study of workplace deception featured in this book. That people lie at work surprises no one. Scholars of white-collar crime do analyze deceptive workplace behaviors, but their focus is usually on deceptions primarily as a horrifying organizational problem or as criminal acts by aberrant or elite protagonists. Deception is viewed, to use Arthur Stinchcombe's description, as an "exceptional act directed at criminal ends rather than as a routine act directed at everyday ends."[2] Studies of insider trading (Reichman 1989), price-fixing (Ross 1992), savings and loans looting (Pontell and Calavita 1993), and patterns of illegal acts by large organizations and their punishment (Clinard and Yeager 1980; Punch 1996; Sutherland 1949) illustrate this focus on criminal ends and elite actors. Studies of low-level deviance by nonmanagers, such as investigations into employee theft and drug use, also emphasize deceptions with criminal aims. Overall, low-level, noncriminal deception within organizations has not been made a central focus of empirical or theoretical inquiry. A systematic analysis of organizational deception is required to study the noncriminal deceptive activities that extant workplace ethnographies document in bits and pieces. Further, the study of moral decision making by managers has not trickled down to studying the moral decision making of entry and lower-level white-collar workers. While managers do give orders about what tasks to perform, the organizational world in which these orders are carried out and products delivered to the clients is accomplished in the world of lower-level workers. There are also more low-level workers than high-level ones, and their numbers and practical relevance warrant attention. My goal for the second case study on workplace deception was to interview people in a range of jobs rather than just the big shots and managers.

In interviewing lower-level workers, I learned about the choices and dilemmas that new workers face when they are socialized into acting deceptively in their particular workplace. Lower-level workers offer a fresh eye into the choices that induce and deter deception, including the power of hierarchical position to compel deception from others. Deciding what to say when something is not understood, whether to question a superior or to notice fast-talking or lying to clients, whether to participate in backstabbing or to acknowledge the first awareness of a vulnerability in an organization's image are all dilemmas that confront new and lower-level workers. What do they think about them? I offer a reconceptualization of lying here as a routine, rather than exceptional, behavior in the workplace, and I examine common workers and not elite ones. To do so I collected both interview and observational data.

Interview Data

I conducted interviews with forty-three mostly lower-level workers in thirty organizations. My research focused on learning what deceptions occur as part of the everyday experience of working. I adopted the "hunt and peck" style of ethnographic research (see Schwartz and Jacobs 1979) to investigate workplace deception. Hunt and peck ethnography is an ethnographic method aimed at "generating examples, of samples of situations, that are useful in their own right for how they instruct about a subject of interest." Hunt and peck ethnography is an exploratory form of qualitative research where ethnographers explore new empirical terrain, which I argue is the case here with deception.

I chose qualitative exploration rather than quantitative certainty. My aim was to produce an exploratory analysis of people's experiences with deception in the workplace. These explorations have yielded relevant analytic themes that quantitative or qualitative researchers might pursue further. My aim was not to produce quantitative accounts of how many lies a person tells each day or experimental simulations where someone creates an incentive to lie and researchers see what happens. Instead I analyzed how people think about and respond to deception during their work.

Interviewee Characteristics: Interns

Interns in their early twenties were an important subset of my sample. Why interns? I had taught an internship program at a university for two years. Through reading journal accounts of work experiences and from listening to interns describe their work experiences in seminar discussions and during numerous office hours, I discovered that many interns observed deceptive acts in their work sites. For example, interns heard boasting about how hard they were working from people who played solitaire on their computers all day. They listened as co-workers bitterly criticized managers privately while never voicing their objections more openly. They saw workers lie to customers. They heard bosses tell them to feel free to ask "any questions," while they also picked up on nonverbal cues that convinced them they should not do so. The overall array of deceptions interns described convinced me that it would be fruitful to talk to them as part of a study on workplace deception.

Interns also occupy an interesting and beneficial structural position in organizations that can enable them to observe and sometimes participate in deceptions. They straddle a hierarchical gulf as people with cultural capital similar to managers but who lack organizational authority over subordinates. Workers below the managerial level usually ended up doing the nuts and bolts of teaching interns. They often instructed them how to get around bureaucratic rules as part and parcel of an intern's accelerated curriculum into "how things are really done." Interns had to be taught quickly so that both high-level and lower-level workers could maximize the temporary availability of their labor. Interns are also eager to please to gain work experience and possibly a reference, and they are usually young and naive about the workplace. Some in the workplace perceive interns as powerless and unthreatening, so interns might hear sentiments and witness actions that subordinates would have concealed from a hierarchical superior, an outsider, or even other co-workers. Alternatively, superiors recognized that interns straddled the hierarchy, so they also sometimes tried to use them as spies. An intern at a bank remarked:

> Many times I wondered if the bankers were using me as a go-between. It seems like some of them had an ulterior motive in wanting to go out to lunch with me. I was fairly close to "Bill" and I often heard comments from some of these bankers about Bill's work ethic. I think they told me those things because they wanted me to pass them along to Bill. A few times I was asked if I thought that a certain person worked hard or not. These were times when I felt as if I was being used as a spy.

Interns, like waiters and taxi drivers, may be considered unthreatening and invisible observers of other people's behaviors. Interns also are asked to do different tasks and work for a variety of people (there were often people vying to unload some of their work on interns), so interns got to observe an array of activities.

Interviewing Interns and Other Informants

Many colleges and universities offer administrative programs that arrange internships for students. These programs place students at diverse internship sites, including advertising firms, arts organizations, banks, government agencies, financial service firms, management consulting firms, and nonprofit social service agencies. Many semester and quarter-long internship programs have their students work full-time at internship sites for at least two months.

After deciding that I would interview some interns for this study, I met with the director and the instructors of the internship program where I worked and from which I wanted to recruit interns. I also met with past students that I had taught in the internship program, to learn how they felt about my interviewing them. My meetings with the program director and present instructors of the internship program, and with my own former students, produced an interview contract and consent form. If I used this form, I would be allowed access through the program to these students. That form also accorded to expected research protocols that guarantee anonymity and the prevention of harm in research. All respondents read and signed an informed consent form prior to interviews.

I imposed several conditions on all interviews, not just those with interns. First, I instructed informants that they were never to identify any workplaces or any individuals from their workplaces by name. As a consequence, there are no specific names of any individuals or organizations that connect to any of the workplace events and behaviors that I present here. I clarified before interviewing every informant that I was not interested in maligning employers or in trying to discover if he or she had done "anything wrong." I always told informants that my focus was to study how people behave within organizational culture and that I had no interest in the actions of any particular organization. I did not want any reader to be able to connect an example of deception in this book specifically to any identifiable organization. While I did ask informants to identify the general type of work their organization did and that they performed, and I did ask questions about the organization's size, I did not report such information in any precise way that could lead to identifying any organizations by name.

Once I received permission from the program director to conduct interviews, I obtained lists of students who had completed the program, and I telephoned them to request interviews. I taped and transcribed all but two interviews. I did not tape one interview at the respondent's request, and during another the tape recorder malfunctioned. I took detailed notes from both interviews. Many respondents had been interns and were now early in their working careers. Thus my sample began to move from talking to people about what they learned as interns to learning more about the deceptions that people encountered in their first few years of work.

I did end up interviewing several people whom I had taught during their college careers through teaching in the internship seminar. That seminar required students and faculty to work closely with one another, spending a full academic quarter together in a very discussion-oriented small-enrollment seminar. This program was the only course a student took during the quarter, so the engagement level with faculty was quite high. Each student worked full time four days a week and came to class on their day off. The background of familiarity that I had with those students enabled a sense of rapport and trust, which I benefited from when I approached those participants for interviews after they had left the seminar, graduated, and became someone's employees. I did not solicit any interviews from people during the time I was teaching in this program, nor did I raise the subject of deception with them during a seminar, unless a student independently brought up examples of lying that they wanted to discuss with the class.

I began all interviews with general questions about the type of work a respondent did. I wanted to check that interviewees did things in addition to performing tasks such as filing or copying that might have kept them isolated from others. I also asked general questions about organizational culture, such as whether people worked in teams, how training operated, and so forth. I then moved on to questions directly related to deception. I asked respondents to define deception and to identify a list of activities that they witnessed at work that illustrated their definition.

I always phrased questions generally and then followed them up with specific inquiries. For example, I asked informants questions along the lines of "is the work you do ever affected by not knowing if other people are being honest?" If an informant said "yes," then I asked follow-up questions to gain a better understanding of what happened.

My general questions about workplace culture and deception often yielded answers that required detailed follow-up questions. Some sample follow-up questions included: How common or routine do you feel these behaviors are? Are the deceptions that you describe associated with one individual or situation? How do you account for people engaging in these behaviors? What motivated them, do you think? How do people actually carry out these deceptions and not get caught? Did the people gossiping ever say how they felt directly to the person they disliked? Did the negative feelings between those people actually come to affect work? How so? So what did he/she do when they didn't meet that goal? What do you mean when you say they were goofing off— what exactly were they doing?

Workers Who Were Not Interns

After starting by interviewing interns, I also began to accumulate a snowball sample with informants who had connections to the internship program. During interviews, as well as miscellaneous conversations with people, I always heard the inevitable: "You know, you really ought to talk to so-and-so. They saw a lot of that stuff." I relied on snowball sampling from respondents and from additional contacts I had in various organizations. I ended up interviewing entry-level, mid-level, and some upper-level workers in order to compare their responses with ones gathered from interns. I thus could contrast the perspectives and incidents of deception that interns described with those reported by workers of greater power, seniority, and involvement in organizational politics.

I asked the same interview questions of all respondents. There were variations in follow-up questions, of course, since respondents would sometimes report deceptions that others did not. For example, some higher-level respondents reported that employers reneged on promises made when hiring or recruiting them away from competitors.

I also achieved "third party" credibility through the respondent vouching for me. I did not simply call up disparate and distant workers; I relied on networks and familiarity to attain the kind of rapport and trust from past connections that are necessary and common practice in conducting these sorts of interviews well. The respondents worked at different locations. Interviewing a variety of workers at a host of different workplaces was important in studying deception as a phenomenon across workplaces. I am wholly confident in the veracity of the data in the second study because of the rapport and trust that came from the familiarity between many of the respondents and myself.

The demographic characteristics of organizations and respondents who participated in interviews is detailed in tables 6 and 7. Table 6 describes the demographics of informants, identifying the distribution of gender, hierarchical level, race, and type of organization in which they worked. Table 7 provides a detailed breakdown of the organizations in which they worked, including organization size, the type of work the organization performs, and how many informants came from each organization.

Table 6. Respondent Demographics by Employment[1], Sex[2], and Rank[3]

	Financial		Nonprofits		Ad./Mkt.		Other		Total
	M	F	M	F	M	F	M	F	
Intern	8	5	I	5	0	3	I	I	24[4]
Entry-level	I	I	I	2	0	2	I	I	9
Middle-level			I			2		I	I	5
High-level				I			4		5
Total	9	6	3	8	2	5	7	3	43

1. "Financial" refers to formal organizations involved in financial work, such as banks, investment firms, and management consultants. "Nonprofits" are not-for-profit organizations, represented here by groups working on a variety of social issues. "Ad/Mkt" refers to advertising, and market research agencies, and political consultants. "Other" refers to respondents from a major airline, a freelance computer software programmer, medical organizations, real estate firms, a large retailer, a television network, and a theater organization.

2. "M" designates male and "F" designates female. There were 22 male respondents and 21 female respondents. One male informant was of mixed race and 1 female informant was of Asian ancestry. Fourteen interns were female and 10 were male. Male interns worked disproportionately in financial services; female interns worked disproportionately at nonprofit organizations. The distribution of female interns across different employers was greater than for male interns.

3. "Intern" refers to respondents who interned at an organization for at least thirty-two hours a week for at least two consecutive months. "Entry-level" refers to respondents who were working as full-time, paid staff in an entry-level position for less than four years. "Middle-level" refers to respondents with some managerial responsibilities for lower-level employees and whose tenure as full-time staff exceeded four years. "High-level" refers to respondents with extensive managerial responsibilities and tenure of at least ten years.

4. I classified respondents as interns if I interviewed them as interns and if they were not employed as full-time workers. However, all of the entry-level workers I interviewed worked in internships before entering their entry-level positions. All of the entry-level workers I spoke with also described their internship experiences during their interviews. In some cases, the entry-level respondents also had been interns for their present employers, prior to accepting an offer of paid employment. Interviews in which informants discussed their internship experiences include 33 intern respondents, 24 with whom I discussed only their experiences as interns and 9 with whom I discussed entry-level work as well as internship.

Table 7. Individual Work Sites by Size, Number of Respondents, and Type of Work

Organizations:	Size[1]	Type of Work	Respondents
Financial			
Firm 1	L	Investment bank	3
Firm 2	L	Investment bank	2
Firm 3	L	Investment bank	1
Firm 4	L	Bank	2
Firm 5	L	Management consultants	2
Firm 6	M	Investment consultants	2
Firm 7	M	Bank	1
Firm 8	M	Investment site	2
Nonprofits			
Group 1	S	Health issues	1
Group 2	L	Environmental issues	3
Group 3	S	Environmental issues	1
Group 4	S	Criminal justice issues	1
Group 5	S	Urban issues	1
Group 6	L	Philanthropy	1
Group 7	L	Education	2
Group 8	L	Philanthropy	1
Advertising/market research			
Firm 1	L	Advertising	2
Firm 2	L	Advertising	1
Firm 3	S	Market research	1
Firm 4	S	Market research	1
Firm 5	S	Political consulting	1
Firm 6	M	Political consulting	1
Other			
Firm 1	L	Real estate	2
Firm 2	S	Real estate	1
Firm 3	L	Retail	1
Firm 4	L	Hospital	1
Firm 5	M	Medical clinic	1
Firm 6	L	Airline	1
Firm 7	M	Television network	1
Firm 8	S	Theater	1
*	*	Technology	1

Totals:

15 Large organizations
6 Medium organizations
9 Small organizations

30 organizations

Total:

43 Respondents

1. L refers to large companies with at least 100 employees. M refers to medium-sized organizations with between 30 and 100 people. S refers to small organizations with 30 employees or fewer.

* This respondent is a freelance computer programmer who works on contracts for multiple companies.

Observational Data

Many internship programs require their students to keep journals in which they record observations about their workplace experiences. This requirement resulted in students writing hundreds of pages of field notes on the daily events at their workplace. Students in such internship programs thus become ethnographic resources on their workplaces. I collected and read hundreds of pages of field notes that represented months of daily workplace observations.

I sampled field notes from interns at both for- profit and nonprofit organizations. These work journals offer a daily record of events occurring at the student's work site. They also describe deceptions that other respondents reported in interviews. Since students took these notes without the knowledge that a researcher might in the future ask them about deceptions, I was glad to see that the work journals generated many of the same deceptions that other respondents mentioned during interviews.

The internship program required students to pick research topics based on their work experiences. All students collected field notes for their own purposes over months of working a four-day week. Those notes showcase the immersion of the students in the field. I accessed some of those field notes for this research and consider them to be excellent sources of information. The students were trained to access field data, wrote dozens of pages every week, and did so with just the goal of getting a day's notable events down on paper.

An additional virtue of these field notes is that no one wrote them with the initial intent of researching deception. It just happened that when they wrote down a day's notable events, examples of deception kept appearing. That happening is noteworthy in that I never asked students to collect field notes on deception for me; they had done so for themselves. That these students gathered so many examples of deception during their daily work shows the abundance of deception in the workplace in general. Put simply, these field notes were detailed and extraordinarily useful because I did not lead the witnesses—the witnesses happened to see important information independently. I did have rapport and trust with many of the interns and lower-level workers in the second case study. I also used some of their field notes for their participant-observation information. I relied on the immersion that those respondents had in their sites, with some confidence that they already knew and trusted me. The benefit of that immersion was to provide an embedded account of a day's work with details that could also be compared to interview-based recollections of work.

Pseudo-focus Groups

The internship programs also require rigorous discussion seminars. These discussions enable students to compare workplace events in diverse places of employment. Students often used class meetings to discuss events in their workplaces that troubled them. For example, many students felt uncomfortable hearing denigrating gossip. Class sessions thus sometimes felt like a focus group on interns' workplace experiences, with instructors as facilitators. Listening to these sessions as de facto focus groups offered me knowledge that informed the findings that I reported here.

Over the course of 240 classroom hours and assorted office hours devoted to listening to interns, I became well educated about the workplace experiences of over 120 interns. This knowledge enabled me to devise good follow-up questions in later interviews with interns, because I knew something about internship experiences in general. I also used the general information I heard during class discussions to identify repeated types of deception. If I heard an intern describe an act of deception that I also heard other students discuss, I concluded that the individual's experience was not a random occurrence.

Further, while I cannot claim casual conversation about people who lie at work as being the same thing as formal interview data, I have had countless informal conversations about deceptions with dozens of people, some strangers, some casual acquaintances, some family and friends. When people ask me what I study and I tell them I study how people lie at work, I always heard the same response: "You should study where I work!" That point often started a long conversation about how people lie at work. Although I cannot claim official social science credit for those conversations, I have ended up talking to many, many people about deception and I have had some of the arguments of this book validated informally from those discussions. I hope that readers see some of their own work worlds here as well.

NOTES

Introduction: Is Dishonesty the Real Policy?

1. For examples, see Bailey 1991; Barnes 1994; Blum 1972; Blumberg 1989; Bok 1978; Broad and Wade 1982; DePaulo 1996; Ekman 1985; Gilsenan 1976; Lewis and Saarni 1993; Mitchell and Thompson 1986; Nyberg 1993; Tefft 1980; Wise 1973.

2. For examples of these orientations, see Aldrich 1989; DePaulo, Stone, and Lassiter 1985; DePaulo et al. 1996; Ekman 1985; Ford 1996; Goleman 1985; Kornet 1997; Lerner 1993; Mitchell and Thompson 1986.

3. See Bok (1978) for an example of "deception is bad" and Nyberg (1993) for an example of "deception can be good."

4. For slightly different but essentially similar wordings see also Barnes 1994, Bok 1978, Ekman 1985, Lewicki 1983.

5. Goffman developed an unsurpassed conceptual vocabulary to map out various dramaturgical processes in social interaction, such as passing, stigma management, front stage and backstage, cooling the mark out, expression games, moral career, frame analysis, total institutions, and defensive and protective practices. With the notable exception of *Asylums*, however, he did not usually specify independent variables that affected people's impression management. People benefit or suffer depending on the types of social resources available to them, such as coaching, education, mentoring, money, past experiences, physical gifts, and training. In *Asylums*, Goffman (1962) does identify social processes that institutions use to transform an individual's identity into an impersonal organizational one. In his 1951 article "Symbols of Class Status" Goffman writes about how legitimate holders of status symbols try to protect them from being appropriated by impostors; hence they develop "curator groups" to help maintain the machinery of status (Goffman 1951, 303). Goffman clearly recognizes structural implications that inform how people adopt techniques of impression management, but he did not always choose to analyze them formally in his writings.

6. For exceptions, see Dalton 1959; Grover 1993a, 1993b; Hunt and Manning 1991; Katz 1977, 1979; Klockars 1984; Ruane, Cerulo, and Gerson 1994; Schein 1979.

7. See, for example, well known ethnographies by Blau 1963; Dalton 1959; Jackall 1988; Kanter 1977; Kidder 1981; Kunda 1992; Morrill 1995. Kanter (1977) describes secretaries lying to clients about their bosses' whereabouts. Jackall (1988) shows managers feigning loyalty to the prevailing party lines of superiors while using insincere flattery and backstabbing gossip to pursue upward mobility. Dalton's ethnographic work (1959) shows, on a routine basis, workers bypassing safety rules and altering records to hide their actions. Morrill's interviews with executives (1995) reveal the frequent use of sabotage and subterfuge to win conflicts with rivals, supervisors, and underlings.

1. Private Detectives and Deception as Official Work

1. We cannot label all secret data "dirty," because there is always some variability in the behaviors that people label "deviant." In this chapter I assume some consensus in defining dirty data because all the types of dirty data that are described here are punished either by law, divorce, or social shaming if they are exposed. They include acts such as having committed adultery, illegal drug use, theft, kidnapping, and lying in hiring contexts.

2. For a more detailed description of enacting, reconstructing, and surfacing see Shulman (1994).

3. This research project uses data from interviews and a participant-observation research methodology. The appendix offers a lengthy description of the research design of the interviews and participant-observations involved in completing both case studies. All names that appear in the interview extracts are pseudonyms.

4. I do not analyze wiretapping and other forms of electronic eavesdropping that were illegal in my research locality. The legality of making covert recordings varies by state. Please consult Lapin (1987, 1989) for explicit professional and technical details concerning wiretapping equipment, installation, and practices.

5. For more details about physical evidence see Buckwalter (1984) and Webb et al. (1981).

6. See Ekman (1985), Royal and Schutt (1976) for inventories of verbal deception cues.

2. Building Believable Lies

1. With the exception of Barnes 1994; Blum 1972; Garfinkel 1967; Goffman 1959, 1963, 1969, 1971, 1974; and B. Jacobs 1992a, 1992b, 1993, the scholarly literature on deception has not addressed the question of what makes a lie believable. There are also special fields where people examine this problem, such as in studies of deception in negotiations (Lewicki 1983), studies of military deceptions (Handel 1973), select organizational ethnographies (Dalton 1959; Jackall 1988), and research on police officers, spies, and undercover operations (see Klockars 1984; Goffman 1969; Hunt and Manning 1991; Marx 1988; Jacobs 1992a, 1992b, 1993).

2. Goffman (1969, 25) used the term "authentication" to describe how spies manage physical props to conduct their work. I use "authentication practices" to describe the

mechanics of creating credible lies. I do not analyze here the authentication practices in lies that people offer to familiars, such as spouses, family, friends, and co-workers. While there might be similarities, private detectives lie to strangers. In chapters describing deceptions among colleagues, I do refer to some authentication practices among familiars.

3. The racial and sexual politics here pose questions about discrimination and economic inequality as to who is selected as a target for investigation. Because I did not interview the targets of investigations or participate in extended weeks of undercover placement, I cannot address these points conclusively here.

4. A converse question is: How much legitimacy is based on the impression management skills in enacting a role, rather than on the ability to perform expert techniques in that role? Bosk (1979) notes that supervising doctors evaluate surgical residents more on how they integrate themselves into the professional role of surgeon than by their technical competency. While Bosk makes it clear that students who repeat technical errors are not tolerated, he also demonstrates that the ability to act like a doctor is a critical factor in supervisors' assessments of how competent a doctor the student will become. Even if a student is an excellent technician, if he or she does not demonstrate the role characteristics that supervisors are looking for, that student will fail to progress in the profession.

3. Justifying Work-Related Deceptions

1. An earlier version of this chapter appeared in *Symbolic Interaction* 23: 259–82.

2. The subjects for this research are usually members of highly stigmatized groups, including male hustlers (Reiss 1964), juvenile delinquents (Sykes and Matza 1957), disgraced professionals (Pogrebin, Poole, and Martinez 1992), and convicted criminal offenders, such as white-collar criminals (Benson 1985) and rapists (Scully and Marolla 1984).

3. See Elliston and Feldberg 1985; Heffernan and Stroup 1985; Hunt and Manning 1991; B. Jacobs 1992a, 1992b, 1993; Klockars 1984, 1985; Peter Manning 1977; Manning and Van Maanen 1978; Marx 1987, 1988; Miller 1987; Sanders 1974; Skolnick 1975; Stenross and Kleinman 1989.

4. See the following for research on the growth of private security: Cunningham and Taylor 1985; Ghezzi 1983; Johnston 1992; Marx 1987; O'Toole 1978; Reichman 1987; Shearing 1992; Shearing and Stenning 1987.

5. For examples of research on accounts, see Benson 1985; Hewitt and Stokes 1975; B. Jacobs 1992b; Klockars 1984, 1985; Mulcahy 1995; Pestello 1991; Reiss 1964; Scully and Morolla 1984; Stokes and Hewitt 1976; Sykes and Matza 1957; Young 1995, 1997.

6. For examples of case litigation, see *Forster v. Manchester,* 410 Pa. 192 A.2d 147, 150; *Pinkerton v. Stevens,* 108Ga App 159; 132 s.e. 2d 119; *Souder v. Pendleton Detectives, Inc. et al.,* 88 So 2d 716. For further legal details, see also Gavison (1980); Geddes (1989); and La Marca (1986).

7. There are several audiences for private detectives' accounts. Some private detectives shared justifications with one another, in camaraderie based on commiserating with peers. Those informal offerings of accounts reflect efforts to preach to the converted about the "misunderstood" nature of private detective work. Other audiences for accounts include juries, when investigative evidence is being considered, and

journalists. State representatives are the audience when state legislatures and regulatory officials consider changes in laws that affect private detective work.

8. For scholarly research on this issue see Gavison, 1980; Geddes 1989; Graham 1987; Linowes 1989; Marx 1988; Rule et al. 1983; Scheppele 1988.

4. The Shadow World of Unofficial Deception

1. Official and unofficial deceptions can both involve illegal behaviors. For example, in official deceptions, police detectives may "entrap" (illegal) in undercover operations instead of covertly observing. Informal deceptions of the goofing-off type may vary similarly—administrative assistants, for example, may tack twenty minutes onto their lunch hours, but failing to perform proper maintenance on an airplane is criminally negligent. I do not address informal illegal deceptions, regardless of their purpose. This is a valuable area of study but beyond the scope of this book.

2. It is an interesting irony that organizational rules and organizational interests may contradict one another. These contradictions are evident in situations where workers break the organization's own rules to serve its interest. One way to explain these contradictions is that organizations have rules that benefit stakeholders other than the organization. If an organizational goal is to make profits, then rules that complicate that goal hurt that organizational interest while serving others. Contradictions between organizational rules and interests also exist when following the rules leads to inefficiencies or other detriments, such as when they prevent innovations or are onerous, such as with excess paperwork.

5. Subterranean Education and Training

1. A professor at another institution described colleagues who distribute "phantom syllabi" on the first day of class that list hundreds of pages of difficult readings due each week and long paper assignments. These supposed marching orders are never implemented once some students have dropped the course. Maybe "scarecrow syllabi" is a better description.

6. Deception as Social Currency

1. In studying belief in magic, famed anthropologists Bronislaw Malinowski and Edward Evans-Pritchard noted a tendency to let one positive event overshadow multiple negative events. If one could argue successfully that magical intervention produced an effect in a single case, that positive outcome was weighted more heavily than accumulated negative ones. In the workplace case I invoke here, a rare work experience is trumpeted as more representative than actual probabilities show. That this moment could and did happen provides a way to make it a truthful claim, since the teller does not advertise its underlying statistical likelihood of being true or even think in those terms.

2. Some informants in for-profit organizations also noted budget diversion as endemic at their workplaces. One general summation on budget strategies from a for-profit manager: "Get money for A, B, C—spend it on D, E, F."

3. See http://www.dilbert.com/comics/dilbert/the_characters/index.html.

4. There is no doubt that boss's complaints about workers would also place highly on the "sure things" list.

8. The Everyday Ethics of Workplace Lies

1. A consistent theme in symbolic interactionist research is dissecting how people deflect unappealing designations of their moral character. Goffman (1959, 1963, 1969, and 1974) in particular conceptualized many different remedial strategies for fending off stigmatization. Other sociologists have identified "accounts" (Scott and Lyman 1968), "aligning actions" (Stokes and Hewitt 1976), "disclaimers" (Stokes and Hewitt 1976), "discounts" (Pestello 1993), "misunderstandings" (Young 1995), "quasi-theories" (Hewitt and Hall 1973), "techniques of neutralization" (Sykes and Matza 1957), and "vocabularies of motive" (Mills 1940) as verbal techniques that reconcile discrediting behaviors.

9. Appreciating Deception in Thinking about Organizations

1. See also Lewis and Weigert 1985; Luhmann 1979; Shapiro 1987a, 1987b; Sitkin and Roth 1993.

Appendix

1. A note on sampling: In the second interview of the private detective study, I was told that private detectives that advertise in the phone book usually offer different investigative services than private detectives who do not advertise in the phone book. "Phone book" private detectives tend to offer more traditional investigative services, such as background checks, missing persons work, and scrutiny of suspected adultery. In contrast, "non-phone book" private detectives usually specialize in one field, such as arson, insurance, and legal investigations, missing persons work, or personal protection (bodyguards). To avoid only sampling "phone book" private detectives, I acquired a list from the state government of all practitioners holding an in-state private detective license. I then took a random sample of every tenth private detective whose name appeared on the books as licensed but who did not advertise in the phone book. Seventeen license holders in the metropolitan area did not advertise in the phone book. Among those, a few did not live at the address I contacted or were no longer in the business, and eight declined interviews or did not respond to my request. I ended up being able to interview four investigators who did not advertise in the phone book.

2. Personal communication with Arthur L. Stinchcombe.

REFERENCES

Abbott, Andrew. 1981. "Status and Status Strain in the Professions." *American Journal of Sociology* 86: 819–35.

———. 1988. *The System of Professions*. Chicago: University of Chicago Press.

Ackroyd, Stephen, and Paul Thompson. 1999. *Organizational Misbehaviour*. London: Sage Publications.

Aldrich, C. Knight. 1989. "Psychiatric Aspects of Lying." *American Journal of Psychiatry* 146: 45.

Arnould, Eric, and Linda L. Price. 1993. "River Magic: Extraordinary Experience and the Extended Service Encounter." *Journal of Consumer Research* 20: 24–46.

Baier, Annette. 1975. "Trust and Antitrust." *Ethics* 96: 231–60.

Bailey, F. G. 1991. *The Prevalence of Deceit*. Ithaca: Cornell University Press.

Ball, Donald W. 1970. "The Problematics of Respectability." In *Deviance and Respectability: The Social Construction of Moral Meanings*, edited by Jack D. Douglas, 326–71. New York: Basic Books.

Barnes, J. A. 1994. *A Pack of Lies: Towards a Sociology of Lying*. Cambridge: Cambridge University Press.

Becker, Howard S. 1967. "Whose Side Are We On?" *Social Problems* 14: 239–48.

———. 1986. *Doing Things Together: Selected Papers*. Evanston: Northwestern University Press.

Becker, Theodore. 1974. "The Place of Private Police in Society: An Area of Research for the Social Sciences." *Social Problems* 21: 438–53.

Benson, Michael. 1985. "Denying the Guilty Mind: Accounting for Involvement in a White-Collar Crime." *Criminology* 23: 583–607.

Ben-Yehuda, Nachman. 1990. "Gathering Dark Secrets, Hidden and Dirty Information: Some Methodological Notes on Studying Political Assassinations." *Qualitative Sociology* 13: 345–71.

Bilmes, J. 1975. "Misinformation in Verbal Accounts: Some Fundamental Considerations." *Man* 10: 60–71.

Blau, Peter. 1963. *The Dynamics of Bureaucracy: A Study of Interpersonal Relations in Two Government Agencies*. 2nd ed. Chicago: University of Chicago Press.

Blum, Richard. 1972. *Deceivers and Deceived*. Springfield, Ill.: Charles Thomas.

Blumberg, Paul. 1989. *The Predatory Society: Deception in the American Marketplace*. New York: Oxford University Press.

Blumstein, Phillip, et al. 1974. "The Honoring of Accounts." *American Sociological Review* 39: 551–66.

Bok, Sissela. 1978. *Lying: Moral Choice in Public and Private Life*. New York: Pantheon Books.

——. 1982. *Secrets: On the Ethics of Concealment and Revelation*. New York: Pantheon Books.

Bosk, Charles L. 1979. *Forgive and Remember: Managing Medical Failure*. Chicago: University of Chicago Press.

Bouchard, Thomas J., Jr. 1976. "Unobtrusive Measures: An Inventory of Uses." *Sociological Methods and Research* 4: 267–300.

Broad, William, and Nicholas Wade. 1982. *Betrayers of the Truth: Fraud and Deceit in the Halls of Science*. New York: Simon and Schuster.

Buckwalter, Art. 1984. *Investigative Methods*. Boston: Butterworth Publishers.

Bulmer, Martin. 1982. *Social Research Ethics: An Examination of the Merits of Covert Participant Observation*. New York: Holmes and Meier.

Carr, Albert. 1968. "Is Business Bluffing Ethical?" *Harvard Business Review* 46: 143–53.

Carson, Thomas. 2001. "Deception and Withholding Information in Sales." *Business Ethics Quarterly* 11: 275–306.

Cassidy-Ervin, Deloris. 1989. "Ethically Speaking." *Security Management* (February): 99–100.

Clinard, Marshall B., and Peter C. Yeager. 1980. *Corporate Crime*. New York: Free Press.

Coleman, James S. 1990. *Foundations of Social Theory*. Cambridge: Harvard University Press.

Connell, Michael. 1989. "Investigator, Know Thyself." *Security Management* (March): 128–32.

Cressey, Donald. 1950. "The Criminal Violation of Financial Trust." *American Sociological Review* 15: 738–43.

Cunningham, William C., and Todd H. Taylor. 1985. *The Hallcrest Report: Private Security and Police in America*. Portland: Chancellor Press.

Dalton, Melville. 1959. *Men Who Manage: Fusions of Feeling and Theory in Administration*. New York: Wiley.

Darley, John M. 1996. "How Organizations Socialize Individuals into Wrongdoing." In *Codes of Conduct: Behavioral Research into Business Ethics*, edited by David M. Messick and Ann E. Tenbrunsel, 13–43. New York: Russell Sage Foundation.

Davis, David S. 1984. "Good People Doing Dirty Work: A Study of Social Isolation." *Symbolic Interaction* 7: 233–47.

Davis, Gerald F., and Walter W. Powell. 1992. "Organization-Environment Relations." In *Handbook of Industrial and Organizational Psychology*, 2nd ed., vol. 3, edited by Marvin D. Dunnette and Leaetta M. Hough, 316–73. h_ Palo Alto, Calif.: Consulting Psychologists Press.

Denzin, Norman K. 1968. "On the Ethics of Disguised Observation." *Social Problems* 15: 502–4.

———. 1970. *The Research Act: A Theoretical Introduction to Sociological Methods*. Chicago: Alden.

DePaulo, Bella M., J. I. Stone, and G. D. Lassiter. 1985. "Deceiving and Detecting Deceit." In *The Self and Social Life*, edited by B. R. Schlenker, 323–70. New York: McGraw-Hill.

DePaulo, B. M., D. A. Kashy, S. E. Kirkendol, M. M. Wyer, and J. A. Epstein. 1996. "Lying in Everyday Life." *Journal of Personality and Social Psychology* 70: 979–95.

Deutscher, Irwin. 1966. "Words and Deeds: Social Science and Social Policy." *Social Problems* 13: 235–54.

———. 1970. *What We Say/What We Do: Sentiments and Acts*. Glenview, Ill.: Scott, Foresman.

DiMaggio, Paul J., and Walter W. Powell. 1983. "The Iron Cage Revisited: Institutional Isomorphism and Collective Rationality in Organizational Fields." *American Sociological Review* 48: 147–60.

Douglas, Donna. 1972. "Managing Fronts in Observing Deviants." In *Research on Deviance*, edited by Jack D. Douglas, 93–115. New York: Random House.

Douglas, Jack D., ed. 1972. *Research on Deviance*. New York: Random House.

———. 1976. *Investigative Social Research: Individual and Team Field Research*. Beverly Hills, Calif.: Sage.

Ekman, Paul. 1985. *Telling Lies: Clues to Deceit in the Marketplace, Politics, and Marriage*. New York: W. W. Norton.

Elliston, Frederick A., and Michael Feldberg, eds. 1985. *Moral Issues in Police Work*. Totowa, N.J.: Rowman and Allanheld.

Emerson, Robert, ed. 1983. *Contemporary Field Research: A Collection of Readings*. Prospect Heights, Ill.: Waveland Press.

Emerson, Robert M., and Melvin Pollner. 1976. "Dirty Work Designations: Their Features and Consequences in a Psychiatric Setting." *Social Problems* 23: 243–54.

Erikson, Kai T. 1967. "A Comment on Disguised Observation in Sociology." *Social Problems* 14: 366–73.

———. 1968. "A Reply to Denzin." *Social Problems* 15: 505–6.

Fallis, Greg, and Ruth Greenberg. 1989. *Be Your Own Detective*. New York: M. Evans and Company.

Farberman, Harvey A. 1975. "A Criminogenic Market Structure: The Automobile Industry." *Sociological Quarterly* 16: 438–57.

Fine, Gary A. 1984. "Negotiated Orders and Occupational Cultures." In *Annual Review of Sociology*, edited by R. H. Turner and J. F. Short, 239–62. Palo Alto, Calif.: Annual Reviews.

———. 1996. "Justifying Work: Occupational Rhetorics as Resources in Restaurant Kitchens." *Administrative Science Quarterly* 41: 90–115.

Ford, Charles V. 1996. *Lies! Lies!! Lies!!!: The Psychology of Deceit*. Washington, D.C.: American Psychiatric Press.

Freidson, Eliott. 1986. *Professional Powers: A Study of the Institutionalization of Formal Knowledge*. Chicago: University of Chicago Press.

Garfinkel, Harold. 1967. *Studies in Ethnomethodology*. New York: Basil Blackwell.

Gavison, Ruth. 1980. "Privacy and the Limits of the Law." *Yale Law Journal* 89: 421–71.

Geddes, Elaine F. 1989. "The Private Investigator and the Right to Privacy." *Alberta Law Review* 27: 256–300.

Ghezzi, Susan Guarino. 1983. "A Private Network of Social Control: Insurance Investigation Units." *Social Problems* 30: 521–31.

Gilsenan, Michael. 1976. "Lying, Honor, and Contradiction." In *Transaction and Meaning: Directions in the Anthropology of Exchange and Symbolic Behavior*, edited by Bruce Kapferer, 191–219. Philadelphia: Institute for the Study of Human Issues.

Gioia, D. 1992. "Pinto Fires and Personal Ethics: A Script Analysis of Missed Opportunities." *Journal of Business Ethics* 11: 379–89.

Goffman, Erving. 1951. "Symbols of Class Status." *British Journal of Sociology* 2: 294–304.

——. 1959. *The Presentation of Self in Everyday Life*. Garden City, N.Y.: Doubleday.

——. 1961. *Asylums: Essays on the Social Situation of Mental Patients and Other Inmates*. Garden City, N.Y.: Anchor.

——. 1963. *Stigma: Notes on the Management of Spoiled Identity*. Englewood Cliffs, N.J.: Prentice-Hall.

——. 1969. *Strategic Interaction*. Philadelphia: University of Pennsylvania Press.

——. 1971. *Relations in Public*. New York: Basic Books.

——. 1974. *Frame Analysis: An Essay on the Organization of Experience*. Cambridge: Harvard University Press.

——. 1983. "The Interaction Order." *American Sociological Review* 48: 1–17.

Goleman, Daniel. 1985. *Vital Lies, Simple Truths: The Psychology of Self-Deception*. New York: Simon and Schuster.

Graham, Jonathan. 1987. "Privacy, Computers, and Commercial Dissemination of Personal Information." *Texas Law Review* 65: 23–70.

Granovetter, Mark. 1973. "The Strength of Weak Ties." *American Journal of Sociology* 78: 1360–80.

——. 1985. "Economic Action and Social Structure: The Problem of Embeddedness." *American Journal of Sociology* 91: 481–510.

——. Forthcoming. *Society and Economy: The Social Construction of Economic Institutions*. Cambridge: Harvard University Press.

Grayson, Kent, and David Shulman. 2000. "Impression Management in Services Marketing." In *Handbook of Services Marketing and Management*, edited by Teresa Swartz and Dawn Iacobucci, 51–68. Thousand Oaks, Calif.: Sage Publications.

Grover, Steven L. 1993a. "Lying, Deceit, and Subterfuge: A Model of Dishonesty in the Workplace." *Organization Science* 4: 478–95.

——. 1993b. "Why Professionals Lie: The Impact of Professional Role Conflict on Reporting Accuracy." *Organizational Behavior and Human Decision Process* 55: 251–72.

Haas, David F., and Forrest A. Deseran. 1981. "Trust and Symbolic Exchange." *Social Psychological Quarterly* 44: 3–13.

Handel, Michael. 1973. "Intelligence and Deception." *Journal of Strategic Studies* 5, no. 1: 122–55.

Hankiss, Agnes. 1980. "Games Con Men Play: The Semiosis of Deceptive Interaction." *Journal of Communication* 30: 104–12.

Harre, Rom, David Clark, and Nicola de Carlo. 1985. *Motives and Mechanisms: An Introduction to the Psychology of Action*. New York: Methuen.

Harrison, Wayne. 1991. *PI School: How to Become a Private Detective*. Boulder, Colo.: Paladin Press.

Hawkins, Keith. 1984. "Creating Cases in a Regulatory Agency." *Urban Life* 12: 371–95.

Heffernan, William C., and Timothy Stroup, eds. 1985. *Police Ethics: Hard Choices in Law Enforcement*. New York: John Jay Press.

Heimer, Carol A. 1985. *Reactive Risk and Rational Action: Managing Moral Hazard in Insurance Contracts*. Berkeley: University of California Press.

Henslin, James M. 1996. *Essentials of Sociology: A Down-to-Earth Approach*. Needham Heights, Mass.: Allyn and Bacon.

Heritage, John. 1984. *Garfinkel and Ethnomethodology*. New York: Polity Press.

Hewitt, John P., and Peter W. Hall. 1973. "Social Problems, Problematic Situations, and Quasi-Theories." *American Sociological Review* 38: 367–74.

Hewitt, John P., and Randall Stokes. 1975. "Disclaimers." *American Sociological Review* 40: 1–11.

Hilbert, Richard A. 1980. "Covert Participant Observation: On Its Nature and Practice." *Urban Life* 9: 51–78.

Hochschild, Arlie. 1983. *The Managed Heart: Commercialization of Human Feeling*. Berkeley: University of California Press.

Hodson, Randy. 1991. "The Active Worker: Compliance and Autonomy in the Workplace." *Journal of Contemporary Ethnography* 20: 47–78.

———. 2001. *Dignity at Work*. New York: Cambridge University Press.

House Committee on Education and Labor. 1939. "Violations of Free Speech and Rights of Labor." *S. Rpt. 6*. Washington, D.C.: Government Printing Office.

Hughes, Everett. 1984. *The Sociological Eye: Selected Papers*. New Brunswick, N.J.: Transaction Books.

Humphreys, Laud. 1970. *Tearoom Trade: Impersonal Sex in Public Places*. Chicago: Aldine.

Hunt, Jennifer, and Peter Manning. 1991. "The Social Context of Police Lying." *Symbolic Interaction* 14: 45–56.

Hunter, Christopher. 1992. "Aligning Actions: Types and Social Distribution." In *Social Psychological Foundations: Readings from the Interactionist Perspective*, edited by Gary Alan Fine, Harvey Farberman, and John M. Johnson. Greenwich, Conn.: JAI Press.

Illinois Department of Professional Regulation. 1992. *Annual Report*. Springfield: State of Illinois.

Jackall, Robert. 1980. "Structural Invitations to Deceit: Some Reflections on Bureaucracy and Morality." *Berkshire Review* 15: 49–61.

———. 1988. *Moral Mazes: The World of Corporate Managers*. New York: Oxford University Press.

Jacobs, Bruce A. 1992a. "Undercover Deception: Reconsidering Presentations of Self." *Journal of Contemporary Ethnography* 21: 200–226.

———. 1992b. "Undercover Drug-Use Evasion Tactics: Excuses and Neutralization." *Symbolic Interaction* 15: 435–53.

———. 1993. "Undercover Deception Clues: A Case of Restrictive Deterrence." *Criminology* 31: 281–99.

Jacobs, Jerry. 1969. "Symbolic Bureaucracy: A Case Study of a Welfare Agency." *Social Forces* 47: 413–22.

Johnson, John, and Jack D. Douglas, eds. 1978. *Crime at the Top: Deviance in Business and the Professions*. Philadelphia: J. B. Lippincott.

Johnston, Les. 1992. *The Rebirth of Private Policing*. New York: Routledge.

Kanter, Rosabeth Moss. 1977. *Men and Women of the Corporation*. New York: Basic Books.

Katz, Jack. 1977. "Cover-up and Collective Integrity: On the Natural Antagonism of Authority Internal and External to Organizations." *Social Problems* 25: 3–17.

——. 1979. "Concerted Ignorance: The Social Construction of Cover-Up." *Urban Life* 8: 295–316.

Kelman, Herbert, and V. Lee Hamilton. 1989. "The My Lai Massacre: A Military Crime of Obedience." In *Crimes of Obedience*, edited by Herbert Kelman and V. Lee Hamilton, 1–20. New Haven: Yale University Press.

Kidder, Tracey. 1981. *The Soul of a New Machine*. Boston: Little, Brown.

Klockars, Carl B. 1984. "Blue Lies and Police Placebos: The Moralities of Police Lying." *American Behavioral Scientist* 27: 529–44.

——. 1985. "The Dirty Harry Problem." *Moral Issues in Police Work*, edited by Frederick A. Elliston and Michael Feldberg, 55–71. Totowa, N.J.: Rowman and Allanheld.

Kornet, Allison. 1997. "The Truth about Lying: Has Lying Gotten a Bad Rap?" *Psychology Today* 30: 52–58.

Kunda, Gideon. 1992. *Engineering Culture: Control and Commitment in a High-Tech Corporation*. Philadelphia: Temple University Press.

La Marca, George. 1986. "Overintrusive Surveillance of Plaintiffs in Personal Injury Cases." *Defense Law Journal* 35: 603–24.

La Piere, Richard. 1934. "Attitudes versus Actions." *Social Forces* 13: 230–37.

Lapin, Lee. 1987. *How to Get Anything on Anybody*. Boulder, Colo.: Paladin Press.

——. 1989. *The Outlaw Reports: Insider Secrets and Tricks of the Trade*. Boulder, Colo.: Paladin Press.

Larson, Magali Sarfatti. 1977. *The Rise of Professionalism: A Sociological Analysis*. Berkeley: University of California Press.

Leidner, Robin. 1993. *Fast Food, Fast Talk: Service Work and the Commercialization of Human Feeling*. Berkeley: University of California Press.

Lerner, Harriet Goldhor. 1993. *The Dance of Deception: Pretending and Truth-Telling in Women's Lives*. New York: Harper Collins.

Lewicki, Roy J. 1983. "Lying and Deception: A Behavioral Model." In *Negotiating*, edited by Roy J. Lewicki and Max Bazerman, 68–90. Durham: Duke University Press.

Lewis, J. David, and Andrew Wiegert. 1985. "Trust as Social Reality." *Social Forces* 63: 967–85.

Lewis, Michael, and Carolyn Saarni, eds. 1993. *Lying and Deception in Everyday Life*. New York: Guilford.

Linowes, David. 1989. *Privacy in America: Is Your Private Life in the Public Eye?* Chicago: University of Illinois Press.

Lowry, Ritchie P. 1972. "Toward a Sociology of Secrecy and Security Systems." *Social Problems* 19: 437–50.

Luhmann, Niklas. 1979. *Trust and Power*. Chichester: John Wiley and Sons.

Maines, David R. 1982. "In Search of Mesostructure: Studies in the Negotiated Order." *Urban Life* 11: 267–79.

Manning, Peter K. 1977. *Police Work: The Social Organization of Policing*. Cambridge: MIT Press.

Manning, Peter K., and John Van Maanen. 1978. *Policing: A View from the Street*. Santa Monica, Calif.: Goodyear.

Manning, Phillip. 2000. "Credibility, Agency, and the Interaction Order." *Symbolic Interaction* 23: 281–98.

Mars, Gerald. 1994. *Cheats at Work: An Anthropology of Workplace Crime.* Brookfield, Vt.: Dartmouth.

Marx, Gary T. 1987. "The Interweaving of Public and Private Police." In *Private Policing,* edited by Clifford D. Shearing and Phillip C. Stenning, 172–93. Newbury Park, Calif.: Sage.

———. 1988. *Undercover: Police Surveillance in America.* Berkeley: University of California Press.

———. 1990. "Notes on the Discovery, Collection, and Assessment of Hidden and Dirty Data." In *Studies in the Sociology of Social Problems,* edited by Joseph W. Schneider and John Kitsuse, 78–113. Norwood, N.J.: Ablex.

Merton, Robert K. 1940. "Facts and Fictitiousness in Ethnic Opinionnaires." *American Sociological Review* 5: 13–27.

———. 1968. *Social Theory and Social Structure.* New York: Free Press.

Metts, Sandra. 1989. "An Exploratory Investigation of Deception in Close Relationships." *Journal of Social and Personal Relationships* 6: 159–79.

Meyer, John W., and Brian Rowan. 1977. "Institutionalized Organizations: Formal Structure as Myth and Ceremony." *American Journal of Sociology* 83: 340–63.

Miller, George I. 1987. "Observations on Police Undercover Work." *Criminology* 25: 27–45.

Miller, Gerald R., Paul A. Mongeau, and Carra Sleight. 1986. "Fudging with Friends and Lying to Lovers: Deceptive Communication in Personal Relationships." *Journal of Social and Personal Relationships* 3: 495–512.

Miller, Gerald R., and James B. Staff. 1993. *Deceptive Communication.* Newbury Park, Calif.: Sage.

Mills, C. Wright. 1940. "Situated Actions and Vocabularies of Motive." *American Sociological Review* 5: 904–13.

———. 1963. "Methodological Consequences of the Sociology of Knowledge." In *Power, Politics, and the People: The Collected Articles of C. Wright Mills,* edited by Irving L. Horowitz, 453–69. New York: Ballantine Books.

Mitchell, Robert, and Nicholas S. Thompson, eds. 1986. *Deception: Perspectives on Human and Nonhuman Deceit.* Albany: State University of New York Press.

Morrill, Calvin. 1995. *The Executive Way: Conflict Management in Organizations.* Chicago: University of Chicago Press.

Mulcahy, Aogan. 1995. "Headhunter or Real Cop: Identity in the World of Internal Affairs Officers." *Journal of Contemporary Ethnography* 24: 99–130.

Nichols, Lawrence. 1990. "Reconceptualizing Social Accounts: An Agenda for Theory-Building and Empirical Research." *Current Perspectives in Social Theory* 10: 113–44.

Nyberg, David. 1993. *The Varnished Truth: Truth Telling and Deceiving in Ordinary Life.* Chicago: University of Chicago Press.

Orbuch, Terry L. 1997. "People's Accounts Count: The Sociology of Accounts." *Annual Review of Sociology* 23: 455–78.

Ostrom, Elinor. 1990. *Governing the Commons: The Evolution of Institutions for Collective Action.* New York: Cambridge University Press.

O'Toole, George. 1978. *The Private Sector: Private Spies, Rent-a-Cops, and the Police-Industrial Complex.* New York: W. W. Norton.

Perrow, Charles. 1986. *Complex Organizations: A Critical Essay.* New York: Random House.

Pestello, Fred P. 1991. "Discounting." *Journal of Contemporary Ethnography* 20: 26–46.

Pfohl, Stephen. 1985. *Images of Deviance and Social Control.* New York: McGraw-Hill.

Pogrebin, Mark R., Eric D. Poole, and Amos Martinez. 1992. "Accounts of Professional Misdeeds: The Sexual Exploitation of Clients by Psychotherapists." *Deviant Behavior* 13: 229–52.

Pollner, Melvin. 1975. " 'The Very Coinage of Your Brain': The Anatomy of Reality Disjunctures." *Philosophy of the Social Sciences* 5: 411–30.

Powell, Walter W., and Paul J. DiMaggio, eds. 1993. *The New Institutionalism in Organizational Analysis.* Chicago: University of Chicago Press.

Punch, Maurice. 1996. *Dirty Business: Exploring Corporate Misconduct.* Thousand Oaks, Calif.: Sage.

Rapp, Burt. 1986. *Shadowing and Surveillance: A Complete Guidebook.* Port Townsend, Wash.: Loompanics Unlimited.

Rathje, William J., and Cullen Murphy. 1992. *Rubbish! The Archaeology of Garbage.* New York: Harper Collins.

Ray, Melvin D., and Ronald L. Simons. 1987. "Convicted Murderers' Accounts of Their Crimes: A Study of Homicide in Small Communities." *Symbolic Interaction* 10: 55–70.

Reichman, Nancy. 1987. "The Widening Webs of Surveillance: Private Police Unraveling Deceptive Claims." In *Private Policing*, edited by Clifford D. Shearing and Phillip C. Stenning, chap. 10. Newbury Park, Calif.: Sage.

———. 1989. "Breaking Confidences: Organizational Influences on Insider Trading." *Sociological Quarterly* 30: 185–204.

Reiss, Albert J., Jr. 1964. "The Social Integration of Peers and Queers." In *Outsiders: Studies in the Sociology of Deviance*, edited by Howard Becker, 181–210. New York: Free Press.

———. 1987. "The Legitimacy of Intrusion into Private Space." In *Private Policing*, edited by Clifford D. Shearing and Phillip C. Stenning, 19–44. Newbury Park, Calif.: Sage.

Reppetto, Thomas. 1978. "The Detective Task: State of the Art, Science, Craft?" *Police Studies* 1: 5–10.

Robertson, Diana C., and Talia Rymon. 2001. "Purchasing Agents' Deceptive Behavior: A Randomized Response Technique." *Business Ethics Quarterly* 11: 455–79.

Roethlisberger, F., and W. Dickson. 1939. *Management and the Worker.* Cambridge: Harvard University Press.

Ross, Irwin. 1992. *Shady Business: Confronting Corporate Corruption.* New York: Twentieth Century Fund.

Ross, Lee, and Richard Nisbett. 1991. *The Person and the Situation: Perspectives of Social Psychology.* Philadelphia: Temple University Press.

Roth, Julius. 1962. "Comments on Secret Observation." *Social Problems* 9: 283–84.

Roy, Donald. 1952. "Quota Restriction and Goldbricking in a Machine Shop." *American Journal of Sociology* 57: 427–42.

Royal, R. F., and S. R. Schutt. 1976. *The Gentle Art of Interviewing and Interrogation: A Professional Manual and Guide.* Englewood Cliffs, N.J.: Prentice-Hall.

Ruane, Janet M., Karen A. Cerulo, and Judith M. Gerson. 1994. "Professional Deceit: Normal Lying in an Occupational Setting." *Sociological Focus* 27: 91–109.

Rule, James B., Douglas McAdam, Linda Stearns, and David Uglow. 1983. "Documentary Identification and Mass Surveillance in the United States." *Social Problems* 31: 222–43.

Sanders, William B. 1974. *The Sociologist as Detective: An Introduction to Research Methods.* New York: Praeger.

——. 1977. *Detective Work: A Study of Criminal Investigations.* New York: Free Press.

Schein, Virginia. 1979. "Examining an Illusion: The Role of Deceptive Behaviors in Organizations." *Human Relations* 32: 287–95.

Scheppele, Kim L. 1988. *Legal Secrets: Equality and Efficiency in the Common Law.* Chicago: University of Chicago Press.

Schwartz, Barry. 1968. "The Social Psychology of Privacy." *American Journal of Sociology* 73: 742–52.

Schwartz, Howard, and Jerry Jacobs. 1979. *Qualitative Sociology: A Method to the Madness.* New York: Free Press.

Schwartzman, Helen B. 1993. *Ethnography in Organizations.* Newbury Park, Calif.: Sage.

Scott, Marvin B., and Stanford M. Lyman. 1968. "Accounts." *American Sociological Review* 33: 46–62.

——. 1970. "Accounts, Deviance, and Social Order." In *Deviance and Respectability: The Social Construction of Moral Meanings,* edited by Jack D. Douglas, 89–120. New York: Basic Books.

Scully, Diana, and Joseph Marolla. 1984. "Convicted Rapists' Vocabulary of Motive: Excuses and Justifications." *Social Problems* 31: 530–44.

Shapiro, Susan. 1983. "The New Moral Entrepreneurs: Corporate Crime Crusaders." *Contemporary Sociology* 12: 304–7.

——. 1984. *Wayward Capitalists: Target of the Securities and Exchange Commission.* New Haven: Yale University Press.

——. 1987a. "The Social Control of Impersonal Trust." *American Journal of Sociology* 93: 623–58.

——. 1987b. "Policing Trust." In *Private Policing,* edited by Clifford D. Shearing and Phillip C. Stenning, 194–220. Newbury Park, Calif.: Sage.

——. 1990. "Collaring the Crime, Not the Criminal: Reconsidering the Concept of White Collar Crime." *American Sociological Review* 55: 346–65.

Shearing, Clifford D. 1992. "The Relation between Public and Private Policing." In *Crime and Justice: An Annual Review of Research,* vol. 15, edited by Michael Tonry and Norval Morris, 399–434. Chicago: University of Chicago Press.

Shearing, Clifford D., and Phillip C. Stenning. 1981. "Modern Private Security: Its Growth and Implications." In *Crime and Justice: An Annual Review of Research,* vol. 3, edited by Michael Tonry and Norval Morris, 193–245. Chicago: University of Chicago Press.

——, eds. 1987. *Private Policing.* Newbury Park, Calif.: Sage.

Shulman, David. 1994. "Dirty Data and Investigative Methods: Some Lessons from Private Detective Work." *Journal of Contemporary Ethnography* 23: 214–53.

Simmel, Georg. 1950. *The Sociology of George Simmel.* New York: Free Press.

Sitkin, Sim, and Nancy L. Roth. 1993. "Explaining the Limited Effectiveness of Legalistic Remedies for Trust/Distrust." *Organization Science* 4: 367–92.

Skolnick, Jerome H. 1975. *Justice without Trial: Law Enforcement in Democratic Society.* New York: Wiley Press.

Spradley, James P. 1980. *Participant Observation.* New York: Holt, Rinehart, and Winston.

Stebbins, Robert. 1975. "Putting People On: Deception of Our Fellow Man in Everyday Life." *Sociology and Social Research* 59: 189–200.

Stenross, Barbara, and Sherryl Kleinman. 1989. "The Highs and Lows of Emotional Labor: Detectives Encounters with Criminals and Victims." *Journal of Contemporary Ethnography* 17: 435–52.

Stewart, James. 1991. *Den of Thieves.* New York: Simon and Schuster.

Stinchcombe, Arthur L. 1990. *Information and Organizations.* Berkeley: University of California Press.

Stokes, Randall, and John P. Hewitt. 1976. "Aligning Actions." *American Sociological Review* 41: 838–49.

Strauss, Anselm. 1978. *Negotiations: Varieties, Contexts, Processes, and Social Order.* San Francisco: Jossey-Bass.

Strauss, Anselm, et al. 1963. "The Hospital and Its Negotiated Order." In *The Hospital in Modern Society,* edited by E. Friedson, 147–68. New York: Free Press.

Sutherland, Edwin H. 1949. *White Collar Crime.* New York: Dryden Press.

Sykes, Gresham M., and David Matza. 1957. "Techniques of Neutralization: A Theory of Delinquency." *American Sociological Review* 22: 664–70.

Tefft, Stanton. 1980. *Secrecy: A Cross-Cultural Perspective.* New York: Human Sciences Press.

Thomas, Ronald L. 1991. "How to Pick a Private Investigator." *Security Management* (June): 65–67.

Tonry, Michael, and Albert J. Reiss Jr., eds. 1993. *Beyond the Law: Crime in Complex Organizations.* Chicago: University of Chicago Press.

Tversky, Amos, and Daniel Kahneman. 1974. "Judgment under Uncertainty: Heuristics and Biases." *Science* 185: 1124–31.

Vandiver, Kermit. 1982. "Why Should My Conscience Bother Me?" In *Corporate and Governmental Deviance,* edited by M. D. Erdmann and R. J. Lundman. New York: Oxford University Press.

Van Maanen, John. 1983. "The Moral Fix: On the Ethics of Fieldwork." In *Contemporary Field Research: A Collection of Readings,* edited by Robert Emerson, 269–87. Prospect Heights, Ill.: Waveland Press.

Vaughan, Diane. 1983. *Controlling Unlawful Organizational Behavior.* Chicago: University of Chicago Press.

———. 1996. *The Challenger Launch Decision: Risky Technology, Culture, and Deviance at NASA.* Chicago: University of Chicago Press.

Webb, Eugene, Donald T. Campbell, R. D. Schwartz, Lee Sechrest, and Janet B. Grove. 1981. *Nonreactive Measures in the Social Sciences.* Boston: Houghton Mifflin.

Weber, Max. 1958 [1946]. *From Max Weber: Essays in Sociology.* Translated and edited by H. H. Gerth and C. Wright Mills. New York: Galaxy.

Williamson, Oliver E. 1975. *Markets and Hierarchies, Analysis and Antitrust Implications: A Study in the Economics of Internal Organization.* New York: Free Press.

Wilsnack, Robert W. 1980. "Information Control: A Conceptual Framework for Sociological Analysis." *Urban Life* 8: 467–99.

Wise, David. 1973. *The Politics of Lying: Government Deception, Secrecy, and Power*. New York: Random House.

Yeager, Peter C. 1992. *The Limits of Law: The Public Regulation of Private Pollution*. New York: Cambridge University Press.

Young, Robert L. 1995. "Misunderstandings as Accounts." *Sociological Inquiry* 65: 251–64.

——. 1997. "Account Sequences." *Symbolic Interaction* 20: 291–305.

Zand, Dale E. 1972. "Trust and Managerial Problem Solving." *Administrative Science Quarterly* 17: 229–39.

Cases Cited

Forster v. Manchester, 410 Pa. 192 A.2d 147 150.

Pinkerton v. Stevens, 108Ga App 159; 132 s.e. 2d 119.

Souder v. Pendleton Detectives, Inc., et al. 88 So 2d 716.

INDEX